Browning

and

Italy

Browning

and

Italy

Jacob Korg

Ohio University Press
Athens, Ohio
London

Library of Congress Cataloging in Publication Data
Korg, Jacob.
  Browning and Italy.

  Includes bibliographical references and index.
    1. Browning, Robert, 1812–1889—Knowledge—Italy. 2. Browning, Robert, 1812–1889—Homes and haunts—Italy. 3. Italy in literature. 4. Italy—Description and travel. 5. Poets, English—19th century—Biography.
I. Title.
PR4242.I82K67   1983   821'.8 [B]   83–8075
ISBN 0–8214–0725–2

Contents

List of Illustrations

Preface

Why is so much of Robert Browning's best poetry occupied with Italy? Ian Jack has provided some answers to this question in a single admirable and far-ranging sentence:

> In Italy Browning found a country where he could be alone with his own soul, a country where the sectarianism of his early surroundings melted away in the sunshine and the history, where men and women and masterpieces of painting and sculpture wooed the eye as they had seldom done in the smoke and grime of early Victorian London, a country where Shelleyan dreams of man as he should be yielded to a fascinated observation of man as he is—where contemplation of the present led naturally to speculation on the past, and in particular on that period of the past which Michelet had described as "the discovery of man," the Italian Renaissance.[1]

In opening Browning's mind to these new worlds of thought and experience, Italy offered him wonderfully vital material. But it also affected his poetry in other, more fundamental ways. I hope to show that the perceptions Italy awakened in him played an important part in determining the kind of poetry he wrote, and in the formulation of his poetic theories.

It is my primary purpose to illuminate Browning's poems, both by analyzing their texts, and by examining those Italian experiences that influenced his general development, his ideas about poetry, and the course of his production. My intentions are mainly critical; nevertheless, I have introduced much biographical and historical information, including comments on the place of Italy in the English tradition, Italian social conditions and political developments, sketches of the friends Browning knew in Italy, and accounts of his travels and the artists and art works he wrote about. Chapters 5 and 8 are nearly entirely concerned with his life rather than his work, because they cover periods of his Italian residence when he wrote little. For Browning, inactivity was often a phase of composition, and it would be a mistake to believe that these fallow periods were unrelated to his writing.

However, I have not attempted to give a complete biographical record, even for the times when Browning was living in Italy. Fortunately, readers can now rely, as I have throughout my study, on the many excellent biographies of Browning that are now available. *The Life of Robert Browning* by W. Hall Griffin and H.C. Minchin (1910; rev. ed., 1938) set a very high standard in this field. Four comparatively recent biographies, *Robert Browning: A Portrait* by Betty Miller (1952), *Robert Browning and His World* by Maisie Ward (1969), *The Book, The Ring and The Poet* by William Irvine and Park Honan (1974), and *Browning's Youth* by John Maynard (1977) have upheld this standard and made the record a very full one. Further information is available in William C. DeVane's indispensable *Browning Handbook* (1955), in the biographies of Elizabeth Barrett Browning, and in the many volumes of letters by both poets which have appeared.

Some readers will be surprised to learn that there has never been an inclusive and focused study of the place of Italy in Brown's poetry. Nearly every book on Browning at least touches on the subject, but it has never had the sort of sustained examination which yields definitive results. *Browning's Italy* by Helen A. Clarke (1907) identifies some of the major themes, and offers some excellent historical research, especially in relation to *Sordello* and *Luria*, but it is essentially a sentimental excursus that devotes much of its space to quoting poems in full. Two of the essays in *Robert Browning*, edited by Isobel Armstrong (1975), "Browning in Italy" by Barbara Melchiori and "Browning and Painting" by Leonee Ormond, treat parts of the subject effectively, as does Melchiori's *Poetry of Reticence*. There are excellent brief comments on it in many studies, including that of Ian Jack already quoted, *Robert Browning* by G.K. Chesterton, *The Flaming Heart* by Mario Praz, and *Browning's Roman Murder Story* by Richard D. Altick and James F. Loucks II, but in general, Browning's experience with Italy has been regarded as an episode of his life rather than a formative influence on his poetry.

In preparing this book, I visited some of the sites in Italy where Browning lived, or which he used as settings. Many of these places remain in the condition in which Browning saw them, some in the condition in which Guido Franceschini and Giuseppe Caponsacchi saw them. I learned a great deal by comparing the physical and historical realities with Browning's imaginative treatment of them, and hope to pass some of this on to my readers, although much of it is not easily communicated.

One of the pleasures of my work has been that of encountering the work of a previous Browning scholar, Professor W. Hall Griffin. The Griffin Collection in the Manuscript Department of the British Library (Add MS 45558-45564) consists of extensive correspondence, extracts, and other papers containing valuable information that could not be used in his excellent biography. Griffin spent much time in Italy, taking photographs of sites and objects mentioned in Browning's poetry. These are now in the Print Room of the Library, and I have used several to illustrate my text.

For help in providing me with resources for this study, I wish to thank the following: Sir Joseph Cheyne of the Keats-Shelley Memorial in Rome, Ian Greenlees of the British Institute in Florence, Darrel Mansell Jr., Michael Mason, Michael Meredith, and Antonio Pace; the following libraries: the Library of the University of Washington, the Berg Collection of the New York Public Library, the British Library, the Library of London University, the Library of University College, the Library of the University of Toronto, the Huntington Library, the National Library of Florence, the civic archives of Arezzo, the Library of Balliol College, Oxford, the British Institute of Florence, the Keats-Shelley Memorial in Rome, the Pforzheimer Library, the Library of the Victoria and Albert Museum, and the Marylebone Public Library, which has its own Browning collection; and the following institutions: the Casa Guidi, the Dulwich Gallery, the National Gallery (London), the Pitti Gallery, the Uffizi Gallery, the Archaeological Museum of Florence, the Civic Museum of Asolo, the Criminological Museum of Rome, the Palazzo Barberini, and the Museum of 18th-Century Art in Venice, which occupies the Palazzo Rezzonico. I am also indebted to my wife, Cynthia, who shared much of the work of writing this book.

Browning's poetry is quoted from the one-volume *Complete Poetical Works of Browning*, Cambridge Edition, Houghton Mifflin Company, 1895.

ONE

Browning and the Tradition of Italy

No English poet has captured the distinctive qualities of Italy as fully as Robert Browning. Henry James, who knew both Italy and Browning, has argued for his superiority in a famous passage which declares that his achievement in this regard "makes the rest of our poetic record pale and abstract. . . . Shelley, let us say in this connection, is a light and Swinburne, let us say, a sound; Browning alone of them all is a temperature. We feel it, we are in it at a plunge, with the very first pages of the thing before us. . . ."[1] But Italy was more to Browning than a source of especially authentic settings for his poems. His consciousness of it had profound effects on his poetic development, his sense of the poet's responsibility, and his conception of the nature and purpose of poetry.

He once said, in his later years, while observing that he would not have done well at conventional educational institutions: "Italy was *my* university."[2] While Italy provided him with material by teaching him much about history, art, and politics, it also formed his poetic sensibility at a deeper level by lifting the veil of familiarity from the human drama, and displaying, in its history and daily life, a fuller range of the possibilities of human nature than he had seen in England. The great lesson of Italy for Browning was that his subject ought to be, not the private emotions he had dealt with in his early poem, *Pauline*, but the concerns of humanity at large.

He learned that he could deal more effectively with the spiritual and moral issues that occupied him if he treated them with detachment, as the problems of people who were different from himself, as the Italians were. His genius was centrifugal; he was attracted to

1

the horizon. In his "Essay on Shelley" Browning maintains that while there are many "subjective" poets who employ the external object for self-expressive purposes, the world also needs the "objective" poet who can tell "what it was before they saw it, in reference to the aggregate human mind. . . ." The two modes may coexist, or may alternate with each other in the history of poetry. When the influence of a great subjective interpreter has been worn thin through imitation, it is time for the objective poet to bring forward new and unassimilated materials derived from the external world which will destroy the old synthesis and ultimately make a new one necessary. Italy offered Browning the opportunity to become a poet of that kind, who, as Nietzsche put it in *The Birth of Tragedy,* attains "deliverance from the self," redeems his art from egoism, and transforms himself into a channel through which reality as a whole can be expressed.

In taking Italian figures, especially historical ones, as representatives of mankind, Browning was compelled to attend to the processes of minds unlike his own, and to explore unfamiliar regions of thought and emotion in a search for elements common to all humanity. This effort clearly played a part in the development of his dramatic style. In addition, the subtle ironic structures that characterize his dramatic monologues owe much to the fact that he approached his Italian subjects from his own point of view, tacitly maintaining a set of values that contrast with, or even oppose, the attitudes he allows them to express.

Italian realities also impressed themselves on Browning's view of his art. The central episodes of Italian history, the Renaissance and the Risorgimento, are conceived as instances of renewal or rebirth. This is the pattern which is the basis of the theory put forward in *The Ring and the Book*—that poetry is not so much an act of creation, as a redemptive process that brings forgotten truths to consciousness again. Browning's admiration for Renaissance art stimulated his enthusiasm for naturalism, and confirmed his belief that poetry ought to maintain a close relation with the physical world, even when it dealt with transcendental or metaphysical themes. As a result, he took the Italian scene in which he was immersed as an arena of moral drama. Its objects, personages, and phenomena maintain their striking individuality as they appear in his poems, but they also project an allegorical aura, in conformity with Browning's method of locating universals within particulars. In this way, Italy acquires the status of a cosmic metaphor, and becomes a fully adequate symbol for reality itself.

While Browning's Italy creates a remarkably authentic impression, as James observed, its relation to the real Italy remains literary rather than reportorial. Browning encloses the recognized Italian realities in a distinctive fictional world that modifies, and sometimes reverses, their conventional significance. His bold deviations from historical fact are only the most obvious instances of a method that illuminates reality by approaching it from a critical, and even ironic point of view.

Much of the strain and oddness of his poetry can be attributed to his efforts to reshape his materials into something of his own by adopting an indirect approach no one else would have thought of. An anecdote transmitted by Edmund Gosse shows how his mind worked. Hearing a story about a young artist who had suffered disappointment, Browning said that it was "stuff for a poem," and

> began to sketch the form it should take, the suppression of what features and substitution of what others were needful; and finally suggested the non-obvious or inverted moral of the whole, in which the act of spirited defiance was shown to be, really an act of tame renunciation, the poverty of the artist's spirit being proved in his eagerness to snatch, even though it was by honest merit, a benefit simply material.[3]

Because he looked for the "non-obvious and inverted moral" in dealing with Italy, as with other subjects, Browning felt very little responsibility for adhering to facts that conflicted with his themes. He asserts in *Sordello* that it is the "healthy spirit" which "Craves aliment in plenty,—all the same/Changes, assimilates its aliment."

Early in their marriage, Elizabeth gratefully took note of Browning's creative relationship with the world of actuality. "It is not so bad a thing, be sure," she wrote to her sister, "for a woman to be loved by a man of imagination. He loves her through a lustrous atmosphere which not only keeps back the faults, but produces continual novelty through its own changes."[4] This selectivity may not seem appropriate to the pursuit of truth, but it corresponds with a view of poetry formulated by John Stuart Mill in an article which appeared in the *Monthly Repository* in the year after Browning's *Pauline* had been reviewed there. Mill contended that poetry does not represent externals or the past, but seeks instead to generate the feelings connected with them through what T. S. Eliot was later to call objective correlatives. Its materials come from actuality, but it "selects and combines, not so much what is an object of sense, as what acts upon the feelings and awakens the sympathies."[5]

Departure from fact was not merely a convenience for Browning, but an artistic principle. Toward the end of his life he wrote irritably to a friend who had asked him to clarify some allusions that "poetry, if it is to deserve the name, ought to create—or re-animate something—not merely reproduce *raw* fact taken from somebody else's book."[6] He approached the resources that fed his imagination in a contentious, dialectic spirit and seems to have adopted toward them some of the attitudes that poets in Harold Bloom's analysis of literary filiations, *The Anxiety of Influence*, are found to assume toward their precursors. As impatient of the controlling influence of facts as strong poets are of the tyranny of their forerunners, Browning plunged into complex, perverse relationships with them, subjecting them to a wide range of "creative misinterpretations" that correspond, in many cases, with those described by Bloom. The thaumaturgic pass at the beginning of *Sordello*, "Ye believe? / Appears Verona . . ." introduces a stratagem that resembles Bloom's "daemonization," for Browning admits that he intends to supplant objective truth with a vision of his own; the effect of such a move, says Bloom, is to humanize the antecedent elements. A counterpart of Bloom's "kenosis," apparent self-denial that surreptitiously minimizes the precursor, is heard in Browning's statement about the documentary source of *The Ring and the Book:* "I disappeared; the book grew all in all."

Browning differed from Bloom's strong poets in directing his revisionist energies against facts or supposed facts rather than earlier writers. And his motive was not the Oedipal animus inherent in Bloom's patterns, but the urge to rescue or redeem whatever seemed in danger of being lost. Browning's theory that poetry "Completes the incomplete and saves the thing" corresponds with Bloom's "tessera," the method of preserving a precursor's values by augmenting, revising, or even contradicting them. Something similar appears in many aspects of Browning's life, from his marriage to a woman who considered herself an invalid and a recluse, to his interest in old books and manuscripts. When he lived in London, he kept on his writing desk a picture showing a rescue, an engraving from a fresco called "Perseus and Andromeda" by the sixteenth-century painter, Polidoro da Caravaggio. The scene shown is described with a fair degree of accuracy in the passage about Andromeda in *Pauline,* and the Andromeda theme became a significant one in Browning's poetry.[7] An announcement that the Paris Morgue was to be demolished called forth a response in the form of a poem beginning "No, for I'll save it!" Even the suicides whose bodies he saw there are described as *"apparent* failures."

For a poet who thought of poetry as an act of reclamation, Italy was an irresistible subject. In Browning's time it was living a shadow life among the remains of its former greatness. It had been the birthplace of modern ideas of nationality and individualism, but was now ignominiously occupied by foreign powers. Everywhere about him, in Roman ruins, decaying palaces, peeling frescoes, importunate beggars, and the general vacancy of intellectual life, Browning saw evidence of its decline from grandeur. Italy became his Andromeda, and he studied it for flickers of vitality that could be breathed into flame. In *Sordello* he dramatized obscure wars in which Italians had exhibited enormous energies and passions; *Pippa Passes* based its insights into the human condition on the wanderings of a poor girl in a humble town; and *The Ring and the Book* was triumphantly erected on the record of a despicable, forgotten crime found in an old book bought from a seller of used goods.

Browning took Italy, as he took everything else, on his own terms, transforming what he saw to suit his needs, and often viewed Italy and Italians with irony. This should not be taken to mean, however, that Italy failed to influence him profoundly. He may have distorted particular facts and rejected specific values, but he gained an indispensable spiritual perspective within which his own feelings and ideas could achieve fuller dimensions. He did not think of Italy as a land of pure beauty and enchantment; it did not cast a lotus-eater's spell on him. He was never tempted to lose himself in its culture, as Lafcadio Hearn did in Japan, and T. E. Lawrence did in Arabia. At Elizabeth's death, after fifteen years' residence in Italy, when faced with the problem of educating his son, who had been born and reared in Florence, Browning wrote that he intended to take the boy back to England so that he could acquire "the English stamp." The comment that he added is a key to the treatment of Italy and Italian figures in his poems. "I distrust all hybrid and ambiguous natures and nationalities," he wrote. "I find, by myself, that one leans out the more widely over one's neighbour's field for being effectually rooted in one's own garden."[8]

He did not make Italy a poetic theme, as Elizabeth did. He had opinions about its people, politics, art, and religion, but he offers no coherent picture or theory, no vision of the whole. On the contrary, it was the diversity and inconsistency of Italian civilization, with its evil and violence on the one hand, and its noble accomplishments on the other, that attracted him. Though he lived in Italy for many years, he could not claim to know it intimately, as his friends T. A. Trollope and William Wetmore Story did. He had few Italian acquaintances of his own class, but lived in a circle of English and American friends. He once remarked that he had never had a conversation with a priest, except for the abbé who tutored his son. His image of Italy was derived from long, observant walks about the streets, hours spent over Vasari's *Lives of the Painters*, relations with servants and tradesmen, travel, general reading, and the study of history and works of art.

He was not strongly influenced by Italian literature. He admired Dante and Petrarch, and his hero, Sordello, is a kind of surrogate for Dante. But he did not follow Italian examples in his work, and the Italian sources of his plots and characters are mainly sub-literary works such as biographies, chronicles, trial documents, and the like. There was certainly little to attract him in the intellectual life of contemporary Italy. He once wrote to his friend Isa Blagden: "I agree with you, and always did, as to the uninterestingness of the Italians individually, as thinking, originating souls: I never read a line in a modern Italian book that was of use to me,—never saw a flash of poetry come out of an Italian *word*; in art, in action, *yes*,—not in the region of ideas. . . ."[9] Not long after the Brownings had settled in their first Italian home in Pisa, Elizabeth wrote that the library had no significant Italian books: "the roots of thought here in Italy, seem dead in the ground. It is well that they have great memories—nothing else lives."[10] It was the "great memories," the general spectacle of Italian cultural history that provided or corresponded with some of the major themes of Browning's poetry.

Browning continued and extended an English tradition of Italy that is nearly as old as English literature itself, and his views are hardly understandable unless that tradition is taken into account.

Its most striking feature is its emphasis on the contradictions to be found in Italy and Italians. We hear that Italy is a land of ravishing art and repellent cruelty; the countryside is beautiful, the people poor; there are priests and churches everywhere, yet immorality is rife; the Italian character is volatile and capricious, and reaches to the limits of human capacities for good and evil. In his widely-read *Italy* (1822), Samuel Rogers wrote that the Italian was

> *Subtle, discerning, eloquent, the slave*
> *Of love, of Hate, for ever in extremes;*
> *Gentle when unprovoked, easily won*
> *But quick in quarrel—through a thousand shades*
> *His spirit flies cameleon-like, and mocks*
> *The eye of the observer.*

The tendency to attribute two distinct sides to the Italian character appears at the very beginning of the English tradition of Italy, and is conveniently symbolized by two medieval Englishmen, each of whom knew Italy in one of its aspects. One was a hardened professional soldier who lived by shedding blood for money, Sir John Hawkwood; the other a genial, observant poet and courtier, Geoffrey Chaucer. Both were in Milan in the summer of 1378. While there is no record of an encounter between the two, they almost certainly met, for Hawkwood was in the service of Bernabò Visconti, the ruler of Milan, and Chaucer, who had been sent to Milan on a diplomatic mission, carried travel documents that named Hawkwood as one of the persons he was to see.[11]

Hawkwood, the younger son of a prosperous Essex tanner, had come to Italy with his formidable White Company of English and German soldiers in 1364, after learning military tactics in France during the Hundred Years' War and receiving his knighthood in the field. He adapted himself perfectly to the atmosphere of guile and violence that prevailed among the incessantly warring Italian cities, and became one of Italy's first and most famous *condottieri*. Chaucer, who had been in Italy before, having spent a year in Genoa on government business in 1372, found there a civilization that was far more advanced and sophisticated than the one he knew at home, and he profited from the full-blooded humanism of its art and literature. While his genius was too powerful to be transformed in any radical way, he did acquire in Italy a wider range of allusion and consciousness of mankind, and helped himself, for purposes of his own, to materials drawn from Dante, Petrarch, and Boccaccio. The two Englishmen focused on contrasting aspects of the complex phenomenon of Italian civilization, and the split survived to shape the tradition that Browning inherited centuries later.

This ambivalence is perfectly apparent in sixteenth-century literature, where Italy is treated, on the one hand, as the homeland of the brigand, the vendetta, Papistry, Machiavelli, and Lucrezia Borgia; and on the other, as the mother of the Renaissance, the leader of fashions in dress and manners, and the source of active ideals of courtliness and love. The Elizabethan dramatists took it as a conventional setting for unspeakable horrors and intense passions, but Shakespeare's Italian comedies exhibit a society where wit, courtesy, and exquisite sensibilities are found. Crimes and noble deeds which could not be imagined as occurring anywhere else might exist—and even coexist—in the disembodied Paduas, Veronas, and Malfis of Webster, Marlowe, and Shakespeare. Milton's knowledge of Italian literature, and his year-long visit to a number of Italian cities in 1638-39, where he met many learned men, including Galileo and the librarian of the Vatican, enabled him to assimilate the spirit of Italian humanism, and to embody it in his work. But he wrote little about Italy itself, and the values he transmitted did not change the image of Italy in the popular mind.

The vogue for collecting Italian paintings which began late in the seventeenth century was ultimately to bring into England abundant evidence of the vitality of Italian civilization, and in the eighteenth century English taste was influenced by fashions in gardening stimulated by Italian landscapes and by the popularity of Italian opera. Giuseppe Baretti's *Account of the Manners and Customs of Italy* (1768) and Mrs. Piozzi's *Observations and Reflections* (1789) helped to dispel the impression that all Italians were Machiavellian by describing daily life and explaining some of the practices that the English misinterpreted. On the other hand, the Gothic novel emphasized the old associations with cruelty and violence by relying on Italian villains and Italian settings to generate its horrors. Gibbon's *Decline and Fall of the Roman Empire* (1776–88) reminded its readers that the ruins and monuments of the Italian landscape were the remains of a great past. And it perpetuated the image of

Italy as a scene of profoundly contradictory elements by describing both the bloody intrigues of Italian dynastic history and the achievements of artists and scholars in the time of the Medici.

In the Romantic period, Italy became the second native land of English poetry. Byron, Shelley, Keats, Landor, Leigh Hunt, and Samuel Rogers lived, wrote, and in some cases, died in Italy, often using the beautiful and historic land as a subject or a setting without idealizing it. The sensational plots of Byron's and Shelley's tragedies exploited its reputation for bloodshed and passion. *Childe Harold's* descriptions of Italy gloomily emphasize the sorrows of the past. Its review of the great Tuscans of history dwells on the injustices they suffered, even after death. Byron admits that the works of art gathered in Florence are overwhelming, but he is more attuned to the mountain landscape with its "horribly beautiful" cataract. Rome appears in *Childe Harold* as a Piranesi-like image of decline, a counterpart of the hero's grandiose, but futile aspirations, and a symbol of the hollowness of the modern world.

All of Shelley's mature poetry was written during his four years in Italy, and Italian sites and their history are an integral part of his symbolic vocabulary. The "wood that skirts the Arno," the scene of the storm described in "Ode to the West Wind," was the Cascine, the parklike area in Florence, and the sea imagery in the same poem reflects impressions gathered at the Bay of Naples. Scenes in Rome, Pisa, Venice, and the Euganean Hills touched Shelley's deepest feelings, and were embodied in important poems. His letters from Italy are full of remarkable descriptions of the places he saw, and he urged Thomas Love Peacock to see them for himself: "Come to Rome. It is a scene by which expression is overpowered: which words cannot convey."[12]

In spite of his enthusiasm, he did not escape the sense of contradiction that travelers in Italy had always felt. To Leigh Hunt he wrote:

> There are two Italies; one composed of the green earth and transparent sea and the mighty ruins of antient times, and aerial mountains, and the warm and radiant atmosphere which is interfused through all things. The other consists of the Italians of the present day, their works and ways. The one is the most sublime and lovely contemplation that can be conceived by the imagination of man; the other the most degraded disgusting and odious.[13]

One day, in the square in front of St. Peter's he saw three hundred convicts in chains hoeing weeds under guard, a sight which he felt essentialized the baffling contrasts of Italy.

> The iron discord of those innumerable chains clanks up into the sonorous air, and produces, contrasted with the musical dashing of the fountains, and the deep azure beauty of the sky and the magnificence of the architecture around a conflict of sensations allied to madness. It is the emblem of Italy: moral degradation contrasted with the glory of nature and the arts.[14]

In the Victorian period the English conception of Italy became both more sentimental and more realistic. By the time Browning made his first trip to Italy in 1838, the Italian tour had become commonplace, not only for aristocrats, as it had been in the eighteenth century, but for middle-class families. After the defeat of Napoleon, the English swarmed into Italy in numbers too large to be accommodated in the existing hotels. English visitors and even residents seldom learned Italian or Italian customs, but carried their own folkways wherever they went. British-style horse races took place in the Cascine in Florence, and a cricket ground was laid out in Naples. By the middle of the century there were well-established English colonies at Florence and Bagni di Lucca (which had an English casino), and the area around the Piazza di Spagna had become an English quarter with English shops and a reading room "where elderly gentlemen in drab gaiters read the 'Times' newspaper with an air of grim intensity."[15]

By the mid-century it was assumed that every well-stocked European and American mind would be familiar with certain works of art, music, and architecture from Italy. The contributions of Italian civilization were so naturalized that there was some danger that the sense of their Italian origins might be lost. The Victorian image of Italy expanded and grew more complex as new information about art, history, politics, and social conditions became available. One new component was sympathy for a helpless land partitioned by foreign powers and struggling for freedom and unity. T. A. Trollope, who spent most of his adult life in Italy, saw much that was absurd, but also emphasized the appearance of freedom in Tuscany in 1848 in the form of a revitalized press and a newly convened Parliament that met in Florence's Palazzo Vecchio. Frances

Power Cobbe, a determined social investigator whom Elizabeth admired, visited schools, army posts, prisons, and courts, and reported that in spite of all difficulties, "There is a human spring reviving in the beautiful land after its long winter of frost-bound oppression."[16]

The Romantic poets had established Italy in the popular mind as a country where emotions and artistic energies stifled in England might be freed. George Eliot sent Dorothea Brooke, the heroine of *Middlemarch*, to Italy on her honeymoon, with consequences that were ultimately beneficial. When the young clergyman who is the hero of James Anthony Froude's *Nemesis of Faith* (1849) admits that he feels doctrinal doubts, and his bishop advises, ". . . go travel, see what men are . . ." he naturally goes to Italy, where he falls in love.

The notion that human nature was more openly displayed in Italian life also became a part of historical doctrine. Jacob Burckhardt was the chief spokesman for the nineteenth-century view that the northern Italian republics of the late Middle Ages and the Renaissance had been cradles of individualism. For the first time in history it had become not only possible, but common, for people to lead self-determined lives, obey private passions and thoughts, and control the course of important events. The reasons given for this development are varied and intriguing. Burckhardt explains that the need for competent administrators in the small states opened a field for vigorous and ambitious men, but that turbulent struggles for power often made it futile to continue in public service, so that independence was encouraged. Exile forced many able men to rely on their own resources rather than those of their country. Within the small states personal capacities were quickly recognized and highly valued. Conditions like these brought forward the whole range of attitudes associated with the Renaissance conception of man: self-consciousness, independence of mind, curiosity about the nature of man and the world, and a taste for fame, display, versatility, and personal distinction. Vasari's comparison of the history of art to the development of the body is an expression of the Renaissance principle that man is the fit measure of all things, a conviction that survives as an everyday force in modern Italian life. "The pleasure of living in Italy," testifies so authoritative a witness as Luigi Barzini, "comes from living in a world made by man, for man, on man's measurements."[17]

Browning's conception of Italy obviously owes much to the complex image built up in English minds over the centuries. Its layers of Renaissance, Romantic, and Victorian feeling are sometimes as visible as the strata in a geological formation. He felt the contradictions, admired the landscape, recognized the greed and cruelty, immersed himself in the art and history, and sympathized with the new libertarian stirrings, very much as others had. Browning's own position is not entirely derivative, however, but makes a significant contribution to the thinking of his time. With respect to the Renaissance, for example, Wallace K. Ferguson has maintained that he corrected the excesses of the Romantic view, achieving a "perfect synthesis" of the Romantic and neo-classical conceptions of the period. In the relevant dramatic monologues, says Ferguson, Browning "presented all the facts of the Renaissance character as the mid-nineteenth century saw them, and made them human and believable. From Browning it is but a short step to Burckhardt."[18]

Burckhardt considered an interest in inward spiritual life and in the natures of great men prominent parts of the Renaissance outlook; and these were subjects that Browning favored. *Sordello*, he wrote in his dedication, was concerned with "incidents in the development of a soul; little else is worth study." In finding that Italian culture exhibited the development of souls far more openly than English culture did, he was concurring with a general opinion illustrated by Nathaniel Hawthorne's observation that "Anglo-Saxons" are prevented from going to extremes by their reserve, but Italians behave otherwise, acting according to "individual will and character," so that "a hundred plots for a tragedy might be found in Florentine history for one in English."[19]

Browning was one of many perceptive English observers who realized that Italian sensibilities often extended beyond their own. Hazlitt, noticing that aristocrats often took part in funeral processions in disguise as a form of penance, interpreted this custom as an acknowledgement of the leveling power of death, and gave them credit for setting an example of sympathy and generosity.[20] Frances Power Cobbe attributed the emphasis worshipers placed on the Virgin to the belief that she understood human weaknesses, and could be appealed to for small, even trivial, services. Cobbe considered this worship a favorable indication, for truly wicked people would prefer to believe in an unrelenting deity; Browning's Caliban is her example.

Browning's attitude toward Italy was, in the final analysis, neither simple nor easily defined. His affection for it, as he expressed it in a letter to Isa Blagden, was composed of a mixture of contradictory feelings. In England, he said, he felt the encroachment of many minds that resembled his own. But in Italy, where people did not reflect, but lived vigorously, developing life to its fullest possibilities for good and evil, he found a clear field for the process of sorting out fundamental ideas which amounts to intellectual self-discovery. He wrote to Isa: "My liking for Italy was always a selfish one,—I felt alone with my own soul there. . . ."[21] D. H. Lawrence had a remarkably similar response to Italy. He wrote, "We ought to look at ourselves and say, 'My God, I am myself!' That is why I like to live in Italy. The people are so unconscious. They only feel and want; they don't know."[22]

The reactions of both writers to the naked elements of human nature exhibited in Italian life had a reflexive effect, opening their own identities to them. Browning makes this double disclosure explicit in a line from *The Ring and the Book* where he says that after reading the record of passion and virtue preserved from seventeenth-century Italy that he was to use as the basis of his poem, he went out on the terrace of Casa Guidi to look down into the street, and felt that "I turned to free myself and find the world." It was as if the spectacle of Italy gave him access to his own feelings and the central themes of his own thoughts. Italian materials influenced him in somewhat the same way as the discovery of the Russian novel influenced the generation that came after him. They enlarged his conception of human nature and deepened his sense of moral life. Things that could not happen in England—or anywhere outside of Italy—could be explained by motives that were latent in human beings everywhere, but were brought to the surface only in the prolific turmoil of the Italian scene.

TWO

The First Italian Tour:

Sordello *and* Pippa Passes

One would not expect to find many foreign influences in the dull southern suburbs of London where Browning was born and brought up. But stray radiations of Italy penetrated to him there. The Italian paintings in the Dulwich Picture Gallery, which was a half-hour walk from the Camberwell neighborhood where Browning lived until he was nearly thirty, must have been the first examples of Italian culture he encountered. The Gallery's Italian collection consisted entirely of fifteenth-century and baroque works, and included paintings (or copies of paintings) by Domenichino, Titian, Guercino, Correggio, Tiepolo, Giorgione, Bronzino, and some anonymous Italian painters.

Browning visited the Dulwich Gallery repeatedly throughout his youth, and later said that he had been strongly impressed by the paintings he saw there. His favorites were dramatic and sententious treatments of Biblical or legendary scenes with some narrative interest. Browning might have read about the Italian artists in the copy of Vasari's *Lives of the Painters* in his father's library, but did not distinguish them from artists of other nationalities. In a letter to Elizabeth written many years later, he mentions pictures by Guido Reni and Giorgione as among the most memorable.[1] The Dulwich Gallery clearly prepared Browning for his future study of Italian painting. Two of its pictures, a *Holy Family* by Del Sarto and a *Judith with the Head of Holofernes* by Cristofano Allori were copies of originals that he was later to see in the Pitti Palace opposite his home in Florence.

14

A stronger and more controlling Italian influence reached him in 1828 or 1829, after his brief enrollment at London University, when he began to take private lessons from an Italian tutor, Angelo Cerutti. In his autobiography (*Vita di Angelo Cerutti,* 2 vols. [Firenze, 1846]), Cerutti does not mention Browning, who had not yet achieved fame, but he does say that one of his pupils at Mrs. Goodson's school in Camberwell in 1828 was a young lady named Browning who had a good mind and looked more Italian than English. It can be supposed that Browning, then sixteen years of age, heard of Cerutti through his sister, Sarianna, and arranged to take lessons from him. In this way Browning came under the influence of a personality who brought considerable ardor to his teaching, and implanted in his pupil a permanent and growing interest in the language and culture of Italy.[2]

In the "Proemio" to his autobiography, Cerutti says that he went abroad in order to demonstrate that the ancient "virtù" of Italy was not exhausted. He was born in 1797 near the Certosa di Pavia south of Milan, one of the eight children of a tenant farmer. He had a good education at a "collegio" in Arona on Lago Maggiore, and went to Paris early in his twenties to take a position at a bank for which he had been recommended. But when the position did not materialize, he moved to London, and taught at the school where he encountered Sarianna.

Cerutti, who believed that the best training for language students was immersion in great literature, put together a book of selections from Tasso, Ariosto, and Boccaccio which Browning must have studied. He complained that most of his English pupils were not serious, but Browning was certainly an exception, for he read Dante with Cerutti, and, very possibly, Petrarch, whose work he came to know in any case. In 1830 Cerutti published another text for his pupils, an edition of Daniello Bartoli's *De'Simboli Trasportati al Morale,* a collection of 124 sermonlike discussions by a Jesuit born in Ferrara who lived from 1608 to 1685 and presented his essays as lessons in moral discipline. Browning spent much time with this book. His name and Sarianna's appear in the list of subscribers. He took his copy with him on his trips to Italy in 1838 and 1844 for practice in reading Italian and wrote "Home Thoughts from the Sea" and "How They Brought the Good News from Ghent to Aix" on blank leaves in it. An allusion in Bartoli's book may have played some part in leading Browning to choose the medieval Italian poet, Sordello, as the hero of the important new poem he began in March 1833. By presenting him as a forerunner of Dante and the father of literary Italian, he was obviously responding to the influence of Cerutti and the *Divine Comedy*.[3]

Sordello

> There is not one drop of British ink in the whole composition. . . . it is all written in Tuscan grape juice, embrowned by the sun.
>
> —from Richard Hengist Horne's review of *Sordello* in
> *The Church of England Quarterly*, October, 1842.

Browning's long and painful effort to complete *Sordello* drove him to make his first visit to Italy. The poem was begun soon after Browning had completed *Pauline*, and before he thought of *Paracelsus*, and was apparently intended at first to be no more than a study of a poet's development, an improved *Pauline*. When John Stuart Mill read Browning's first effort as an autobiographical poem, identifying the poet with his bewildered *persona*, Browning decided to prevent this in his new poem by dramatizing the spiritual conflicts through a surrogate, the thirteenth-century troubadour, lover, and warrior. It was a simple, even a transparent device, but a vital step toward the objective presentation of subjective processes which became Browning's mature manner.

Browning probably first encountered the figure of Sordello while reading Dante with Cerutti. The lonely, proud poet of Cantos VI–IX of *Purgatorio* who welcomes Virgil as a fellow Mantuan and then condemns the negligence of princes is no more than an extrapolation on Dante's part from some of Sordello's verses. The real Sordello's most conspicuous deed was the abduction, probably for political reasons, of Cunizza, the wife of Count Riccardo di San Bonifazio of Verona in or about the year 1226. After making many enemies in northern Italy, he migrated to Provence, where he wrote famous verses, served in the wars, and died at an advanced and prosperous old age. In *De Vulgari Eloquentia*, Dante praises Sordello as one who wrote well in different genres and combined various dialects into an improved Italian, accomplishments Browning would have approved; but the only extant poems attributed to Sordello are in Provençal.

Sordello exhibits a shift in Browning's poetic loyalty from Shelley to Dante; it is much more a tribute to the Florentine than to the troubadour whose name it bears. In its first pages Browning continues the conversation with the spirit of Shelley, the "Sun-Treader," begun in *Pauline,* asking him not to witness this new poetic effort. Later in Book I he breaks off his narrative to address Dante, declaring that he has chosen Sordello as his protagonist because he was a part of Dante's tradition, and that he intends to distinguish Sordello's gentler light within the radiance of the greater poet who assimilated him. There is no evidence that Browning, who searched so widely for sources, read any of Sordello's verses. If he did, he was not impressed, for he makes no use of them. The song Sordello is described as composing in Book III is Browning's work. The character's speculations on poetic theory do not correspond with the real Sordello's works, which were performances in a specialized, aristocratic mode without any claim to democratic appeal.

Browning was also indebted to Dante for the heroine of his poem. In Book V of *Sordello,* he refers to Dante's treatment of Cunizza da Romano (called "Palma" in Browning's poem), who had numerous husbands and lovers, but showed compassion by freeing the slaves she had inherited. Perhaps for this reason, perhaps because he may have known her, Dante placed her in *Paradiso,* where she appears, appropriately, in the sphere of Venus, among lovers whose earthly passions have been purified, providing Browning with a prototype for his own virtuous heroine.

During the time *Sordello* was in progress, Browning's intentions shifted and broadened, leading him to introduce material about his protagonist's environment, friends, loves, and deeds, and to narrate his participation in the historical events of his time, simultaneously pursuing the original aim of psychological analysis. The result was the strained, self-interrupting, chaotically fertile work critics have so often complained of. But it was also the corridor that led Browning from the enclosed room of lyric introspection to his true subject, the thoughts and acts of others.

Browning's conception of *Sordello* was probably changed by three interruptions which took place while he was working on it. In 1834, he set the poem aside to write *Paracelsus;* in the winter of 1836 he helped his sick friend, John Forster, complete a prose *Life of Strafford;* and later in the year he wrote his own play, *Strafford.* He had to gather historical facts for these projects, and incorporate them into what he wrote. The two verse plays resulting from this process were successful, while *Sordello,* after three years, was still on his writing desk. That experience may have suggested that facts liberated his powers, and that it was best to take them from documentary or reportorial sources, where he would not have to compete with the inventions of another writer. It would have been entirely natural for him to apply this lesson to *Sordello,* and to see that he ought to stiffen a poetic fabric that probably consisted largely of limp speculation with firm historical substance.

The intention of making his poem a definition of Sordello's contribution to poetry therefore receded as Browning, following the method used in writing his plays, continued to gather information. He probably consulted the entry on Sordello in the *Biographie Universelle, Ancienne et Moderne* (1825) by one Daunou, as soon as he chose his subject, for it was easily accessible in his father's library. This entry assembled the facts and traditions about Sordello by surveying the sources, including Dante, the two extant *vidas,* and a number of commentators and chronicles. When Browning followed Daunou to these sources in Ludovico Muratori's great compilation of documents, *Rerum Italicarum Scriptores* in the library of the British Museum, then to a history of the Romano family and other works, *Sordello* entered a new phase of development, becoming a historical poem as well as a psychological study.

Other influences were moving it in this direction as well. Forster's *Life of Strafford,* to which Browning had made a substantial contribution, was published in May 1836, and his play about Strafford had the first of five performances at Covent Garden on May 1, 1837, and was published as a volume on the same day with the notice "Nearly ready. *Sordello,* in Six Books." While he was working on these projects with the uncompleted *Sordello* in mind, Browning might well have begun to feel that the moral issues involved in politics could not be excluded from poetic theory, and as a result, he planned to make *Sordello* a widely ranging narrative of love and war as well as an examination of the poet's task. But the facts about the tangled history of northern Italy's thirteenth century that he had been gathering from books apparently refused to come to life. He felt the need to touch them directly. On April 13, 1838, nearly five years after beginning *Sordello,* he left abruptly for Italy, writing to a friend, "I sail this morning for Venice—intending to finish my poem among the scenes it describes."[4] His ship anchored at 4 P.M. on Wednesday, May 30 at Trieste, where Browning first set foot on Italian soil. The next day he left by steamer for Venice, arriving on June 1, and the following day took lodgings at Casa Stefani, Calle Giacomozzi, San Moise 1139, just to the west of the Piazza San Marco, and about a third of a mile from the Palazzo Rezzonico, where he was to die fifty-one years later.

It was two weeks before he was able to leave Venice behind. On June 17, he traveled forty miles northeast, through Treviso and Castelfranco to Bassano, the center of the region where the Romano family had held power, and where he found a few thirteenth-century ruins and place names that fed his imagination. But he was diverted from these sites by the delightful discovery of Asolo, a town in the hills at the edge of the plain where the Romanos had ruled. He spent three days there, charmed by its people, its countryside, and its history, neglecting his responsibilities to *Sordello* for a time. After Asolo, the route back to England lay through Vicenza, Padua, Venice, and Verona, the territory of the Lombard League, whose wars were the subject of his poem.[5]

This itinerary shows that Browning had not yet planned his poem's full historical dimensions. The fact that he did not go to the sites of its most important actions, Goito, Mantua, and Ferrara, must mean that he did not think of them until after the Italian visit. When he returned to England, he felt that he needed to learn more about the places he had seen, and through this additional reading great amounts of history entered the poem.

Far more important than these researches, however, was his direct experience of Italy and Italian life. He was immediately captivated by them. He felt what Chesterton has accurately called "the love of those whom we do not know." Every commonplace detail seemed radiant and significant, "new flowers, new stones, faces, walls, all new."[6] He took delight in small events that exhibited the peculiarities of human nature: an old woman at Possagno lighting a propitiatory candle at every peal of thunder during a storm, putting it out when the thunder died, immediately relighting the candle when the thunder returned; people eating in the open at Trieste, driven indoors by a sudden storm:

> you are in glorious June-weather, fancy, of an evening, under green shock-headed acacias, so thick and green, with the cicalas stunning

you above, and all about you men, women, rich and poor, sitting, standing and coming and going—and thro' all the laughter and screaming and singing, the loud clink of the spoons against the glasses, the way of calling for fresh "sorbetti"—for all the world is at open-coffee-house at such an hour—when suddenly there is a stop in the sunshine, a blackness drops down, then a great white column of dust drives strait on like a wedge, and you see the acacia heads snap off, now one, then another—and all the people scream "la bora, la bora!"—and you are caught up in their whirl and landed in some interior, the man with the guitar on one side of you, and the boy with a cageful of little brown owls for sale, on the other. . . . out comes the sun—somebody clinks at his glass, all the world bursts out laughing, and prepares to pour out again. . . . Such things you get in Italy. . . ."[7]

This delight in witnessing the passing crowd and the details of everyday life has an obvious relation to the verisimilitude and study of character which are the strengths of Browning's mature poetry. Yet he had apparently never experienced this feeling in England. By opening his mind to the value of commonplace people and events in this way, Italy enabled Browning to fulfill an ambition he had expressed through one of the characters in *Paracelsus*, that of writing poetry which embodied the concerns of humanity in general.

The Italian tour, instead of helping him to complete his poem, deflected him. He had intended to write, but instead observed, writing almost nothing. He meant to finish *Sordello;* instead he found the material for *Pippa Passes*. He came to search for the past, but was far more impressed by what he saw of the present. The misery, color, and vitality of Italian life aroused feelings that led him to still another revision of *Sordello*, and ultimately to a new kind of poetry. In this way Italy shouldered its way into the center of his consciousness, becoming an active and transforming force.

The most obvious reflection of Browning's first journey to Italy in *Sordello* is the account of his meeting with the beggar girl in Book III. I will discuss this passage before turning to the poem as a whole. The most important part of *Sordello*, it stands outside the poem's fictional frame, moves abruptly from the past to the present, deals with personal experience rather than historic materials, and is meditative rather than narrative in style. It is also a bridge between opinions Browning had brought from England and motivations formed in Italy. As in Books I and XII of *The Ring and the*

Book, the poet drops his dramatic stance here to speak directly, and to incorporate the story of the genesis of his poem into the poem itself.

Taking advantage of a moment when Sordello is asleep in his palace, the narrator tells us that a poet has a life separate from, and greater than that in his poem. Accordingly, he interrupts his story to say that he will turn from the elements of his poem that were planned in England to seek sources of poetic energy in his own experiences, and asks the reader to look through his eyes at contemporary Venice. He is seated on "a ruined palace-step at Venice," asking himself what female figure he should take as a source of inspiration.[8] He looks at the attractive peasant girls working beside the canal, but turns away from them because, seeming happy enough, they offer no opening to his reforming impulses. He takes instead a beautiful but tattered girl who comes up to him with trembling lips and tearful eyes, and transforms her into a symbol of the dispossessed, a love that replaces older loves, a representative of irresistible moral claims.

There is reason to believe that this event actually occurred, forming one of Browning's first impressions of Italy, and that it became a turning point in his poetic development as well as a source of convictions that had to be included in *Sordello.* When Fanny Haworth asked him to explain the passage, he wrote a summary of it which sounds like an account of an actual and important experience:

> . . . as I stopped my task awhile, left off my versewriting one sunny June day with a notion of not taking to it again in a hurry, the sad disheveled form I had just been talking of, that plucked and pointed, wherein I put, comprize, typify and figure to myself Mankind, the whole poor-devildom one sees cuffed and huffed from morn to midnight, that, so typified, she may come at times and keep my pact in mind, prick up my republicanism and remind me of certain engagements I have entered into with myself about that same, renewed me, gave me fresh spirit, made me after finishing Book 3d commence Book 4th. . . .[9]

Browning's remark that the girl turned from less promising pedestrians to accost him strikes a credible note of realism. The details of the scene may be arbitrary, mere standard Venetian properties, but they correspond fairly well to the spot where the Rio San Trovaso joins the Canale della Giudecca. His reaction to the girl does not mean that he was uniquely sensitive. Many years later, George Eliot wrote to a friend that on her second day in Rome "a little crippled girl seated at the door of a church looked up at us with a face full of such pathetic sweetness and beauty that I think it can hardly leave me again."[10]

There is another piece of evidence which suggests, not only that this meeting actually occurred, but also its date. To examine it, we must move forward to a day in 1863 when Moncure D. Conway, a neighbor of Browning's in Warwick Crescent, asked the poet for an autograph that could be sold at a philanthropic bazaar in America. Browning took the wrapper from a bundle of his early manuscripts, and presented it to Conway, who, finding some notations on it, carefully copied them before sending it on.

They consisted of a group of quotations in classical Greek, Biblical Greek, English, and Latin, and some dates. The dates, listed together without any explanation, go from Saturday, May 27, 1837, to February 23, 1840, and are followed by four Greek capitals, Theta, Delta, Epsilon (or Eta) and Alpha. To the left, and given special prominence because it is spread over three lines and enclosed in a box, is the notation "Today Venezia June 2, 1838." Michael Mason has hypothesized that the dates mark phases in the composition of *Sordello* (though *Sordello* was not among the manuscripts inside the wrapper), and the final Greek quotation supports this view. Conway translates it: "As travellers rejoice to see [how far they have come?], and mariners to see the port, so scribes see the end of the book."[11]

According to Browning's itinerary, he arrived in Venice on June 1, and on the second took lodgings in Calle Giacomozzi. This is the last entry for this visit to Venice; it is also the date written so conspicuously next to the skeleton record of the composition of *Sordello*, as if it were the most important of all. It might well have been the day recorded in *Sordello*, when Browning, newly arrived in Venice and exceptionally responsive to the novel sights around him, had the encounter that struck him as a revelation of his poetic mission.

Browning's reaction to the beggar girl encompasses a convergence of the English moral conscience and Italian social realities. As *Pippa Passes* shows, Browning learned from this experience and others like it to find meaning in the lives of ordinary Italians, espe-

cially, but not exclusively, those of poor women. Other writers of
the nineteenth century who were moved to indignation by poverty
and social injustice might express their feelings by direct protest, as
Byron and Shelley did, or might, like Morris and Ruskin, channel
their compassion into political action. Instead of expending itself in
mere sympathy, Browning's sense of moral responsibility became
the first phase of a growing consciousness of the external world
which penetrated to the roots of his art. It must have played a sig-
nificant part in leading him to reject the Romantic, meditative
mode of *Pauline,* to turn to externals in a spirit of comparative real-
ism and objectivity, and to construct a moral universe in which his
convictions could be tested against minds and actions based on ac-
tuality.[12]

The assimilation of Browning's humanitarianism into the tech-
nical resources of his poetry is well illustrated in the passage from
Book IV of *The Ring and the Book* where "Tertium Quid" describes
Violante's visit to the prostitute from whom she intends to buy the
unborn child who will become Pompilia. Having made her deci-
sion, Violante

> Posts off to vespers, missal beneath arm,
> Passes the proper San Lorenzo by,
> Dives down a little lane to the left, is lost
> In a labyrinth of dwellings best unnamed,
> Selects a certain blind one, black at base,
> Blinking at top,—the sign of we know what,—
> One candle in a casement set to wink
> Streetward, do service to no shrine inside,—
> Mounts thither by the filthy flight of stairs,
> Holding the cord by the wall, to the tip-top,
> Gropes for the door i' the dark, ajar of course,
> Raps, opens, enters in: up starts a thing
> Naked as needs be—"What, you rogue, 't is you?
> Back,—how can I have taken a farthing yet?
> Mercy on me, poor sinner that I am!
> Here's . . . why, I took you for Madonna's self
> With all that sudden swirl of silk i' the place!
> What may your pleasure be, my bonny dame?"
> Your Excellency supplies aught left obscure?
> One of those women that abound in Rome,
> Whose needs oblige them eke out one poor trade
> By another vile one. . . .

In this sophisticated, disciplined, and understated narrative vignette, everything emerges naturally from the historical setting and the story which is being told. The woman's degradation is disclosed indirectly through the details of her room, lightly touched, but enormously suggestive, through her allusion to her pimp, and her reaction to the well-dressed bourgeoise who has come to see her. In the most masterly touch of all, the accompanying tone is not Browning's sympathy, which lies far beneath the surface, but the smirking facetiousness of the cynical courtier who is telling the story. This resourceful and inventive passage amounts to a devastating condemnation of poverty far more effective than any direct expression of sympathy or indignation could be.

We naturally wonder why home conditions failed to generate this growth in Browning's powers while those of Italy did. In the *Sordello* digression he explains that he has been an idealist about social reform in the past, hoping for universal happiness, but that his encounter with the peasant girls in Venice has led him to accept reality, and to turn to less extravagant hopes.

> *I ask youth and strength*
> *And health for each of you, not more—at length*
> *Grown wise, who asked at home that the whole race*
> *Might add the spirit's to the body's grace,*
> *And all be dizened out as chiefs and bards.*
> *But in this magic weather one discards*
> *Much old requirement. Venice seems a type*
> *Of Life—'twixt blue and blue extends a stripe,*
> *As Life, the somewhat, hangs 'twixt naught and naught:*
> *'Tis Venice, and 'tis Life. . . .*

The importance of this inconspicuous passage as a clue to the position Italy held in Browning's feelings and in his poetry can hardly be exaggerated. In it the image of Venice becomes a metaphor for something he had never met with in England, the "stripe" of an intractable external reality that contrasts with the "naught and naught" of subjectivity, a substantive "somewhat" distinct from private emotions, an embodiment of "Life."

Venice becomes a microcosm again in "Fifine at the Fair," a poem written thirty-three years later, where Don Juan says, after seeing Venice in Carnival time,

> *There went*
> *Conviction to my soul, that what I took of late*
> *For Venice was the world. . . .*

Italy, the larger Venice, was to remain Browning's surrogate for the world outside the self, where, as the revised version of *Sordello* says, he found an archetype of reality,

> *the evil with the good*
> *Which make up Living, rightly understood.*

In writing to Fanny Haworth that his meeting with the beggar girl had aroused his "republicanism" and reminded him of "certain engagements I have entered into with myself," Browning was referring to the liberal ideas he had first learned from Shelley, which had been more fully developed through his association with W.J. Fox. He had known Fox when he was a boy, but his friendship with him dated from 1833, when he sent Fox some copies of *Pauline* to be reviewed in the journal he edited, came to call, and became an intimate of his wards, Sarah and Eliza Flower. Fox, who was known as an orator and writer on religious and political subjects, had two outlets for his opinions, which he used with superlative skill: the pulpit of the Finsbury Unitarian Chapel, better known as the South Place Chapel, where he led a large and distinguished congregation, and the *Monthly Repository*, a religious publication that he transformed into a vigorous journal of liberal opinion.

As a Dissenter, Fox naturally favored religious liberty, but he had much wider reforming interests. He sympathized with many causes advocated by the Philosophical Radicals, supported repeal of the Corn Laws, free national education, and reform of the Poor Laws, and was active in the campaign for the Reform Act of 1832. But he went further than most contemporary Radicals in advocating universal suffrage, female emancipation, and freedom of divorce. His major divergence from Benthamism lay in the direction of a more humanitarian and flexible approach to social problems. Fox's most distinctive theme was perhaps his emphasis on free access to knowledge and on intellectual liberty, and he thought that poetry ought to address itself to the great social questions and take part in promoting progress. The most famous articles on poetry published in the *Monthly Repository*, the three essays by John Stuart

Mill that are known as "The Two Kinds of Poetry" take a different view, but many of Fox's contributions to the journal between 1832 and 1835 discuss poetry as one of the legitimate instruments of social reform.

While Browning may not have agreed with all of Fox's opinions, it seems clear that the humanitarianism with which he responded to the Venetian beggar girl was derived from the modified Benthamism that prevailed in Fox's circle and the *Monthly Repository*.[13] His earlier efforts to serve the cause of social reform in his poetry only exposed his uncertainty about the relationship he thought they ought to have with each other. In *Pauline* the faith in liberty and the perfectibility of man he had learned from Shelley are treated as a phase of his hero's development, soon left behind in a cloud of turbulent emotions that lead to a determination to do better. There is a somewhat more decisive note in *Paracelsus*. Aprile, the poet who comes to teach the scientist, Paracelsus, the value of love and intuition, makes Browning's first statement of his new poetic by declaring that the creator must include in his view of life the varied passions and daily activities of man:

> *Marts, theatres, and wharfs—all filled with*
> > *men,*
> *Men everywhere!*
> . . . .
> > *no thought which ever stirred*
> *A human breast should be untold. . . .*

The audience must be democratic too:

> > *for common life, its wants*
> *And ways, would I set forth in beauteous hues:*
> *The lowest hind should not possess a hope,*
> *A fear, but I'd be by him, saying better*
> *Than he his own heart's language.*

But Aprile's commitment to plebeian interests is brought into question when he asserts that "clay, once cast into my soul's rich mine, / Should come up crusted o'er with gems," and admits, further, that his program has been a failure because he has surrendered to passions that control instead of obeying him. The effort to serve the needs of humanity through Romantic poetry, in accordance with Fox's view of poetry as a medium of social reform, subsides into abstract, self-indulgent idealism. The formation of the new poetic was postponed until Browning's meeting with the Venetian beggar girl; then, as happened to Sordello himself when he saw the poor suffering during the wars in Ferrara, "Old memories returned with new effect."

Let us now turn to *Sordello* as a whole. It was Browning's first serious attempt to apply the theory of poetry later set forth in *The Ring and the Book:* the poet seeks out dying or imperfect things, restores them by injecting his energies into them, "adds self to self," and "start[s] the dead alive" so that "something dead may get to live again." Having found in the *Purgatorio* the figure of the half-forgotten poet who had denounced tyranny, he followed up the sources given in the *Biographie Universelle* and went beyond them until he had surrounded himself with an ever-widening circle of historical personages and events. Most of them came from Muratori's *Rerum Italicarum Scriptores,* although there is evidence that he consulted other records as well.[14]

One of his main sources was *Storia degli Ecelini* by Giambattista Verci (1779), which traced the history of the family Sordello had briefly identified himself with, and may have suggested to Browning the usefulness of visiting the places it mentioned, for his route through northern Italy seems to have been strongly influenced by his interest in the Romano family. As he visited sites associated with them, he found that the thirteenth century was not entirely forgotten. At Bassano, where he went after leaving Venice, he could have seen the Torre di Ezzelino, a characteristic square, battlemented tower with three arched apertures on each side. Remains of the castles occupied by the Ezzelini are visible both in Bassano and in the nearby town of Romano d'Ezzelino, which is approached by a road named after Cunizza da Romano.

To the east, the town of San Zenone degli Ezzelini marks the site of the barbaric slaughter of Alberic, the last of the Romanos, and his family, an event described by Verci and mentioned by Browning. Browning also refers to the tomb in Solagna, two miles north of Bassano, whose lid bears the recumbent figure of a Benedictine monk, said to be a portrait of Alberic's father, Ezzelino II. Browning saw San Zenone, and may also have visited Solagna, but the language he uses in both passages is nearly a translation of what Verci says, as if his researches gave him little to add. On the other hand, the discovery of a skeleton supposed to be Alberic's, which is mentioned in *Sordello*, came from information Browning picked up in the neighborhood.

Returning from Italy with his head full of historic scenes and a desire to know more about them, he turned to the British Museum, and Volume VIII of Muratori's compilation, which contained several accounts of the north Italian wars. He placed his story within a comparatively minor episode of the long struggle between the Este and Romano families which was itself a part of the Guelf and Ghibelline wars between Emperor and Pope. In 1224, the year of the poem, the Guelf leader, Azzo d'Este, with the aid of his ally, Count Riccardo di San Bonifazio of Verona, was besieging Taurello Salinguerra, an ally of Ezzelino da Romano, who held Ferrara. Salinguerra invited Count Riccardo to Ferrara to negotiate peace, then took him prisoner; the news of this "trap" reaches Verona at the beginning of *Sordello*, and inspires a renewed attack on Ferrara.

Browning begins the action of his poem at the time when a crowd in the market square at Verona learns that their leader, Count Riccardo, has been trapped in Ferrara. Verona's ruling council meets to plan its next move. In a distant room of the same palace, Sordello is asleep, while Palma, who is the sister of Ezzelino da Romano, and the betrothed of his enemy, Count Riccardo, but really in love with Sordello, stands over him.

In these passages, Browning may well be projecting imagined actions on a scene he had actually visited. When he was in Verona, he could have seen the market place where his crowd is discussing the capture of their lord. It had become the courtyard of the Palazzo della Ragione, but was still called the Mercato Vecchio. From it he could have seen a square tower with small windows that adjoined the palazzo but was obviously of earlier construction, a surviving portion of the very palace in which his lovers had their tryst.

A noise in the square wakens Sordello; the story now breaks off and goes back in time. A long flashback that runs from the middle of Book I to line 174 of Book III narrates the story of Sordello's childhood, early accomplishments as a poet, and ensuing doubts, and ultimately circles back to the room where Palma and Sordello are talking, and to Verona's crisis. Palma proposes that she and Sordello go to Ferrara in disguise to parley with Riccardo's captor,

Salinguerra. When they come to the besieged town, Sordello experiences two revelations: he feels a profound sense of responsibility for the people whose lives have been ravaged by war, a fictional counterpart of Browning's reaction to the poor of Italy; and he is impressed by Salinguerra, a man of action who does not fail to carry out his purposes.

Sordello acts according to his new standard of morality by trying to persuade Salinguerra to support the people against the power of the Emperor by going over to the Guelf cause. But Salinguerra tries to subvert him by offering the badge of leadership of his own forces. At nearly the same moment, Palma reveals that Sordello is Salinguerra's son. Sordello, tempted to give up an idealized future for the sake of an imperfect present, moves to accept Salinguerra's offer, but he dies before he can speak, the badge beneath his foot.

Since most of these events are fictional, we may wonder why Browning brings so much historical background into his poem. The reason is to be found in Sordello's meditations on his craft, which contain an apologia that is also a first justification of Browning's practice of organizing a poem around a nucleus of reality without surrendering the rights of the poetic imagination. These correspond, in some detail, with the ideas about poetry Browning encountered while he was a member of Fox's circle. As a boy, Sordello promises himself that one day his deeds will rival those of "grown-up men and women." The inconspicuous phrase attracts no attention here, or in other places where Browning reverted to it from time to time, but the fact that it ultimately became the title of his best book of verse suggests that the earlier uses of it quietly signal his idea of the right subject for poetry. After passing through a phase of egotistic lyricism, Sordello tries to establish rapport with his audience by pleasing them, but realizes that he has the more serious responsibility of leading them in words as others do in deeds. This was one of Fox's principles. He had said, in a *Monthly Repository* book review of 1832, that "poetry is no longer a plaything, or a mere drawing-room ornament," but a "weapon of strife" in the social conflict.[15]

Sordello finds that if he is to use poetry in this way, he must speak to the people in concrete terms, must "include a world in flesh" that he now grasps only in spirit. "The highest order of poetical association," Fox had written, "must, after all, be sought in natural objects and human emotions." The common people, Sor-

dello sees, are too benighted to respond to the ideal of a new
Rome, but their capacities can be built up gradually. He realizes
that he must use the collective experience of the past by teaching
the people to recognize their feelings in those of historical fig-
ures, and by speaking to them in terms drawn from this common
ground. "The effect of allusion in poetry," Fox had written, "is like
that of a combination of mechanical powers. It invests one man
with the strength of many." Universal ideas are not deflated if they
are embodied in mundane details; in fact, a particular setting is es-
sential. "The life and soul of poetry are always the same; but to
make them visible and tangible, they must become incarnate in
various forms, which forms bear the peculiar features of age, class
or country."[16]

Ideas of this kind are the basis of the poetic program Sordello
puts before Salinguerra, as he says that he intends to create a new
poetic idiom based on a knowledge of the past.

> *To-day*
> *Takes in account the work of Yesterday:*
> *Has not the world a Past now, its adept*
> *Consults. . .?*
> . . . .
> *My art intends*
> *New structure from the ancient. . . .*

The poet must prepare his public by introducing it to historical fig-
ures of the kind Browning himself had encountered in his reading,
and dramatizing their moral and emotional experiences. Once a
community of knowledge has been established in this way, readers
will be ready for poetry that operates by referring to it, so that

> *a single touch more may enhance,*
> *A touch less turn to insignificance*
> *Those structures' symmetry the past has strewed*
> *The world with, once so bare. Leave the mere rude*
> *Explicit details! 'tis but brother's speech*
> *We need. . . .*

When the poet does this, as Browning asserted in an impertinent
riposte to his critics which was inserted into the later editions of the
poem, "he writes *Sordello!*"

The history embodied in *Sordello* is therefore intended to be a referential field for a poetic of suggestion and allusion. Much of the poem is devoted to filling in this background in vivid, rapid narrative verse, so that it may serve both as a subject and a communicative medium between poet and reader. For example, a long passage in Book I formulates the conflict between Emperor and Pope in the image of a cliff threatened by a growth of seaweed. But once facts have been established in this way, Browning may revert to the second, allusive idiom described by Sordello, one that "Takes in account the work of Yesterday," and compels the reader to draw upon his knowledge of the time and its people:

> *our lingering Taurello quits*
> *Mantua at last, and light our lady flits*
> *Back to her place disburthened of a care.*
> *Strange—to be constant here if he is there!*
> *Is it distrust? Oh, never! for they both*
> *Goad Ecelin alike—Romano's growth*
> *So daily manifest that Azzo's dumb*
> *And Richard wavers . . . let but Friedrich come!*
> *—Find matter for the minstrelsy's report*
> *Lured from the Isle and its young Kaiser's court. . . .*

In such passages, historical information is employed rather than reported. Through a transformation more easily recognized by us than by Browning's contemporaries, things that were once signified become signifiers themselves; Italian history, once a message, becomes a medium. This language is able to deal with the "veritable business of mankind" by observing historical figures as they

> *disengage*
> *Their forms, love, hate, hope, fear, peace make, war wage*
> *In presence of you all!*

But it obviously fails to communicate unless the reader assimilates a body of facts that lie outside the normal range of what Browning called "the aggregate human mind." The trouble was that the research Browning undertook to achieve control of the historical background gained its own momentum. He found the materials attractive. The poet of "Porphyria's Lover" always turns a steady, perceptive gaze on violence. He puts the atrocities of the

siege of Ferrara and the cruelties of Guido in *The Ring and the Book*
before us because they offer penetrating insights into the potential-
ities of human nature. The Italian chronicles and histories he read
recorded passions and conflicts more intense than any Browning
had encountered earlier. Azzo d'Este and Riccardo di San Bonifazio
were carrying on a war that had been waged by their fathers before
them. A girl who was supposed to have been married to Salinguer-
ra to promote an alliance of the families was kidnapped. A period
of fighting followed in which power changed hands ten times, and
one side burned the houses of the other to the ground. Trickery
and deception appeared everywhere, often involving women who
were abducted and forcibly married. Salinguerra's entrapment of
Riccardo was an exact repetition of a trick he had played two years
before. Riccardo's ally, Azzo d'Este, had gone to parley with Salin-
guerra and had been taken prisoner; incredibly, Riccardo fell into
the same trap. The display of human nature which he found in his
sources must have fascinated Browning, for he worked much of it
into his poem in the colorful, but largely unintelligible accumula-
tion of detail that is one of the most taxing features of Sordello.[17]

Many of these enigmatic details can be brought to life by refer-
ring to Browning's historical sources. In Book III Sordello, telling
Palma that the soldiery of Verona are moving on Ferrara, says they
are "armed to march / with Tiso Sampier," a person not otherwise
identified. Browning had read, in Rolandino's *De Factis in Marchia
Tarvisina*, the story of a young Guelf noble, Tisolino di Camposan-
pietro, who had been surrounded during the fighting at Ferrara
two years before the action of *Sordello*, but had refused to surrender
to any but a man "de sanguine Militari." Since no one of proper
rank appeared, he fought to the death. His enemy, Salinguerra,
was so impressed by this display of courage, that he gave him an
honorable funeral (though Browning thought Salinguerra had
killed him). Hence, Sordello is saying that the departing soldiers
are motivated by a heroic example.

Similarly, in Book IV, a horrible story is told as a warning that the
wells of besieged Ferrara have been contaminated with dead bod-
ies. A soldier named Cino sits on the edge of a well, humming and
stamping his feet harder and harder until one kick brings up his
own mother's head, "caught by the thick / Grey hair about his
spur!" Browning seems to have invented this incident, but not the
words that Cino hums, "Za, za, Cavaler Ecelin." Rolandino reports

that the forces of Ezzelino da Romano cried out "Ad arma, ad arma, za, za cavaler Ecelin" as they attacked. (At least one editor of Muratori considered "za, za" unfamiliar enough to footnote it as meaning "ecco.") The irony of the incident is immensely reinforced by the presence of the swaggering battle cry.

In explaining that the hero of his poem cannot go astray because he lives at the beginning of a new age, Browning introduces some facts about art history, making his first use of Vasari:

> Born just now,
> With the new century, beside the glow
> And efflorescence out of barbarism;
> Witness a Greek or two from the abysm
> That stray through Florence-town with studious air,
> Calming the chisel of that Pisan pair . . .
> If Nicolo should carve a Christus yet!
> While at Siena is Guidone set,
> Forehead on hand. . . .

Browning had not yet seen the work of the artists mentioned here, Nicola and Giovanni Pisano and Guido da Siena. He had learned from Vasari that Nicola had met some Greek sculptors in Pisa (rather than Browning's Florence), and that he and his son freed both sculpture and architecture from "the clumsy and ill-proportioned Byzantine style." Nicola was an excellent example of Browning's "efflorescence," because he learned naturalism from the bas-reliefs on Roman sarcophagi, thus anticipating the reversion to antiquity characteristic of the Renaissance. In exclaiming "If Nicolo should carve a Christus yet!" Browning is using hindsight gained from Vasari to allude to the foreshadowing of Renaissance humanism seen in Pisano's treatment of religious subjects.

Browning's method of immersing himself in the historical records and then allowing his imagination full play raises the question, which has a general relevance to his use of all Italian materials, of whether the poem has any relation at all to the reality on which it claims to be based. As a record of facts, *Sordello* is grossly inaccurate. The historical Sordello did not play any role in the war, though he was probably at Riccardo's court in Verona while it was going on. He did not die in Ferrara in 1224, but lived to abduct Cunizza two years later, and to receive some castles in the Abruzzi in return for services rendered to Charles of Anjou in 1268, forty-

Nicola Pisano, *Crucifixion*, Detail of the Pulpit, Baptistry, Pisa (Archivi Alinari)

"If Nicolo should carve a Christus yet!"

four years later. Cunizza was not Riccardo's intended in 1224, but had been married to him for two years. No historian suggests that Sordello was the son of Taurello Salinguerra, and there is no evidence that they knew each other. Most important of all, the interplay of ideas that arises from his spiritual perplexities and political awakening is entirely anachronistic, and can be meaningful only in a nineteenth-century context.

On a critical level, *Sordello* is vulnerable to the objections Gyorgy Lukács has made to the "historical novel of democratic humanism," which expresses a desire for some affiliation with the common people, but fails to take common life as the basis of history, relying instead on surface realism or subjective invention.[18] Browning is guilty of the error that Lukács calls "modernization," the idea that past and present are not radically different, and that the past can be effectively evaluated according to modern standards. Lukács observes that the "subjectivism" of Nietzsche's superman theory and the "modernization" of Croce's view of history would, if put into verse, produce a mythic, exotic, and thoroughly ephemeral view of the past.

The relevance of these comments to *Sordello* means, not that Browning had lost touch with his materials, but that he saw them within the framework of contemporary ideas about history. If allowances for his Victorian perspective are made, *Sordello* can be seen as an accurate reflection of some aspects of the medieval spirit, just as his Italian poems in general project a striking authenticity in spite of the coloration his attitudes impose upon his materials. He was not entirely wrong to make political liberty one of the issues in the wars that raged in northern Italy. The cities of the Lombard League and Tuscany had developed a republican form of government which enabled them to resist the power of the Holy Roman Emperors. The Verona council, called "the Twenty-Four," that appears in *Sordello* was typical of the committees they elected to govern themselves; these were so open to dissension that the government apparatus required the added services of a *podestà*, a foreigner appointed for a limited term as supreme magistrate, to be workable. This form of government hardly satisfied the standards of Victorian liberalism, but it did preserve individual freedom.

Lukács is critical of the "great men" theory of history whose influence in the nineteenth century is illustrated by Burckhardt and Renaissance historians in general, and which *Sordello*, with its emphasis on heroes and leaders, unconsciously follows. However, this emphasis is not entirely unjustified. By the period of the poem, the republican systems had begun to give way to the dominance of powerful nobles. The period was ideal for demonstrating the view expressed in Carlyle's *Heroes and Hero-Worship,* that the course of history is determined by the energies of Great Men, and Browning is right to describe the wars as contests between powerful figures.

His hero thinks of himself as a great man, a trait that is acceptable as a medieval one; but his notion that this implies the responsibility of leadership and service to the people is Victorian. The two alternatives for action he considers—that of the troubadour, and that of the military leader—are historically authentic, and Browning is realistic in allowing him to reject idealism in favor of fleshly pleasures in his final soliloquy. Sordello, we see, has at last begun to think like a man of his time, too late to redeem himself as an authentic figure of the Middle Ages.

Salinguerra, on the other hand, is quite successful, both as a representative of a time dominated by powerful men, and as a living and complex character. He is a warrior who fights for passion and self-interest, not for principle, and his main passion is hatred. Unlike Sordello, he is a man of action, has a pragmatic outlook, and knows people. When power is offered to him, he is wise enough to know that his acceptance of it will only serve someone else's purpose. One of his resources, Browning tells us, is a cynical indifference which enables him to maintain his self-possession. He is—not surprisingly—unmoved by Sordello's impassioned harangue on the political importance of poetry, and calmly hears Palma's story about the survival of his wife and child at Vicenza. But his later reactions, when he sketches wild dreams of conquest through an alliance with Palma and Sordello, are marked by hysteria, as if a long-suppressed lust for power were being released. Salinguerra, like all of Browning's characters, is primarily an imagined creation, but in this case the imagination is faithful to the conception of the thirteenth century Browning drew from his sources.

If Sordello's view of the function of poetry is Victorian, his ideas about poetic language can, with some accuracy, be associated with medieval Italy. There is evidence to suggest that the poem as a whole is meant to emulate the *Divine Comedy.* Near its beginning, Browning says that he intends to make the moral qualities of his characters especially plain. This principle reappears in Book V when Sordello says that one stage of his poetic must present "Life's elemental masque," which is conceived as a vivid display of good and evil in Dante's mode. He must, says Sordello,

> *Apprehend*
> *Which sinner is, which saint, if I allot*
> *Hell, Purgatory, Heaven, a blaze or blot.*
> *To those you doubt concerning! I enwomb*
> *Some wretched Friedrich with his red-hot tomb;*
> *Some dubious spirit, Lombard Agilulph*
> *With the black chastening river I engulf!*
> *Some unapproached Matilda I enshrine*
> *With languors of the planet of decline. . . .*

He will, in short, take the *Divine Comedy* as his model in depicting character.

The aim of writing allusive poetry accessible to a broad public—"brother's speech" as Browning's Sordello calls it—is much more suitably identified with Dante than with Sordello. The "troubadour" poetry of Provence was the popular poetry of Italy in the time of Frederick II, but Sordello was not one of those who took the revolutionary step, as some of his contemporaries did, of writing in Italian. Dante, on the other hand, was the first powerful advocate of the use of the vernacular for serious poetry. Italian had been used for lyric poetry for nearly a century, but Dante set out to make it a medium suitable for noble themes. In *De Vulgari Eloquentia* he analyzes the poetic capacities of Italian, evaluates the various dialects (dignifying the subject by writing in Latin), and proposes to seek a language based on standards common to all of Italy, naming Sordello as a forerunner in this effort.

The language of the *Divine Comedy* is simple, direct, vigorous and sometimes even colloquial, an idiom close to common life and based on actual speech, yet capable of expressing exalted feelings and complex ideas. Dante defined his poem as a comedy in his letter to Can Grande precisely because, being in the vernacular, it is written in a modest and unpretentious style. The *Divine Comedy* (and perhaps Dante's speculations about language, which Cerutti may have called to his attention) might well have encouraged Browning to undertake the systematic deviations from linguistic conventions that characterize *Sordello*. He could not have meant to emulate Dante's style directly, for his strained and distorted word order, and the nervous movement of his verse create an impression totally unlike that of Dante's smooth and natural language.

Nevertheless, Dante is an important presence in *Sordello*, both as an influence on Browning's ideas about poetry and as a source of characters and images. The poem had its origin in the Sordello passage of the *Purgatorio*, and returns to Dante near its end when it observes that Dante succeeded where Sordello failed by taking "that step Sordello spurned." Perhaps a Dantean contempt can be heard here, and in the passage where the hero, arguing that his impotence is preferable to war, says, "I have done nothing, but both sides do worse / Than nothing." This is an echo of the reason Dante's Virgil gives for his exclusion from Heaven, "Non per far, ma per non far" (*Purgatorio*, VII, 25); the parallel has the effect of exposing Sordello's moral bankruptcy. Years after he had completed *Sordello*, Browning found in Dante a good summation of his character's fate. He translated the passage for Elizabeth, at a pinch, in this way:

> And sinners were we to the extreme hour;
> Then, *light from heaven fell, making us aware,*
> So that, *repenting us and pardoned, out*
> Of life we passed to God, at peace with Him
> Who fills the heart with yearning Him to see.[19]

Pippa Passes

In *Sordello*, Browning tells what the poet ought to do: "Behoved him think of men, and take their wants . . . As his own want which might be satisfied. . . ." He first began to follow this principle in writing *Pippa Passes* in 1839, when he had come back from Italy, turning from the Romantic conception of poetry as an exposition of the poet's soul to the dramatic presentation of "men and women," the mode he was to employ in the central body of his work. This change is inescapably connected with his visit to the village of Asolo, the setting of *Pippa Passes*.

He went to Asolo because it had been one of the places conquered by Ezzelino da Romano, and stood at the edge of the region he had controlled, in the *colli Asolani* that interrupt the plain stretching northward from Venice. After walking the ten miles from Bassano, Browning spent three days there, from June 19 to June 21; Asolo unexpectedly became the most vital memory of his tour, eclipsing even Venice. And, like Venice, it forced its way into *Sordello*, in the description of the boy singing on the hillside at the end of the poem.

Browning recalled Asolo, in his old age, as "the *first* spot of Italy I ever set my foot in, properly speaking," though he came to it after Trieste, Venice, and Bassano, and spent only three days there, not the week he spoke of.[20] The place impressed him powerfully. In another late recollection, the Prologue to *Asolando*, he wrote

> *my Asolo,*
> . . . .
> *I found you, loved yet feared you so—*
> *For natural objects seemed to stand*
> *Palpably fire-clothed!*

Asolo, like Venice, had its poor, its history, its politics, its art, and a troubled and contentious humanity, but all on a small and accessible scale. Most important, perhaps, it was free of the intervention of other minds. No one had written about Asolo since Cardinal Bembo in the fifteenth century. It was not familiar to English tourists, and was mentioned, but not described, in the *Murray's Guides* of the time. Browning did not think of Asolo as poetic material while he was on the spot. The idea of *Pippa Passes* came to him when he was back in England, and then, as he said in a sentence that applies to much of his best poetry, "I made use of Italian memories."[21]

In *Pippa Passes* Browning accomplishes what he was unable to do in *Sordello:* he identifies with the common people of Italy, and fashions their lives and feelings into poetry. He was one of the few English visitors of his time who saw more than a component of Italy's picturesqueness in the poverty that was visible everywhere. He realized that, as George Stillman Hillard put it, the most important features of a countryside "are those growing out of the relation of humanity to the soil on which we gaze," and that it is wrong "to overlook all these relations, to surrender ourselves, without question or protest, to the magic of lovely scenery, in spite of the shadow of human suffering which may rest upon it. . . ."[22] Browning, who disliked Hillard's book, nevertheless agreed with him fully on this point, as *Pippa Passes* shows. He attentively observed the suffering and injustice he saw about him, and channeled his feelings into the objective presentation of people and their concerns which now became the style of his dramatic poems. In *Pippa Passes*, the people rise vividly before the reader to speak for themselves, while the author seems absent.

Pippa fits into several of Browning's imaginative patterns. As an innocent who is capable of curing evils she knows nothing about, she resembles the boy at the end of *Sordello* and the figure of David in "Saul." She also illustrates his favorite figure of the victimized young girl, like Phene, and the Asolo girls who sit gossiping on the steps. But she is more than a type, and it is not hard to believe that she is based on some original Browning may have seen among the factory girls in Asolo. Pippa's poverty, her cheerfulness, her envy of the town's great people, and her practice of singing in the streets, are all perfectly plausible as traits Browning might have observed.

More doubtful is the story of her past. Is it possible that in the nineteenth century, even in a small town, a man would order his niece to be killed in order to gain possession of her property, and that the villain charged with the task would keep the girl alive as a blackmail threat? That there would be a plan afoot to have her seduced by a visiting Englishman, and sent off as a prostitute to Rome, where she would be sure to die in a short time? Browning was no doubt guilty of exploiting sensational traditions about Italian treachery and violence. But many of the elements of the play, such as rapacious landowners and bishops, the corruption of young women, and the stews of Rome, did exist in an impoverished Italy oppressed by foreign rule, and were legitimate subjects for social criticism.

The play's finest expression of social consciousness is the short scene of the "poor girls" on the steps. Their conversation reveals that they are not only poor, but prostitutes, and Browning deserves recognition for ignoring Victorian moral taboos here and elsewhere in *Pippa Passes* by confronting the theme of sexual exploitation. But the main value of the scene is its revelation of injustice through an informed, particularized realism that reflects sympathetic and attentive observation. Women who would ordinarily be dismissed as mere degraded objects are seen as people with familiar feelings and even virtues, and the injustices they have suffered are illuminated through brief allusions to episodes of their daily lives. The setting is established through a handful of brilliant details, such as the good dinner with which a girl is rewarded by her lover, and the wasps eating paper hung to keep off the birds. The scene is objective, and, on the surface, non-committal, but it clearly originated in feelings that came to Browning at his meeting with the beggar girl in Venice.

Browning's contemporaries tended to take the moral squalor of Asolo as a background setting off Pippa's piety and optimism, and regarded her song, "God's in his heaven, / All's right with the world," as an expression of the play's theme. Modern readers, on the other hand, are likely to feel that Browning's merciless penetration into the daily life of an apparently innocent town is the real subject, and that Pippa's optimism is brutally (if sympathetically) undercut by what is going on around her in "The cheerful town, warm, close / And safe. . . ."

The characters and actions are so intimately entwined with the physical setting of *Pippa Passes* that the town and its inhabitants form a single fabric. In *Sordello,* as we have seen, Browning played fast and loose with historical facts. In *Pippa Passes,* on the other hand, he records even small details about Asolo with startling accuracy. Written a year after he had left Italy, in the seclusion of his writing room in South London, the play shows that his three day visit to Asolo and its neighborhood remained extraordinarily clear in his memory. He could not have expected this accuracy to impress his readers. Rather, Asolo, in all its glowing detail, was itself the substance of his conception, and emerged lucidly in the finished poem.

The social structure of Asolo is the structure of *Pippa Passes.* The variety of people Browning saw—or learned about—provided him with the device of the social cross section. And the layout of the town gave him a pattern for linking the different scenes together as Pippa moves about.

When I visited Asolo, I was able to identify most of the scenes mentioned in the play, even though the town has changed a great deal, and to follow Pippa's movements, though some of them did not seem very plausible. Lucca Gaddi's villa, with its separate shrub house, must have been one of the large houses that lie along the road she took to town, commanding a view of the Trevisan plain, where Padua and Vicenza lie. Soon after passing this, Pippa comes to the town itself, and turns into its main street, now called Via Roberto Browning, which leads to the central market square; she goes diagonally across it to the Via Canova, which takes her to the road leading out of the town to the Orgagna valley on the north (called Orcana by Browning), and Possagno beyond it. Possagno is six miles from Asolo, but Browning treats it as an integral part of his scene, and sends Pippa to the house of Jules in or near it, so that she is able to sing her song outside his window at noon. Her return to Asolo is circuitous, for the "Turret" where she is heard by Luigi and his mother in the evening is an old fortress set high on a hill over the town. She descends from it by a long flight of broad, shallow steps paved solid with pebble that takes her back to the market square. She crosses the square again, this time leaving it by way of a flight of steps that leads down to a small open area in front of Asolo's Cathedral, where she encounters the group of gossiping girls.

This spot, the present Piazzetta Santo Pio X, became charged with imaginative possibilities for Browning. He was as responsive to specific scenes as Byron's Manfred, who lingered in the Coliseum, opening his imagination to thoughts of the past and the beauty of the present until "the place / Became religion." This sensitivity to locale appears again in Browning's use of the Piazza Santissima Annunziata in Florence in "Andrea del Sarto" and "The Statue and the Bust," and the Piazza San Lorenzo and the main street of Arezzo in *The Ring and the Book*. The Asolo piazzetta became a kind of stage setting which enabled him to visualize his characters and their actions, and is, in reality, the imaginative center of *Pippa Passes*.

It consists of a small rectangular area lying partly in front of the Cathedral, together with a short, narrow street leading along the Cathedral's south wall. At its northwest corner is a side wall of the palazzo—the present Palazzo Municipale—in one of whose rooms Browning's Bishop and his Intendant have their meeting. Opposite is the Cathedral, and between them is a flight of steps that goes up to the town's main square. These are the steps of Part III, Scene 2, where the "poor girls" in the play sit talking.[23] On the southeast corner is the "bishop's brother's house," Pippa's last destination for the day.

In the narrow street between this house and the south wall of the church is one of the details Browning used in his play. In the first scene of Part I, the troubled Ottima sees "Benet the Capuchin" passing the house, feels haunted by him, and recalls:

> *always in one place at church,*
> *Close under the stone wall by the south entry,*
> *I used to take him for a brown cold piece*
> *Of the wall's self, as out of it he rose*
> *To let me pass—at first, I say, I used:*
> *Now, so has that dumb figure fastened on me,*
> *I rather should account the plastered wall*
> *A piece of him, so chilly does it strike.*

At the specified spot, near a finely carved small porch that ornaments the south door of the church, a long bench is built against the wall. The wall itself is brick; it has no doubt been stripped of the plaster that still covers the rest of the church. There is nothing notable about this bench, but because it was in the piazzetta that had taken firm root in Browning's memory, he used it to envision Ottima's disturbing encounter with the Capuchin.

Pippa Passes shows that art and artists were a conspicuous part of Browning's first visit to Italy. He had obviously encountered art students of the kind he shows harassing Jules in his play, and was apparently impressed by the high-spirited frivolity of these groups, which were quite different from anything else in Italy, although they were a part of the general scene. Jules, who is French, and evidently joined the predominantly German group shown in the play in Munich, has a solemn temperament and becomes the group's butt. Sebald, who is lodging in Lucca Gaddi's house, is another student of the same kind.

The students have come up for the day from Venice, not to Asolo, but to Possagno, six miles to the north, the birthplace of Antonio Canova, the sculptor whose sentimental classicism was universally admired in the first part of the nineteenth century. The gallery the play refers to, the Gipsoteca Canoviana, was being established in Possagno at just this time. Browning undoubtedly saw it, and revisited it in later years. It contained a large collection of models, plaster casts, and sketches by Canova, and was an excellent place to study his work.

Of the two pieces by Canova mentioned by Browning's art students, the *Pietà* is a rather original female figure with drapery thrown over her head and falling in vertical folds along her body.

There is no Christ with her, perhaps because the piece is, as the students say, unfinished. The other, the *Psiche-fanciulla*, a graceful and sensuous figure of a young girl draped from the hips with one leg idling, holding a butterfly in one hand and shading it with the other, was widely celebrated as a masterpiece. Hence, Jules's display of condescension toward it may have helped to earn him the resentment of the other students. But he probably also reflects the opinion of Browning, who wrote that he had been disappointed in Canova during his tour.[24]

Realizing that he will never see the girl he loves again, Luigi says, "We were to see together / The Titian at Treviso." There are two Titians in Treviso, but Luigi can hardly mean the portrait of Speroni, the Renaissance humanist, that hangs in the museum. He must refer to the fresco of the Annunciation in the Duomo. Browning could have seen this work when he was in Treviso on Sunday, June 17, 1838, en route from Mestre to Bassano. It shows the angel facing the Virgin across a checkered floor; behind him are the vigorous clouds and sunrays from which he has descended. A wall ornamented with pilasters displays the perspective and leads the eye toward a mysterious old woman who is sitting or crouching on the floor. It is an eventful picture, full of attractive colors and exciting forms, both natural and geometric. Browning uses it as an emblem of the joys of life that Luigi is giving up, and a measure of his sacrifice.

With *Pippa Passes* references to art and artists began to form a sublanguage, based mainly on the Italian context, that eventually became a feature of Browning's style. *Pippa Passes* also broaches a Browning image that owes much to his Italian experiences: the use of art as a metaphor for life as a whole. The problems Jules discusses have the resonance of moral issues that confront mankind in general, so that he foreshadows such figures as Andrea Del Sarto and Fra Lippo. When Pippa's song about Catherine of Cornaro recalls him from his decision to kill the students who have been persecuting him, and reminds him that he can create rather than destroy, he sees that

> *there is clay*
> *Everywhere. One may do whate'er one likes*
> *In Art, the only thing is, to make sure*
> *That one does like it—which takes pains to*
> *know.*

And we later learn that he has in fact acquired this self-knowledge, when the Bishop reads his letter announcing that he is turning from sculpture to painting in order to escape traditional influences.

Pippa Passes is Browning's first treatment of Italian political themes, and the first expression of his sympathy with the Risorgimento. Luigi, the would-be assassin, is presented as a naive and selfless young man blinded by his passion to free his country from the Austro-Hungarian domination imposed on it by the Treaty of Vienna in 1815. He places himself politically by using the name of a Roman revolutionary to test the echo in the turret where he meets with his mother, and by mentioning contemporary libertarians. The one to whom his mother refers, Silvio Pellico, was a popular poet who had been arrested and imprisoned in 1820, and the author of a well-known book about his prison experiences, *Le Mie Prigione* (1832). The policeman's plan for sending Luigi to Venice and then to Spielberg probably reflects Browning's reading of Pellico's book, which describes periods spent in the dreadful *Piombi*, the cells under the lead roof of the Ducal Palace in Venice, and at the fortress of Spielberg in Moravia.

The seizure of Luigi's passport by the police illustrates a practice no traveler in Italy could ignore. The suspicious foreign regime controlled all movements carefully. The need to present and validate traveling papers (usually with the accompaniment of a bribe) as travelers moved from one small jurisdiction to another was a major nuisance of the time. In 1845, Ruskin complained that he had been stopped eleven times on a journey between Bologna and Parma to show his papers or to make some payment.[25]

The "turret" where Luigi and his mother go for their secret conversation is one of Asolo's most prominent features. Called "La Rocca" locally, it is an irregularly oval enclosure, about forty yards long, consisting of a wall of fitted stone some thirty feet high, said to have been built on pre-Roman foundations. It stands on the highest point of Asolo's hill, overlooking the town and countryside. The interior is without interest, except for its relation to *Pippa Passes*. The magnificent view is cut off by the high wall; all that is visible is the sky overhead and the weedy, irregular stretch of ground inside the enclosure. Nevertheless, Browning went to see it on his first morning in Asolo, was strongly impressed by it, and recalled it vividly when he wrote *Pippa Passes*. The echo he discovered, the "ridge"—a rising, moundlike area—and the stonecrop growing in the wall are used for significant touches in his scene.

One of the few things known about La Rocca is that the "archway" Luigi mentions was rebuilt in the Gothic style by Ezzelino da Romano, the background figure of *Sordello*, who ruled Asolo for a time.

With Pippa's song about Catherine of Cornaro we come to another aspect of Asolo that deeply interested Browning. The lines spoken by Jules following Pippa's song in Scene 1 of Part II strongly suggest that Browning had heard an actual song about Catherine and a page who languished for her love, a relic of the period between 1489 and 1509 when Catherine actually lived and held court in Asolo. The remains of the castle she lived in and its garden are still in use. They consist of a main section and two outlying towers. But the most interesting parts of the site, historically, are the gardens on the hillside just below, for they are the setting of *Gli Asolani* (1505) by Cardinal Bembo, a series of imaginary discourses and entertainments that reflect the life at Catherine's court.

As Jules's remarks show, Catherine was a figure who is easily romanticized. The daughter of a prominent Venetian family, she was married at the age of eighteen to the king of Cyprus. Widowed after a year, she maintained an uncertain dominance over her kingdom for fifteen years, but was then forced to abdicate as Cyprus fell into the hands of Venice. She settled in Asolo, where she established a lively court. Here, according to Cardinal Bembo, the time was passed in music, singing, and dancing, and young people carried on discourses about love in the beautifully designed garden while the queen retired to her afternoon siesta. Browning of course read Cardinal Bembo, either before or after his visit to Asolo. He owned a portrait supposed to represent Catherine, and in later years bought some of the property attached to her palace.[26] The dramatic situation of the witty and compact song Pippa sings about her, in which the queen's maid tries to keep her from knowing that a lowly page is singing of his love for her, became the subject of a painting by Dante Gabriel Rossetti entitled *Kate the Queen*.[27]

The realities of Asolo, some historical, some actual, provided the bones of *Pippa Passes*, but many aspects of the play, such as the wonderful scene between Ottima and Sebald, cannot be accounted for externally, and must be regarded as Browning's inventions. And parts of it, such as the speeches of Pippa, Jules, and Luigi, do not seem to have profited from Browning's new sense of rapport with reality. In spite of this, it is clear that *Pippa Passes* opened a new phase in Browning's development: in it he mastered the art of presenting strikingly individualized characters against the background of their environment, an art he learned by observing the daily life of Italy.

THREE

The Second Italian Tour

Between his two Italian journeys, from July 1838 until August 1844, Browning lived with his parents in Surrey and worked hard to continue the career begun with the comparative success of *Strafford* and *Paracelsus*. Part of his time was spent in the seclusion of the writing room in the cottage at New Cross, Hatcham, to which the Brownings had moved in December 1840, and part of it in the colorful milieu of London's theaters, where he met writers and actors, and tried to enlarge his foothold as a playwright by submitting play after play to William Macready, the theatrical manager. His accomplishments and his resistance to discouragement during these years are equally impressive. *Sordello* was completed and received with bafflement and derision. *Pippa Passes* won considerable praise when it appeared in 1841 as the first in the sequence of pamphlets called *Bells and Pomegranates*, but his first short poems, including some which later became famous, were totally ignored. Of the four plays he wrote for the theater, two were produced; *Strafford* had five performances, and *A Blot in the 'Scutcheon* only one.

Browning's friend, Alfred Domett, emigrated to New Zealand in 1842, and in the letters he wrote to Domett, Browning, no doubt freed from restraint by the distance between them, opened his thoughts and feelings with exceptional candor. He said that he was trying to see, once and for all, whether he could expect to succeed as a writer; he considered that it was the public, not he, that was on trial; and he thought it was possible that he might ultimately fail, even after a long effort. Italy played a part in these thoughts. He wrote to Domett that he expected to wait ten or twelve years before doing "any real thing," and complained that he was out of touch with readers, that he did not know "what men require." England suffocated him. He felt that he could accomplish something only by "*going to New Zealand*—partial retirement and stopping the ears against the noise outside; but all is next to useless—for there is a creeping, magnetic, assimilating influence nothing can block out. When I block it out, I shall do something."[1] The phrase about New Zealand is metaphoric. Browning's New Zealand was Italy. This became clear in the summer of 1844 when, after a long period of intense work and persistent discouragement, he wrote to Domett that he needed a change, and would go to Italy.

Some of the pieces he wrote before he left show that his first visit had already had a profound influence on his choice of subjects and his manner of writing. "My Last Duchess," which is, astonishingly, either his first dramatic monologue or his second (after "Porphyria's Lover") exhibits the economy, control, and objectivity Browning developed during a period of careful self-discipline when, as he said, using the phrase that encoded his new subject, he caught himself "grudging my men and women their half-lines, like a parish overseer the bread-dole of his charge."[2] It leads directly to the question of the relation between his Italian experiences and the form which was to be his most characteristic vehicle. Browning believed that Italians, in spite of their sensitivity, lacked self-consciousness, and could not perceive their own qualities or interpret themselves as well as foreign observers could. The dramatic monologue, in its most developed form, reflects a situation of that kind, one in which the limited consciousness of the speaker is enveloped in the more inclusive one of the author (and reader).

During his life in Italy, Browning kept his distance, and did not surrender his opinions, his national characteristics as an Englishman, or his religious beliefs. At the same time, he was a sympathetic and affectionate observer who recognized the merits of certain attitudes he could not share and the aspects of universality in what he saw. This state of mind corresponds to the structure of his best dramatic monologues: an intricate interplay of sympathy and judgment (to use Robert Langbaum's terms) which culminates, not in a moral decision, but in an indefinite deferral that prevents the character and his problems from collapsing into the elements of a moral allegory.

Enfolded into the self-disclosing surface of the dramatic monologue is an awareness superior to that of the speaker, which is shared by the author who speaks through him and the reader whom he is addressing. This duality has its moments of unanimity, when the views and language of the speaker and the author coincide, but its main fabric is a closely bound compound of contradictory attitudes; the speaker's voice is accompanied by a silent commentary from the author or reader, who obviously—and often, not very obviously—must see things from a different point of view. The Duke of "My Last Duchess," who links art with murder and cruelty with connoisseurship, is the first of many similar characters in Browning's work, figures who command our admiration in some way, and whose strength, grandeur, taste, or intelligence would persuade us to see things as they do, if their general moral vision were not unacceptable. It is not hard to tell where Browning first experienced divided feelings of this kind. Many years later he wrote of Guido Franceschini, the villain of *The Ring and the Book:* "all *great* (conventionally great) Italians are coarse—showing their power in obliging you to accept their cynicism."[3] It would seem that the double consciousness of the dramatic monologue owes something to his experience of seeing Italy through English eyes.

Browning believed that a poem should supply everything needed for comprehension within itself, and "My Last Duchess" certainly meets this requirement. It swims superbly in its own melting. Nevertheless, certain of its implications are linked to its external relations, and to the fact that Browning intended it to be an expression of his consciousness of Italy. When it was first published in the third number of *Bells and Pomegranates*, it was titled simply "Italy," and was paired with "Count Gismond" under the heading "Italy and France." Its superscription, "Ferrara," identifies its Duke with Alfonso II of Ferrara, a sixteenth-century representative of the Este dynasty, whose thirteenth-century fortunes are treated in *Sordello.*[4] The marriage between Browning's Duke and his ill-fated young Duchess corresponds closely with that between Alfonso and Lucrezia, the daughter of Duke Cosimo de' Medici of Florence in 1558. Alfonso was exactly the sort of proud, cultured, jealous, and cold-hearted figure Browning depicts. The marriage was a political one, the bride being fourteen, the groom, who was heir to the Dukedom at the time, twenty-five. Alfonso left for France three days after the wedding, did not return to Ferrara until after his father's death the following year, and did not send for his bride until three months after that. She entered the city accompanied by a gorgeous procession; less than a year and half later she died, probably from natural causes. The allusion to the statue of Neptune by the fictional "Claus of Innsbruck" links Browning's Duke firmly with Alfonso, for Innsbruck was the home of Barbara of Austria, the prospective wife whose dowry he is negotiating, and the native town of the envoy he is talking to. The "nine-hundred-years-old name" of which the Duke boasts was, of course "Este."

Alfonso is remembered as the oppressor of the poet, Torquato Tasso, and "Ferrara" leads directly to the passage in *Childe Harold* where Byron gives his romanticized version of the relation between the Duke and the poet. After the apostrophe, "Ferrara!" it condemns "the antique brood / Of Este," "patron or tyrant," of whom it says, "Tasso is their glory and their shame," naming Alfonso, and subjecting him to two stanzas of savage invective. Tasso, in fact, may have been the point of departure of "My Last Duchess" in Browning's mind. The so-called "Essay on Chatterton," written for John Forster's *Foreign Quarterly Review* in 1842, was a review of a book on Tasso. The task of writing it may have taken Browning back to the family that had figured in *Sordello*, and to its sixteenth-century descendant.

The Romantics considered Tasso an archetype of the alienated, oppressed poet, and the version of his story that descended to Browning and his contemporaries through such treatments as Goethe's *Tasso* (1789) and Byron's "Lament of Tasso" and *Childe Harold* had it that he fell in love with Alfonso's sister, Leonora, and that the Duke retaliated by imprisoning him.[5] *Tasso Reading His Poem Before Alfonso, Duke of Ferrara* is the subject of a painting by Elia Honoré Montagny executed in 1815, which shows an arrogant-looking and well-dressed Duke listening to the poet in the company of his Duchess.[6] The cell in Ferrara called "Tasso's dungeon" was a favorite sight for visitors. Byron saw it and called upon his readers to "see . . . where Alfonso bade his poet dwell"; Shelley saw it and sent Peacock a piece of wood from the door; he also searched out some of Tasso's manuscripts in a library and noted their flattering allusions to Alfonso. Browning's illogical reply to the question of what the Duke meant by "I gave commands" to the effect that he might have had the Duchess "shut up in a convent" may show that the connection with the imprisoned Tasso was at the bottom of the poet's mind. Even if "Ferrara" did not identify Browning's Duke for his readers, its associations with Tasso would have prepared them for his portrait of a man who combined cruelty with a taste for art, and whose pride would consist in stripping others of their idealism.

As DeVane says, "Soliloquy in a Spanish Cloister," which was published in *Bells and Pomegranates* in 1842, was probably a result of Browning's first Italian trip. There is something to be said for the argument that "Spain" in this poem, in "The Confessional" of 1845, and in "How it Strikes a Contemporary" of 1855 is a surrogate for Italy. Browning knew nothing of Spain, and the specific conditions and general atmosphere in all three are perfectly appropriate to Italy. The "Soliloquy" owes much of its vitality to details that Browning could only have seen in Italy. It corresponds with his other Italian poems in a number of ways. Most significant is its mastery of the processes of a commonplace, if energetic, mind, the sort of consciousness Browning learned to interest himself in when he visited Italy and wrote *Pippa Passes*. But it is also critical of a phenomenon Browning thought he often saw in Italian Catholicism—the effect of perverted or excessive religious zeal. The monk's plan to revenge himself on his hated rival by religious means recalls the Italian myths of the Elizabethan dramatists and the Gothic novelists, but Browning's Protestant sensibility expresses itself through an uproarious humor that is almost affectionate, rather than through horror.

Browning's second visit to Italy, which took place between August and late December 1844, was more conventional than his first. He traveled for pleasure, not in search of information, and went to the usual places tourists visited, not the out-of-the-way regions he had penetrated in 1838. Betty Miller suggests that he was following Shelley's path, and the trip may have been a literary pilgrimage of the kind that was common in the post-Romantic years. The cities he visited, Naples, Rome, Pisa, Leghorn, and Florence, were places where Shelley had lived, and he spoke with Edward Trelawny, who had been present at Shelley's funeral and left a famous account of it. While he was in Rome, he went to the Protestant cemetery, where the graves of Keats and Shelley were to be seen, and where people Browning himself knew were later to be buried. He visited the fountain of Egeria, the subject of a passage in *Childe Harold*, where he gathered fennel seeds that turned out, when he planted them in his garden in London, to be hemlock. He also saw St. Praxed's Church, an obscure place that could hardly have been the goal of a deliberate pilgrimage, but suggested one of his greatest poems.

Pisa, his next stop, had even more associations with Shelley and Byron than Rome. Browning went to nearby Leghorn to talk with Edward Trelawny, hoping, no doubt, to hear some reminiscences of the Romantic poets, but the conversation seems to have been confined to Trelawny's difficulties in having an old bullet removed from his leg. Pisa was to mean much to Browning in a short time, for it was his first home with Elizabeth. Their permanent home was to be in Florence, and it is odd to think of Browning visiting it for the first time, unconscious of the part it was to play in his future life. He may have thought of Shelley, who had lived in Florence for four months. During the time Shelley lived there his son, Percy, was born, and he took a memorable walk in the Cascine before going home to write "Ode to the West Wind."

By December Browning was back in London, thinking, as he later wrote to Elizabeth, of making arrangements to return to Italy. The journey had done him good, after the years of frustration connected with his writing for the theater and the unheralded *Bells and Pomegranates*. About two months after his return he dined with Joseph Arnould and H.F. Chorley, and the former reported, in a letter to Domett, that Browning was in better health and spirits, that he was "full of Venice, Rome, Naples and enthusiasm," and had plans for "a successful poem."[7]

The 1844 tour generated a number of shorter poems that appeared in the seventh number of *Bells and Pomegranates*, some on political themes. Browning had seen signs of political espionage and oppression in Lombardy and Venetia, which were under direct Austrian control in 1838, but conditions in Naples were worse, especially at the time of his visit. After 1815 the Kingdom of the Two Sicilies had been restored to the Bourbons, who maintained their power by collaborating with the Austrians. There had been a revolt in 1820, and the south of Italy remained the most restive, oppressed, and backward part of the country. In the summer of 1844, just before Browning's trip, a new episode focused attention on conditions there.

In June 1844 a group of nineteen patriots led by Attilio and Emilio Bandiera, the sons of an admiral in the Austrian navy, landed in Calabria to carry on guerrilla warfare against the monarchy.

They were misled by spies and captured after being allowed to wander aimlessly about the countryside for a time. Seven of them, including their leaders, were shot on July 23. There was an intensely dramatic scene at the execution. The firing squad was in tears, and was unable or unwilling to fire accurately. After the first round of shots had missed, the condemned men called to them, "Courage, do your duty! We too are soldiers." At the second fusillade, they shouted, "Viva la libertà! Viva la Patria!" Reports of this event naturally created a sensation; the Bandiera brothers were enrolled in the list of Italian martyrs, and the patriotic sentiments aroused by their deaths went far to promote the cause of liberty. Browning might well have heard much about this episode when he arrived in Naples the following month. It forms the immediate background for "The Italian in England," his most vigorous treatment of Italian patriotism.

Not all Englishmen shared Browning's enthusiasm for Italian independence. During the Napoleonic wars the British, while taking an active part in fighting the French in Italy, naturally sympathized with the victims of French oppression, and advocated self-government in certain regions—notably Sicily. After 1815, however, when Austria was given direct control of the northern provinces and indirect control of the rest of the country, while the Papacy ruled the middle of the peninsula, the British government followed a policy of discretion. It acknowledged that Austria was despotic and repressive, and that it maintained its power through spies, imprisonment, and outright violence, but the British government could not encourage resistance movements that were prevailingly republican, and preferred not to disturb the European balance of political power. The British were satisfied to recommend that Austria adopt more moderate methods, and did not call for it to surrender its power.

English people themselves held very mixed attitudes. They might wish that Italy could be free, but they might also be skeptical about the capacity of the Italians to govern themselves. Pro-Italian sentiment was discouraged by the persistent failure of revolutionary uprisings, and by the lack of agreement among the revolutionaries. In H.F. Chorley's *Roccabella* (1859), a novel critical of Italian expatriates, a sturdy Englishman says that the Italians don't deserve better government because they are always quarreling among themselves; "the Italians," he declares, "make famous opera-singers;—but very rubbishy patriots, *I* think." Browning quotes Carlyle as avowing that the Italians deserved German rule because they were ignoring their opportunities for spiritual renewal and went on "verse-making, painting, music-scoring."[8]

Browning was never as ardent an advocate of Italian independence as Elizabeth was to become, and sometimes changed his mind about the practicality of actual measures, but he never felt any difficulty in accepting its principles. As a student and admirer of Cerutti, and an adherent of W.J. Fox's school of Benthamism, he of course favored political liberty. He also felt, through Carlyle, the influence of Mazzini.

Mazzini is commonly thought to be the speaker of "The Italian in England," and while the identification must remain a very loose one, the poem certainly reflects his sentiments, and he may well have served as the inspiration for it. Mazzini liked the poem, read a translation of it to his supporters, and sent it to his mother in Italy —in parts, to evade the censorship. It is likely that Browning heard a good deal about Mazzini from the Carlyles, and may also have seen something of him in London in the early forties. In 1845, Browning lent Elizabeth a copy of Mazzini's book about the Bandiera expedition, *Ricordi dei Fratelle Bandiera*. However, no meeting is recorded until Jane Carlyle took him to see the Brownings in London on July 17, 1852, and reported that they made "such a fuss" over him.[9]

Mazzini gained special prominence just before Browning's 1844 journey to Italy by the revelation that the British government was spying on his mail. The Bandiera brothers had written to him for advice about their expedition—he counseled delay—and Mazzini suggested that the British had caused their deaths by opening his correspondence with them and transmitting advance information about their plans to the Austrian authorities. He demonstrated that his mail was being opened by enclosing grains of sand in letters sent to himself, and dramatically showing, before witnesses, that they were missing when the letters arrived. The accusation precipitated a great controversy in the press and a noisy debate in Parliament, and resulted in the admission that Mazzini's charges were substantially true. The affair made Mazzini famous, and identified him, in the minds of readers, with Browning's "Italian in England."

The episode narrated in the poem, though fictional, was undoubtedly put together from anecdotes that could have been picked up for the asking anywhere in spy-ridden Italy. Browning may have located the action near Padua rather than Naples, where the idea of the poem probably occurred to him, because that enabled him to show Austrian soldiers hunting the refugee. He may well have witnessed a hunt of this kind in the north, with the troops combing the countryside and lighting signal fires at night. The speaker's emotional declamation is less effective as an expression of love for Italy than the little description of the peasants on their way to work in the fields, or the imagined scene of his talk with the peasant woman, though this is less particularized, and is spoiled by sentimentality. There is a convincing realism in the directions for transmitting a message through the confessional booth, and in the suggestion that the girl and her lover do not agree about politics.

The figure of "Charles," who has betrayed the cause, brings to mind "Giles" of "Childe Roland to the Dark Tower Came," suggesting that this far more significant poem may owe something to Browning's thoughts of Italian revolutionary bands. A long quest through hostile, enigmatic countryside, the death of comrades, suggestions of torture—nothing in Browning's knowledge approaches this fantasy more closely than the guerrilla warfare carried on by Italian patriots.

The more radical effects of Browning's Italian experiences are found in the inner form and substance of "The Italian in England." It is a dramatic monologue that depicts a character and spiritual situation of some complexity. As the revolutionary imagines the home and family the girl is probably enjoying, he seems to feel regret that he is denied these things. He himself has sacrificed love of woman for love of country, yet he might have learned, from the very episode he is describing, that the two are not incompatible with each other. As in Browning's later monologues, the speaker himself fails to grasp the meaning of what he is telling us. It was in Italy that Browning learned to attend to the thoughts of "men and women" in this way.

Although it is marked "Spain," "The Confessional" is based upon conspiratorial activities of the kind described in "The Italian in England," which Browning could have encountered only in Italy. The poem might well have been conceived as a companion piece to "The Italian in England," because it deals with a girl who unintentionally betrays a revolutionary instead of preserving him, and becomes a tortured prisoner rather than a happy wife and mother. The speaker has been urged by a priest to recount her lover's subversive activities during confession, so that the priest may pray for him; instead, he betrays the revolutionary and has him executed. The girl is thrown into prison, where her monologue is spoken. The poem brings forward the potential irony in the situation of the revolutionary who believes that his struggle against secular power is sanctioned by divine authority. The man was exposed because the girl, after spending a night of passionate love with him, felt penitent, and dutifully went to the priest to confess it. All of the elements of the poem are natural to Italy, where Browning might have observed them and he seems to have located them in Spain simply to pair the poem with "The Laboratory" as a couple that could be called "France and Spain."

Browning returned to the ironies of the revolutionary's career and to the link between liberty and religious sentiment in "The Patriot," a poem written some years later (apparently in 1849), while he was living in Florence, and after the Italian liberation movement had suffered some serious reversals. The speaker, who is walking to his execution with his wrists bound while the people of the town throw stones at him, recalls that they welcomed him joyfully a year ago when he came to liberate them, and bitterly calls this reversal "An Old Story." The situation moves him to turn to higher authority. The ingratitude of human beings gives him, in death, a claim upon God. "I am safer so," he reflects. In the original version of the poem, published in *Men and Women*, the scene was identified as Brescia, but Browning removed this name in order to prevent identification of the speaker with Arnold of Brescia, and to keep the poem from being related to a medieval rather than a contemporary setting.

Although their titles seem to connect them with each other, "The Italian in England" and "The Englishman in Italy" are unrelated, and it is misleading to regard them as a pairing. It is true that both have contemporary Italy as their subjects and begin as impromptu reflections, but they are entirely different in purpose and tone. "The Englishman in Italy" is primarily a description springing from a casual occasion; the speaker is trying to entertain a bored child. On this pretext, Browning puts together a series of remarkable vignettes that form a string, like the child's rosary beads, not a structure. He has wonderfully chosen a rainy day for this paean to the landscape of Italy. The sirocco has brought a storm; how to keep the child amused? We can easily believe that she is transfixed by these vivid descriptions of town and country scenes she knows well. They culminate in a picture of the sea and sky viewed from a rocky wind-swept height that is introduced with the line, "Oh heaven and the terrible crystal!" an allusion to the opening vision of the Book of Ezekiel that identifies the sky with the platform of God's throne. Before this presence, the beautiful landscape seems to cower, crouch, and bend beneath the mountains. A condemnation cruel in its casual dismissiveness is at hand. "All is silent and grave," says the speaker, "How fair! But a slave. / So I turned to the sea."

He now sees the Galli, the islands the ancients called the Sirenusae, where the Sirens are supposed to have sung to Ulysses, which lie off the peninsula of Sorrento, and asks Fortù whether they shall go there. His description shows that he knows them already. In fact, Browning drew a sketch of the largest of these islands in a letter to Elizabeth, saying, ". . . you have the green little Syrenusa where I have sate and heard the quails sing."[10] The speaker in his poem equates the birds with the singers who told Ulysses the secret of life, and playfully claims that he has heard it too—"I hear and I know." The sinister atmosphere of the mountain has been relieved by this description of the islands, but the two places share a sense of some impending disclosure.

The recital is interrupted when the sun comes out, and the speaker asks the child to come to the town to see the preparations for the next day's *festa*, all described with wonderful details. But she remains sulking and will not come. So he proposes that they go at least as far as the garden wall, where he will drive out an angry scorpion for her amusement.

The conclusion, in which the poet repels the potential accusation that the things he has been talking about are trivial by referring to the Corn Laws, is usually regarded as the main point of the poem.

Elizabeth thought it unified the whole—which otherwise does need a concluding note—but it is actually entirely out of keeping with it, an obvious offering to spurious relevance, and probably an afterthought added on impulse. The scorpion is the right place to end. It may seem an odd source of diversion, even as a desperate measure, but Browning once wrote to Elizabeth: "I always loved all those wild creatures God '*sets up for themselves*' so independently of us, so successfully, with their strange happy minute inch of candle, as it were, to light them; while we run about and against each other with our great cressets and fire-pots."[11] The speaker of the poem feels the same love for the scorpion and for the self-contained vitality of the village. He praises the capacity of both to sustain a limited, but independent way of life.

Mario Praz has asked, not without irony, who but Browning "has observed so much, nay discovered so much in the Neapolitan landscape."[12] He has these perceptions because he looks at Italy with English, perhaps with specifically Wordsworthian sensibilities. In the natural setting that enfolds the village, his speaker discovers intimations of terror and sublimity the villagers themselves do not feel. The human and the natural, the limited and the infinite, exist side by side, in the incongruity that often puzzled travelers in Italy, and the poem finds it possible to celebrate both.

"The Englishman in Italy" earned Browning the most encouraging praise he had yet heard. Walter Savage Landor, after reading it in *Bells and Pomegranates,* published the verses called "To Robert Browning" in the *Morning Chronicle* of November 22, 1845. Landor and Browning had met at the supper given after the first performance of the play *Ion* by Serjeant Talfourd in May 1836, and Landor had followed Browning's work and predicted great things for him in letters written to John Forster. Now the older poet expressed his admiration in a poem that was as superbly controlled as it was generous:

> *There is delight in singing, though none hear*
> *Beside the singer; and there is delight*
> *In praising, though the praiser sit alone*
> *And see the prais'd far off him, far above.*
> *Shakspeare is not our poet, but the world's,*
> *Therefore on him no speech; and short for thee,*
> *Browning! Since Chaucer was alive and hale,*
> *No man hath walk'd along our roads with step*

So active, so inquiring eye, or tongue
So varied in discourse. But warmer climes
Give brighter plumage, stronger wing; the breeze
Of Alpine heights thou playest with, borne on
Beyond Sorrento and Amalfi, where
The Siren waits thee, singing song for song.

The allusion to Italy is more than symbolic. Landor had lived in
Fiesole for ten years, had written *Imaginary Conversations* there, and
might well have understood that Italy opened to Browning Chau-
cerian powers that could not emerge in England. The poem is, of
course, irresistibly prophetic: it appeared at the time when Brown-
ing and Elizabeth had begun to think of Italy as a refuge; it was the
prelude to the long association between Browning and Landor—in
Italy; and it predicted that Italy would inspire Browning's best
work.

The most significant poem resulting from the 1844 journey was
"The Bishop Orders His Tomb at St. Praxed's Church." Its
authenticity—as distinguished from its accuracy—is due to Brown-
ing's general feeling for the historical period rather than to his
knowledge of the setting, for it could have been written by a poet
who had never been to Rome, and its connection with the actual
church of Santa Prassede is altogether dispensable. There is no real
evidence to show that Browning ever entered it, and it might well
have been an arbitrary choice.[13] A church was first built on the site
in 499, over the grave of St. Praxedes, a female saint supposed to
have been helpful to oppressed Christians during the reign of An-
toninus Pius.[14] The original church was destroyed in 822, then re-
built, and, after a long period of neglect, restored in the fifteenth
and sixteenth centuries.

It is not especially ornate, fails to correspond with the details in
the poem, and has some striking features that Browning does not
use. The most important are the ninth-century mosaics in the apse
showing God flanked by three saints, one of them being St.
Praxed, and the chapel of St. Zeno, which is colorfully decorated in
a style that the Renaissance Bishop would have found dreary and
"Gothic." The frescoes that cover large parts of the church walls
are imitations of marble in paint, *trompe-l'oeil* efforts to create a
three-dimensional effect at little expense by continuing the marble
pilasters and wainscoting; they would have offended the marble-

loving Bishop. Much of the ornamentation was added since his time, so that the church might have been even plainer then.

The tombs in the church are not remarkably elaborate. As Ian Jack has pointed out, the search for the original of the Bishop's tomb is bound to be futile; the Bishop knows that he is pleading in vain, and realizes that no tomb of the kind he describes will be built. William Lyon Phelps thought of looking for the original of *Gandolf's* tomb, and chose a possibility, a tomb against the south wall.[15] But, if we can assume that Browning actually knew the church, there is another tomb that might have suggested one of the details in the poem. The Bishop reviles Gandolf for seizing "the corner south"; the Latin inscription on the tomb in the southwest corner of Santa Prassede does not contain the famous "Elucescebat" (the probable source of this word is elsewhere), but has a word that may have suggested it: *fluctuatione,* "disturbances" or "waverings," which, like *elucescebat,* is an unusual, pretentious, relatively late form that might have caught Browning's eye and suggested that an equivalent be attributed to the tomb of Gandolf.[16]

The poem gives remarkable life to the love of physical sensation which the Victorians attributed to the Renaissance. The Bishop feels that there are no contradictions between paganism and Christianity, love of art and love of life, the appetite for beauty, wealth, manuscripts, and mistresses on the one hand, and the hope for salvation on the other, because he believes that the various states of man form a single whole. His spiritual naiveté is hard to accept, but it is explained by Burckhardt's engaging view that both the virtues and vices of the time originated in its imaginativeness. Gambling, vendettas, and adultery are, after all, imaginative projects; such crimes as banditry and assassination assert feelings of independence, self-sufficiency, and freedom from authority. Burckhardt admits that these were harmful, but claims that they were also symptoms of the development of individualism, and were necessary to the evolution of modern moral standards.

Ruskin praised "The Bishop Orders His Tomb" in the fourth volume of *Modern Painters* because it expressed imaginative sympathy with Renaissance esthetic feeling and portrayed the corruption of spirit to which the love of beauty had led. Unlike Shakespeare, who ignored mountains and said little about art, Browning understood the Italian love of building materials quarried in mountains—

stone and gems—in contrast to the English love of wood, especially oak. From this specific example of Browning's grasp of his material, Ruskin passes to the famous acknowledgement that the poem says as much about the "Central Renaissance" as he had been able to say in thirty pages of *The Stones of Venice*.[17]

A later critic has insisted, however, that the conception of the Renaissance to which Browning subscribed was an invention of the nineteenth century with little historical validity. Arnold Hauser, in the first volume of *The Social History of Art*, contends that such ideas about the Renaissance as its sharp break with the Middle Ages, its discovery of nature, and its emphases on individualism, sensualism, self-determination, and personal liberty were part of a mythology perpetrated by such historians as Michelet and Burckhardt. Browning certainly participated in propagating this view of the Renaissance, and if Hauser is right, we are forced to the conclusion that his poems expose, not a Renaissance sensibility, but a Victorian one. This should not be considered disturbing. Browning was not a historian, but a poet who both felt and shaped the intellectual currents of his time, including its estimate of the Renaissance. More accurate than Ruskin's praise for his authenticity is the observation of W.K. Ferguson who, we recall, said that Browning helped to formulate the nineteenth-century view by harmonizing previous conceptions of the Renaissance with each other. Browning, he said, restored "sanity" to a field where exaggerations had prevailed.[18]

Another poem in the sixth number of *Bells and Pomegranates*, "Pictor Ignotus," is connected with Italy through the note "Florence, 15——." J.B. Bullen has identified the primary source of this poem as Vasari's account of Baccio della Porta, known as Fra Bartolommeo.[19] Bullen's evidence for this identification is strong, and is further supported by a comment in one of Elizabeth's letters. Complaining that Browning expected his readers to know too much, she said, in a letter dated March 24, 1846, that Vasari was not universally familiar. The only poem Browning had written up to that time to which this could apply was "Pictor Ignotus"; apparently, Browning had told Elizabeth of its basis in Vasari, a relation which has escaped Browning students for more than a century. It is the first of his poems drawn from this fertile source, and the first of his artist's monologues, if Jules's speech in *Pippa Passes* is excluded.

Browning's unknown painter says that he was once ambitious for worldly success, but that "a voice" changed him, so that he is now content to decorate churches with traditional, uninspired pictures that few notice, and that are bound to be destroyed by time. His pride is his independence; "at least no merchant traffics in my heart." His pictures do not have to court public favor, but can perish quietly in the churches to whose walls they are affixed. The poem seems to suggest a more definite situation than it actually reveals, and when it is put side by side with the career of Fra Bartolommeo recorded in Vasari and other sources, a plausible factual background appears. Baccio was a Tuscan of religious temperament and great accomplishment as a painter who did some work at the monastery of San Marco in Florence, where he came under the influence of Savonarola, and actually consigned some of his pictures showing the nude to one of the fires that marked Savonarola's purges of profane works of art. Though a layman at this time, he was residing at the monastery of San Marco on the night of April 18, 1500, when a mob attacked it in an effort to bring Savonarola down. Terrified by the violence, Baccio swore that he would join Savonarola's order, the Dominicans, if his life were spared, and later entered a monastery in Prato, near his birthplace, taking the clerical name by which he is known. He stopped painting, but after a few years was brought back to Florence, where he was persuaded to continue.

There are, as usual, obvious differences between Browning's figure and its model. Fra Bartolommeo did not paint in the spirit of resignation that dominates Browning's artist, but gave art up altogether after his conversion. When he continued with his painting, he showed no signs of using it as a means of spiritual discipline, but did his best work. Vasari's obscure comment that he gained "the wished for power of accompanying the labour of his hands with the uninterrupted contemplation of death" seems to have suggested the element of self-abnegation in Browning's portrait. The question of preserving artistic independence that arises in the poem did not trouble Fra Bartolommeo; though said to be unassuming, he apparently had no objection to fame, and collaborated with Raphael and other well-known figures. Finally, he did not paint monotonous Madonnas, but a wide variety of religious subjects, and did not limit himself to doomed frescoes, but put his work on permanent and portable bases, such as wooden panels, so that they could be moved and sold. They survived perfectly well, and can be seen today, in a good state of preservation, in the Uffizi and Pitti galleries and elsewhere.

Fra Bartolommeo is, therefore, not the subject of "Pictor Ignotus." The value of identifying him with Browning's figure, as Bullen observes, is that the "voice" is seen to be something more than a vague prompting of conscience; Savonarola has called the painter's attention to the needs of his soul and its fate in the afterlife. His impression that the world of men appears "like revels through a door / Of some strange house of idols at its rites" is an excellent rendering of Savonarola's vision of worldly life.

The painter's vivid image of himself cringing before the judges of his art, "Shrinking, as from the soldiery a nun," seems excessive but can be explained (if not fully justified) by what Browning learned about Fra Bartolommeo from Vasari. The attack on the monastery of San Marco flickers in Browning's line. The timid painter was on the scene, and was badly frightened. It was no small affair. The mob's assult on both church and monastery lasted far into the night, the doors were burned down, a hundred people were killed or injured, the houses of Savonarola's supporters were attacked, and some of their inhabitants—including women, if not nuns— were put to death.

By identifying Browning's model, Bullen has also identified something even more important to our understanding of the poem —its conflict. We now see that the painter has been forced to choose between the spirit of Raphael and the spirit of Savonarola, between access to human passions and praise, and indifference to this world for the sake of salvation in the next.[20] By choosing the latter course, Browning's painter, unlike his original, set himself apart from the main current of the Renaissance.

FOUR

From Wimpole Street to Pisa

When he entered Miss Barrett's room at 50 Wimpole Street for the first time at 3 P.M. on May 20, 1845, Browning was unconsciously taking the first steps of his return journey to Italy. He would have gone back in any case. He later told Elizabeth that when he first wrote to her in January 1845 his state of mind was such that he was "scheming how to get done with England and go to my heart in Italy."[1] It was obvious from his poems, and from the allusions and examples that occur in his letters to Elizabeth, that Italy continued to attract him.

During that most remarkable and most fully documented of Victorian courtships—91 conversations in the same room, analyzed and annotated in the 573 letters of Kintner's edition—Italy began as a topic of remark, developed into a serious theme, and eventually engulfed the whole drama. Elizabeth fully shared Browning's interest in Italy. Like him, she had studied Italian when she was young, translated Dante for practice, and wrote Italian verses under the guidance of an Italian master. The epigraph of her first book of verse was a line from Tasso. During their life in Italy, she was more militant than he in supporting Italian freedom, and devoted much of her poetry to the theme of Italian nationalism. The tablet placed over the door of Casa Guidi by the Italian government commemorates Elizabeth, not Browning, as the friend of Italy.

Browning's feelings about Italy at this time were complex and intensely personal; some of them are expressed in a letter to Elizabeth in which he tried to explain how he could like Italy, yet criticize the Italians. He was replying to Elizabeth's praise of Hans

Christian Andersen's novel, *Improvisatore.* Having read some of its descriptions of Italy excerpted in reviews, Browning impatiently wrote that it confirmed him in his belief that "Italy is stuff for the use of the North," and that in Italy itself "pure Poetry there is none"—not even in Dante or Alfieri.[2] When Elizabeth objected, he undertook to explain himself more fully, and wrote a wild medley of impressions and reactions that must be quoted at length:

> I intended to shade down and soften off and put in and leave out, and, before I had done, bring Italian Poets round to their old place again in my heart, giving new praise if I took old,—anyhow Dante is out of it all, as who knows but I, with all of him in my head and heart? But they do fret one, those tantalizing creatures, of fine passionate class, with such capabilities, and such a facility of being made pure mind of. And the special instance that vexed me, was that a man of sands and dog-roses and white rock and green sea-water just under, should come to Italy where my heart lives, and discover the sights and sounds . . . certainly discover them. And so do all Northern writers; for take up handfuls of sonetti, rime, poemetti, doings of those who never did anything else,—and try and make out, for yourself, what . . . say, what flowers they tread on, or trees they walk under,—as you might bid *them*, those tree and flower loving creatures, pick out of *our* North poetry a notion of what *our* daisies and harebells and furze bushes and brambles are—"Odorosi fioretti, rose porporine, bianchissimi gigli." And which of you eternal triflers was it called yourself "Shelley" and so told me years ago that in the mountains it was a feast "When one should find those globes of deep red gold—Which in the woods the strawberry-tree doth bear, Suspended in their emerald atmosphere." So that when my Mule walked into a sorb-tree, not to tumble sheer over Monte Calvano, and I felt the fruit against my face, the little ragged bare-legged guide fairly laughed at my knowing them so well—"Niursi-sorbi!" No, no,—does not all Naples-bay and half Sicily, shore and inland, come flocking once a year to the Piedigrotta fête only to see the blessed King's Volanti, or livery servants all in their best, as tho' heaven opened? and would not I engage to bring the whole of the Piano (of Sorrento) in likeness to a red velvet dressing gown properly spangled over, before the priest that held it out on a pole had even begun his story of how Noah's son Shem, the founder of Sorrento, threw it off to swim thither, as the world knows he did? Oh, it makes one's soul angry, so enough of it. But never enough of telling you— bring all your sympathies, come with loosest sleeves and longest lace-lappets, and you and yours shall find "elbow room," oh, shall

you not! For never did man, woman or child, Greek, Hebrew, or as Danish as our friend, like a thing, not to say love it, but I liked and loved it, one liking neutralizing the rebellious stir of its fellow, so that I do'n't go about now wanting the fixed stars before my time; this world has not escaped me, thank God. . . .[3]

The center of this whirling circle of emotions is the "sights and sounds" of Italy, and its theme is the complaint, often voiced by Browning, that the Italians themselves are incapable of doing justice to them. It was not an Italian poet, one of those "eternal triflers," who wrote so vividly about the sorb trees that he recognized them when his mule stumbled into them, but Shelley. The Italians, he rages, are occupied with *festas* where fancy uniforms can be seen, and with superstitions like the story of Shem's swimming to Sorrento. Yet, when he tells Elizabeth that her sympathies will find roots in Italy (adopting the unbuttoned imagery of loose sleeves and long lappets from her last letter), the *festa* and the red velvet robe Shem discarded somehow do double duty as instances of those entrancing "sights and sounds." The last sentence is a microcosmic reflection of the change Italy brought about in Browning's aims as a poet. He no longer aspires to the transcendental, but has grasped the value of "this world."

Once Browning and Elizabeth had decided to leave England, whether separately or as a married couple, there was never any question that they would go to Italy. Their first thought of being together in Italy—the germinal conception of the future Browning household in Florence—arose toward the end of August 1845 when Elizabeth, unwilling to face another London winter, thought of going to Pisa for her health, together with one of her brothers or sisters. Browning said that he was ready to follow her, or even precede her. Their relations went into a new phase, for he now wrote with increased ardor, and she felt compelled to discourage him, because she believed that her bad health was an obstacle to marriage; "if you are wise and would be happy," she wrote, ". . . you must leave me—these thoughts of me, I mean. . . ."[4] Routes and costs for her journey to Italy were discussed, and Browning told her what to expect.

In the middle of September, Mr. Barrett vetoed the plan. With winter, the question of an actual journey to Italy receded; but at the same time, Italy—or "Pisa" or some other code word—became the symbol of the future union they envisioned. Promising Elizabeth deliverance from Wimpole Street, Browning would write, "Why, we shall see Italy together!" or "we may walk on the galleries round and over the inner court of the Doges' Palace at Venice," or "We can go to Italy for a year or two and be happy as day and night are long." By January 1846 he was urging her to think of a definite time for carrying out her "promise" to bring "this state of things" to an end; her reply was to assign the responsibility to him. On March 3 he suggested that she renew her demands to go to Italy, but she said it would be impossible. In the meantime Italy as a fact rather than a symbol played a significant part in their thoughts and correspondence. They exchanged views about Italian books and pictures, many of their acquaintances were planning trips to Italy, and Elizabeth learned of gossip which had it that she was planning to go herself. In addition, the two plays with which Browning was occupied at this time, *A Soul's Tragedy* and *Luria*, were set in Italy of the fifteenth and sixteenth centuries respectively.

By the spring and summer of 1846 they were discussing towns where they might live and ways of carrying out the journey, though still rather speculatively. Florence was "English-ridden," and the water was said to be bad. Sorrento and Pisa were preferable. Ravenna, said Browning at one point, was cheap and free of the English. He reminded Elizabeth that she would have to go somewhere, for she could not expect to survive another winter in London. Since he had committed himself to the principle "ubi Ba, ibi RB," the place did not matter, but there had never been any doubt that it would be Italy. This led them to the question of which of them had first suggested Italy, and they agreed that it was Elizabeth.

In the meantime, the kindness of Elizabeth's friends began to make the need for action more pressing. When her intention of going to Italy became known, several acquaintances offered to accompany her, the most persistent of these being the redoubtable Anna Jameson. Mrs. Jameson first mentioned the possibility in February of 1846, renewed her offer in May, and eventually was so intimately and innocently involved in Browning's and Elizabeth's plans that she threatened to spoil them. As things turned out, however, she became an indispensable accessory.

When she was introduced to Elizabeth by John Kenyon in 1844, Mrs. Jameson was well known in London literary circles, and had just embarked on her career as an interpreter of art with her *Memoirs of the Early Italian Painters* (first published serially in the *Penny Magazine* in 1841). She had many literary acquaintances, including Browning, whom she had met some years before, and whom she continued to see frequently[5] in 1845 and 1846, during the period of the courtship. The lovers often felt very awkward with her, for while she was intimate with both of them, they saw her separately and kept her in the dark about their relationship. She was planning to return to Italy with her niece, Gerardine Bate, to gather material for her book, *Sacred and Legendary Art,* and her repeated offers to take Elizabeth meant that they would form a party of three ladies. It was an attractive prospect; Elizabeth would enjoy both freedom and security, for Mrs. Jameson was a perfectly competent traveler.

She must have been puzzled, therefore, when Elizabeth persistently declined to go with her. The situation was, in fact, full of ironies. Mrs. Jameson praised Browning to Elizabeth, and praised Elizabeth to Browning, apparently without realizing that they were acquainted. As her relations with Elizabeth grew closer and the lovers grew clearer about their intentions, a situation worthy of a novel by Henry James developed. By June of 1846 Elizabeth felt that Mrs. Jameson would be offended when she learned that they had not trusted her enough to tell their secret, and asked whether it would not be better to take her into their confidence. This raised the question of Elizabeth's cousin, John Kenyon, who had brought them together, and who also ought to be told. Browning advised against telling either, and silence was maintained, but Elizabeth's reports of the behavior of both friends suggest that they had suspicions. The code word for the secret was the same one Elizabeth and Browning used: "Italy." Mrs. Jameson persistently asked about Elizabeth's plans for going to Italy, and Kenyon, assured by her sisters that she would find a way, stubbornly asked what this could be.

As if to whet Elizabeth's appetite for Italy, Mrs. Jameson took her to see the famous art collection of Samuel Rogers on one of the rare occasions when Elizabeth felt well enough to leave her room. Elizabeth's letter describing her visit breathlessly throws out the names of Michelangelo, Raphael, Tintoretto, and Titian as well as those of Rubens and Rembrandt.[5] Elizabeth's conversations with Mrs. Jameson now became exquisitely suggestive minuets of inquiry and evasion, exactly like the dialogue in a James novel. Asked if she had decided to go, Elizabeth could only say "Perhaps"; asked if she would have a suitable companion, she said "Yes." When she said obscurely that her means of making the trip was courage, Mrs. Jameson replied, even more obscurely, "Oh, now I see clearly!" On another occasion, when Elizabeth said that no planning was needed because her departure would be sudden, Mrs. Jameson ominously described the idea as "an elopement." "I was obliged to laugh," wrote Elizabeth, reporting this to Browning.

The impetus that finally led the lovers to make their move began to gather in midsummer. They realized that it would be wise to take Elizabeth Wilson, Elizabeth's maid, who was willing to accompany them. Small events built up the pressure to leave. On August 6, Mrs. Jameson pointedly cross-questioned Elizabeth about her travel plans. Her old nurse, Miss Tripsack, casually predicted that she would to to Italy and be married. As if to prepare her, Kenyon took her to see (but not to ride on) her first railroad train, "the great, roaring, grinding Thing." Browning wrote that Smith, Elder had made a very generous offer to publish any poem of his *about Italy*. On August 30, Elizabeth wrote that she felt optimistic— despair was behind her, and Italy ahead. She bought flannel-lined shoes to wear on cold Italian floors, and boots for outdoor wear. They were nearly ready to go.

They were finally moved to act by Mr. Barrett's decision to send the family to the country while the Wimpole Street house was redecorated. In spite of Elizabeth's feelings that it was still too soon, Browning consulted schedules, made arrangements, and sent her details. After the famous secret wedding at the high altar in St. Marylebone Parish Church on Saturday, September 12 between 10:45 and 11:15, Elizabeth returned to Wimpole Street for a week. On the following Saturday the newlyweds, accompanied by Wilson and Flush, Elizabeth's dog, took the train at Vauxhall Station, bound for Southampton and Paris with Pisa as their ultimate destination.

In *Sordello*, Browning describes the font his hero admired in his youth, and in which, we later learn, his mother has been buried, as encircled with bas-reliefs of caryatids, captive maidens bearing burdens. These figures are anachronistic, but they reflect Browning's life-long concern with women who were unjustly treated. No doubt he was too preoccupied on his wedding day to examine the architecture of St. Marylebone Parish Church, but if he had lifted his eyes to the lantern on its tower, he would have seen, circling it high in the air, and glowing with gilt paint, a ring of caryatids.

Before he left England, Browning completed two plays with Italian settings. Both represent something of a regression in his use of Italian materials. He had begun to excel in fictionalizing specific historical events and personalities, but *A Soul's Tragedy* and *Luria* make use only of general characteristics associated with Italy, and have no identifiable models.

A Soul's Tragedy is probably a product of his first Italian trip. Toward the end of February 1845 he wrote to Elizabeth as if it were already completed. It is unlikely that he wrote it during the 1844 journey, or in the two months since he had returned, and there is some evidence that it was written as early as 1842. The soul whose tragedy is unfolded (the title is heavily ironical) is that of Chiappino, a rebel against the Papal rulers of sixteenth-century Faenza, who becomes the town's hero through a trick of fate. His friend, Luitolfo, has gone to the town's Provost to plead against a decree of banishment pronounced on Chiappino, and has killed the man in anger. Chiappino generously takes responsibility for the crime, but finds that the people hated the murdered man, and now glorify his supposed assassin. In the second of the play's two acts, which takes place some months later, we find that Chiappino has gained favor with the authorities, has taken leave both of his revolutionary principles and of the sweetheart he won from Luitolfo, and is about to be made Provost himself. When he expresses concern about reversing himself in this way, the Pope's legate, Ogniben, assures him that inconsistency and falsehood are essential to the world as it is, and prepares to confer his office on him. But when the Pope's emissary imposes the condition that the murderer of the old Provost must be punished, Luitolfo comes forward to admit his guilt, and the ambitious Chiappino is forced to go into exile after all.

Apart from a few local allusions which might have been gleaned from a guidebook or descriptions of Faenza, the only elements in the play that Browning and his contemporaries would have identified with Italy are the violence of the first act, the superficiality of Chiappino's moods, and the sophisticated cynicism of Ogniben's speeches.

The action of *Luria* seems to take place during the 1405–6 war between Florence and Pisa, but the situation and actions of the play are invented, and the characters are all fictional, without historical counterparts. Its reflection of history is so vague that almost any account of the 1405–6 war (or, in fact, of any war among the Lombard States) would have served as a source.

In any event, the main source of *Luria* is not history, but *Othello*. Its hero is a Moorish general who leads the Florentine army, and is removed from his command by a suspicious government, in spite of his success. His antagonist is a functionary named Braccio, who distrusts the foreigner and has him removed out of a sense of civic duty. Actually, Luria is perfectly loyal to Florence, more devoted, as he claims, than native sons. The Secretary, who has watched him carefully, declares, "That man believes in Florence, as the saint / Tied to the wheel believes in God."

The reasons for this devotion are not made convincing. Luria says he is committed to Florence as a place where the work of scholars, painters, and sculptors may resume when the war is finished, but he speaks as a naive outsider from a backward culture. Braccio exhibits Florentine cynicism when he refuses to believe in Luria's devotion, and vows:

> *Brute-force shall not rule Florence! Intellect*
> *May rule her, bad or good as chance supplies:*
> *But intellect it shall be. . . .*

Florence's claim to cultural superiority is thoroughly undermined by her suspiciousness and racial prejudice. The Florentines are willing to use Luria, but will not accept him or trust him because he is black and a foreigner, and cannot fully share Florentine traditions. Luria has casually drawn a sketch of the Florence Duomo with a Moorish facade on the wall of his tent, and Braccio, seeing this, indignantly observes, "A Moorish front ill suits our Duomo's body."[6] Ironically, the noble aspirations Luria thinks he is serving are the cause of his destruction. Braccio argues that everyone must be sacrificed to Florence's ideal of perfection, "She's a contrivance to supply a type / Of man, which men's deficiencies refuse." Luria's Moorish compatriot puts it more plainly: "A savage, how shouldst thou perceive as they?" Luria refuses to turn his army on ungrateful Florence because the spectacle of the city controlled by a "hireling Moor" would be degrading; at the end, he concurs in the right of Florence to use and then discard him by taking poison.

The best that can be said about the lack of generosity with which Italian character is treated in these plays is that Browning seems to be relying on the traditions about Italy rather than his own judgment and experience. Their villains are prototypes of a figure he excels in presenting, the man who combines taste and discrimination with cynicism and cruelty, a figure Browning felt to be quintessentially Italian.

As soon as he and Elizabeth arrived in Paris on September 22, Browning went to find Mrs. Jameson, who had already left on the trip Elizabeth had so often been invited to join. In a note consisting of a single short sentence he left her word that they were married and in Paris. After overcoming her profound surprise, Mrs. Jameson had them move to the hotel where she and Gerardine were staying, and when Elizabeth had rested for a week, they continued their journey as a party of four. They paused to pay a preliminary homage to Italy by visiting Vaucluse, where Petrarch's Laura had lived, then embarked at Marseilles. Elizabeth had her first sight of the Italian coast and its mountains, and on October 12, when the ship stopped at Genoa, she went ashore and took her first short walk through the streets of an Italian city.

When the party arrived in Pisa, Mrs. Jameson and Gerardine went to a hotel, and the Brownings, after a few days in temporary lodgings, moved into a flat in the Collegio Ferdinando, a stately building just a few yards south of the Duomo and the Leaning Tower, and overlooking the busy Via Santa Maria. The building had significant associations for Browning; it had been designed by Vasari, and bore a notice that Daniello Bartoli had once taught there. It had two flats on each of its floors, and the Brownings, together with Wilson and Flush, occupied one consisting of a sitting room and three bedrooms.

Nineteenth-century observers uniformly describe Pisa as a dull, slow place. Mrs. Trollope was told that it retained only about a quarter of the population it had had in the sixteenth century, and found it "tame," "desolate," and "melancholy." She thought the enormous buildings left over from its great days resembled ornamental tombstones.[7] To Elizabeth the place had "rather the repose of sleep than of death." Once popular as a fashionable health resort for English people, it had become a backwater by the forties, though a number of English were still in residence, and a certain amount of English social activity stirred.

The Brownings avoided all this; Pisa's dullness suited them. Elizabeth, though much improved, was not strong enough to spend much time outdoors, especially since it often rained, and Browning was happy to sit with her, so that the rooms in the Collegio Ferdinando became the scene of a "very perpetual tête-à-tête." Meals, ample and cheap, were sent up from the nearby *trattoria*. The couple explored Italian novels, then turned to French ones, saw almost no one after Mrs. Jameson and Gerardine left early in November, and could almost have been living anywhere in the world but in Italy. Elizabeth must have feared that she was isolating Browning, and thought they ought to have visitors. But Browning, afraid of taxing her strength, argued that their happiness might be spoiled if others were admitted. He seemed to want to perpetuate their Wimpole Street interviews as a way of life.

But Italy penetrated their nest a little at a time. They had one Italian visitor, a Professor Ferucci, who opened the university library to them, and supplied them with a copy of Vasari, a book indispensable to Browning, especially since it described many things to be seen in Pisa. The street life of Via Santa Maria, which led to the Leaning Tower and the Duomo, was just outside their window. One day a funeral passed by, with chanting monks, torches, and the corpse laid out with its veiled face turned to the sky. Elizabeth retreated from the window in revulsion, and called Browning away, but he could not stop looking. "I can't help it, Ba," she quotes him as saying, "—it *draws* me."[8]

There had been poets in Pisa before. Shelley had lived in the city and its neighborhood during the two years before his death, and had been joined by a group of friends, including Byron, Trelawny, and Leigh Hunt. Not far from the Collegio Ferdinando was the Convent of Santa Anna, where Emilia Viviani, the subject of his "Epipsychidion," had been confined while her parents arranged for her marriage. Shelley, Mary, and Claire Clairmont all visited her there repeatedly in 1821. The subject of another of Shelley's poems, "The Tower of Famine," once stood nearby in the Piazza dei Cavalieri, and Browning was able to point out that Shelley had put the tower in the wrong location. Shelley had summered at the Bagni di Pisa at San Giuliano, lived for a time at Lerici on the coast nearby, and had met his death in the Gulf of Spezia further north. He had written some of his best poems, and his two best prose works, *A Philosophic View of Reform* and *A Defense of Poetry* in Pisa and its neighborhood, and lived the most settled part of his married life there. *Adonais*, as Browning might have known, first saw the light in Pisa; Shelley wrote it in San Giuliano, and had a small trial edition printed before its publication in England.

Shelley persuaded Byron to move to Pisa in November 1821, and secured for him the Casa Lanfranchi, a handsome palace diagonally across the Arno from his own residence, the Tre Palazzi di Chiesa. Byron's palazzo became a center of social life for his English friends, and Shelley often joined the dinners, billiard games, and conversations that took place there, and rode out with the group that went with Byron to practice pistol shooting in the country. When Leigh Hunt came to Pisa to help start the journal the poets were planning, he moved into the ground floor of Byron's palazzo with his antiaristocratic wife and six lively children, who were very much in Byron's way.

Byron's work, like Shelley's, prospered in Pisa. He overcame Countess Guiccioli's objections to *Don Juan*, continued with the sixth canto, and wrote some of his plays there. Hunt has described how Byron, after working late into the night, came down into the garden of the Lanfranchi in the morning, singing an aria by Rossini, and sat conversing with Hunt while the Countess Guiccioli came to join them under the orange trees. Hunt and Shelley explored the town together, and went to the cathedral and talked. Shelley left for the seacoast the next day, and on July 11 word came that he had been lost at sea. About a week later a party of English people went out to the shore to attend the burning of his body. Afterwards, Byron and Hunt got drunk and laughed and shouted in the carriage that took them back to Pisa.

That moment in the history of English poetry must have manifested itself vividly to Browning as he wandered about the town. It was only twenty years since the Lung'Arno Mediceo had echoed to the sound of horses' hooves as Byron, Shelley, and their party rode out for pistol practice. Browning walked along the Arno past the houses where "Epipsychidion," *Adonais*, and parts of *Don Juan* had been written. He and Elizabeth went into the garden where Leigh Hunt and Byron had sat and talked. It is not unreasonable to believe that his thoughts of the poets who had lived in Pisa gave a deeper resonance to his own presence there. As we know from the first book of *The Ring and the Book*, he had a tendency to regard the present consciousness of past events as an extension of the past, another episode in a single chain. To think of Byron and Shelley, and to see the places where they lived and wrote, was to be included in their history.

Browning had seen Pisa on a previous visit, but the winter of 1846–7 gave him his first chance to examine its art and architecture in detail, probably using Vasari as a guide. When Browning alluded to Nicola Pisano in *Sordello* as an initiator of post-Byzantine art, it was entirely on Vasari's authority, for he had never seen any of his work. By the time he wrote "Old Pictures in Florence," in which he declared, "My sculptor is Nicolo the Pisan," he had had the opportunity of seeing other works, but the first he could have known (and he would not have missed the chance to examine it repeatedly) was the marble pulpit in the Baptistry at Pisa. It is a curious and original fabrication (like the other pulpits he later produced on the model of this one), with four of its vari-colored marble columns resting on the backs of lions, an eagle supporting its lectern with spread wings, and all of its surfaces covered with bas-reliefs of figures, drapery, and animals. By borrowing some of his forms from the reliefs on Roman sarcophagi that could be seen in Pisa, Nicola had, as the authoritative Victorian history of Italian art put it, made "pagan form subservient to Christian ideas."[9] The vigorous naturalism and heroic postures which Nicola brought to the New Testament scenes he depicted were exciting anticipations of a new age that was in touch both with history and the world of immediate experience, and was capable of relating them to each other.

The cloisters of the Campo Santo, the quadrangular burial ground that adjoins the precincts of the Duomo, is decorated with frescoes by numerous artists, including Giotto, Benozzo Gozzoli, Simon Memmi, Buonamico Buffalmacco, and others—attributions have varied. Many of them are large, panoramic works, often representing Biblical and allegorical scenes that display the activities, clothing, and manners of times contemporary with their painters. Ruskin, who was in Pisa in May 1845, just eighteen months before the Brownings arrived, was awed by the Campo Santo frescoes. "You cannot conceive the vividness and fullness of conception of these great old men," he wrote to his father, ". . . all are there, the very people, real, visible, created, substantial, such as they *were*, as they must have been. . . ."[10] Leigh Hunt, who gives a fine de-

Nicola Pisano, *Fortitude*, Detail of the Pulpit, Baptistry, Pisa
(Archivi Alinari)

"pagan form subservient to Christian ideas" — Crowe and Cavalcaselle

scription of the frescoes in his autobiography, was moved by their elemental vigor, variety, and truth. He compared them to Chaucer, and wrote: "They are like a dream of humanity during the twilight of creation."[11]

Vasari describes a cycle of twenty-four Old Testament scenes (the only one based on the New Testament shows the adoration of the Magi) by Benozzo Gozzoli which covered one wall of the cloister. Like other works by Gozzoli, these pictures contain crowds of people portrayed with loving attention to their clothing, the utensils they use, and the architecture around them. Displayed within a religious framework, this realism humanizes devotion, articulating it on an intimate, immediate plane. It was too early for Browning to regard paintings that were still condescendingly considered "primitive" with the respect he felt for the Renaissance artists. But this may have been an advantage. He may have looked at them, instead of merely admiring. If his reactions were like those of others who saw the Campo Santo frescoes, he responded to the vital realism they brought to their representations of people of all ages and conditions, and we can imagine that there was some relation between them and the new kind of poetry he had begun to write.

During this period, Browning applied himself to the first literary work he had ever done in Italy, a revision of *Pippa Passes*. In February Elizabeth wrote that he was putting "so much golden light into 'Pippa' that everybody shall see her 'pass' properly . . . yes, and surpass."[12] Browning did, in fact, make numerous local changes, and a few substantial additions, nearly all for the sake of achieving greater clarity. Some lines inserted into Pippa's introductory speech bring forward his significant phrase, as if he were now asserting more firmly the poetic intentions he attached to it:

> *All other men and women that this earth*
> *Belongs to, who all days alike possess,*
> *Make general plenty cure particular dearth. . . .*

Jules's lines praising Phene's beauty were inserted at this time:

> *Look at the woman here with the new soul,*
> *Like my own Psyche—fresh upon her lips*
> *Alit, the visionary butterfly,*
> *Waiting my word to enter and make bright,*
> *Or flutter off and leave all blank as first.*

They are apparently an allusion to Canova's *Psiche-fanciulla,* the figure of a girl holding a butterfly, and reveal that Jules has responded to Canova, in spite of the contempt he has displayed for him. The plot to have Bluphocks seduce Pippa was even more lightly touched in 1841 than in the later version, for the last two sentences of Part III, in which the 3rd Girl tells Pippa that the Englishman has fallen in love with her, were added in the revision.

The last scene contains the only revision that is possibly crucial. As the text now stands, Uguccio makes his infamous proposal, asks "Is it a bargain?" and the Bishop remains silent while Pippa's song is heard. But in the original version, he replies, "Why if she sings, one might . . . ," suggesting that he is about to assent to Uguccio's suggestion, an idea that has been completely removed by the cancellation of the line. This change obviously entails a shift, if not a reversal, in the conception of the Bishop's character.

Their seclusion in the Collegio Ferdinando did not bring the Brownings security from domestic disturbances. In late January, Wilson had a stomach complaint, the English doctor had to be sent for, and remedies were applied. In March, Browning suffered what may well have been the most profound emotional ordeal he had yet experienced. After a period of pain and discomfort, Elizabeth miscarried. She reported that Browning wept afterward, and it is easy to understand that nothing in the comparatively placid life he had led so far had disturbed him so deeply. They had taken the flat in the Collegio Ferdinando for six months; in mid-April 1847, when the doctor said that Elizabeth was well enough to travel, they left for Florence, where they expected to see Mrs. Jameson again.

Little is known about Browning's thoughts during the time he lived in Pisa, but it is clear that he had made a commitment to Italy. About two weeks before leaving Pisa, he wrote to Monckton Milnes, who was a member of Parliament, asking to be mentioned for a secretarial post if the government decided to send a minister to represent it at the Vatican. He assured Milnes that he was financially independent, and meant to continue writing; he claimed that he had paid attention to Italian politics while in Pisa, and had been a student of Italian literature. "Whatever comes," he wrote, "I hope to remain in Italy for years. . . ."[13]

FIVE

Florence, 1847-1851

When the Brownings arrived in Florence on April 20, 1847, they did not expect to make it their permanent home, but thought of staying for a month or a year before moving on to Venice, Rome, or half a dozen other places that were mentioned. Their long association with the flat in the Casa Guidi was almost an inadvertence. They occupied it temporarily for a time, then lived elsewhere before returning to it. Even then they usually summered in other places, and left Florence for periods that lasted as long as a year and a half to live in London, Paris, or Rome. Although Elizabeth was officially considered an invalid, they traveled frequently—almost incessantly—so that only a part of their fifteen years in Italy was spent at Casa Guidi.

Browning had written to Elizabeth, while they were discussing places where they might live, that parvenus in Florence thrust themselves on people who would not associate with them at home, then claimed friendship when they returned to England. He also observed that the water was bad, to which Elizabeth replied, "As to Florence, the flood of English is the worst water of all in the argument. . . ."[1] The metaphor still served after she had lived in Florence for nearly two years, when she wrote to a friend, ". . . we would *rather not* make general acquaintance . . . it being our object to live quietly and to keep clear of the turbid waters on each side of us called Florentine society."[2] This society was nearly entirely non-Italian. It was dominated by English and American people, with occasional participants of other nationalities, but included only those Italians who had intermarried with the foreigners.

By the 1840s when the Brownings arrived, Florence was no longer a fashionable resort.[3] It had been popular with the English too long. Even Mrs. Trollope, whom Browning thought unbearably

80

vulgar, lamented that the English Florentines were only middle class and lacked style, and wondered whether they profited from their experience with the city's culture. Her son, Thomas Adolphus Trollope, a long-time resident, who left a vivid account of Florence in *What I Remember* (1887), reports that—as the Brownings quickly learned—it was a very economical place to live. He adds that English people of modest station could attend the balls and concerts given every week by the Grand Duke, Leopold II, at the Pitti Palace and the Casino dei Nobili, and could even be assured of being presented to the Grand Duke himself by the minister, Lord Holland. Gambling, dancing, and dining were popular. As a society, says Trollope, it was "frivolous, gay, giddy, and . . . for the most part very unintellectual."[4] The Brownings, he said, were far superior to most Anglo-Florentines; he regarded Elizabeth as an exalted spirit, and referred to Browning with awe.

In his biography of Browning's friend, the American sculptor, William Wetmore Story, Henry James drops his skepticism about the adventures of Americans in Italy long enough to take a favorable, nostalgic view of life in mid-century Florence. It was a time and place where the plane of art and culture overlapped that of daily life. People frequented the opera and ballet, and at home Story modeled while his wife read to him from Monckton Milnes's *Life of Keats*, "lent by Browning." Solid comforts were available. In the evening Mrs. Story could drive to the Cascine with the wife of another American sculptor, Mrs. Horatio Greenough, then attend the play, then hunt for a *trattoria* afterward. It was even possible to go home for supper during the intermissions at the opera. James is delighted at the vitality and intimacy of all this. "The whole scene hangs together," he declares. He is sorry to find Mrs. Story calling the members of Florentine society "vulgar and ignorant people" in her letters, but sets this aside as "a discrimination."[5]

In the midst of this colorful social scene, the Brownings cultivated seclusion. During their first period in Florence, between 1847 and 1851, they never attended the Grand-Ducal functions where anyone who was English was admitted, and where middle-class English people could dine and dance in the company of English and Italian nobility; they never dined out or drove to the Cascine at six in the evening to take part in the popular gatherings where ladies remained seated in their carriages while gentlemen moved about visiting them, and flower girls threw bouquets into their laps. In 1849, Elizabeth wrote to a friend, ". . . we live so very much like snails in a shell," and said that Browning had not spent a single evening out of the house.[6] They passed the time reading, talking, writing, and playing on the piano they had acquired.

But the fact that they did not pay calls or take part in the activities of the English colony did not mean that they were isolated, for they were always hospitable to visitors. In their first years in Florence they made a large number of English and American acquaintances, some of whom were to become permanent friends, and were to play important parts in their lives. Of these the most significant in relation to Browning's work are the two American sculptors, Hiram Powers and William Wetmore Story.

Powers and Story were among the many American sculptors who came to Italy in the middle of the century, seeking not only its artistic traditions, but good marble and skilled workmen. Powers, who lived near Casa Guidi, called on the Brownings very soon after they arrived in the fall of 1847, and was a welcome visitor. A self-taught man, and a rather eccentric figure, he had begun his career as a clockmaker in Cincinnati, and soon combined this skill with his modeling talents to devise wax figures that were moved by clockwork. He had a first great success in America when, with the advice of Mrs. Trollope, who had come to Cincinnati to support her family by conducting a bazaar, he constructed a representation of Dante's *Inferno* that caused a sensation. After this unpromising beginning, he moved to Florence in 1837, and became a serious sculptor, ultimately gaining worldwide fame with his *Greek Slave*, a female nude in chains that became the subject of a poem by Elizabeth. Powers had many inventive ideas about sculpture and other matters which he expressed in an exceptionally direct and forthright manner, and if Browning's reactions to Powers resembled those of Hawthorne, who spent much time with him in Florence, he found something agreeable and stimulating in his original, practical mind.

William Wetmore Story was the most intimate personal friend Browning had in Italy, and the man with whom he felt he could best discuss questions of art, morality, civilization, and the like. Story was a man of numerous accomplishments. Born in Salem, Massachusetts in 1819, he was seven years younger than Browning. The son of a man who was a Supreme Court judge and a distinguished legal authority, he became a judge himself before the age of thirty, and was the author of significant works on the law, as well as poetry, criticism, and a life of his father. He was also an amateur sculptor, and after his father's death he was given the assignment of providing a statue for his monument. In order to prepare himself for this work, he went to Italy, and as a result of his visit decided to abandon America and the law in favor of Italy and sculpture.

He returned to Rome in 1847 and met the Brownings in Florence early in 1848, while on a visit from Genoa. The friendship was continued later that year, when Story and his family returned to Florence to live, and the two families were often together at Bagni di Lucca, Siena, and Rome in later years. Story was both a serious artist and a man of many interests. Browning found him an attractive companion, spent many hours in his Florence studio, and after Elizabeth's death intended to move into an apartment adjoining Story's quarters in the Palazzo Barberini in Rome. He learned sculpture from Story, and once went so far as to describe himself, in a letter to his mentor, as "SCULPTOR and poet."[7] The Storys visited Browning in 1889 during the holiday he spent in Asolo not long before his death; Mrs. Emelyn Story recalled that when he said good-bye to them for what was to be the last time, he said, "We have been friends for over forty years without a break."[8]

Another faithful friend, one for whom Browning felt great affection, was Isa Blagden, a sociable English spinster attracted to Florence by its cheapness, who hospitably received parties of her friends in her various villas. She first encountered the Brownings during an initial stay in Florence in 1849–50, and became a close friend on subsequent visits and during her long residence in the city. Initially an acquaintance of Elizabeth's, she also came to know Browning well when he made it a practice to spend evenings with the company she gathered at her house. She supported Browning sympathetically at the time of Elizabeth's death, and his correspondence with her, kept up until the time of her own death in 1873, remained a link with Florence.

Seymour Kirkup was the most colorful and eccentric member of the English colony at Florence. He was the subject of vivid descriptions by numerous visitors, who came to see him as if he were one of the monuments and included him in the memoirs that were nearly obligatory for literate travelers to Italy. He was an untidy old man who lived in two rooms of the decrepit old Casa Caruana at the foot of the Ponte Vecchio. His apartment was a scene of picturesque squalor, choked with books, pictures, manuscripts, and cobwebs, but in it lived his pretty mistress and a cheerful, enchanting little daughter. He was an artist and art historian who discovered some important lost paintings, and was regarded as an authority. In his late poem, "Of Pacchiarotto, and How He Worked in Distemper," Browning refers to Kirkup by name as one who shared his knowledge of Italian art.

Kirkup was also one of the leaders of Florence's spiritualist circle, communicated with the spirit of Dante through his mistress and his daughter, and often reported strange phenomena at his apartment. He was a serious Dante scholar, and when his library was sold after his death, it was disclosed that his two crowded rooms had housed several hundred editions of Dante and many other valuable books and manuscripts. Browning shared many interests with Kirkup, whose collection included a copy of Filippo Baldinucci's *Notizie de'Professori del Disegno*, one of Browning's sources, a manuscript of Pietro d'Abano, the subject of a poem in *Dramatic Idylls*, and a copy of a Vatican library manuscript recounting the Cenci story, an item related to Browning's poem, "Cenciaja."

Writing to a friend more than a year after he had come to Florence, Browning said that, apart from some visitors, "we know no English-speaking people."[9] This did not mean that they knew any Italians, except servants and tradesmen. It must be remembered that although Browning and Elizabeth spoke Italian, and Wilson also learned to speak it fluently, if not accurately, Browning never established a permanent friendship with any Italian.

His first Italian acquaintances were apparently the Carduccis, old friends of his father, whom he met first in Rome, and then in London. He saw Mazzini from time to time at social functions in London. But the Italian he knew best was Pasquale Villari, the distinguished historian and political figure, who mingled freely with the foreign community in Florence, and was introduced to the Brownings by Margherita, the English wife of the Greek painter, George Mignaty. Villari was a Neapolitan by birth, a scholar, and an ardent libertarian, who had been arrested and exiled for political activism in 1848. He lived in Florence between 1848 and 1859, and returned to an academic post there in 1865 after a period spent at the University of Pisa. He was the author of important works on Savonarola, Machiavelli, and Florentine history, and in later years became a member of the Italian Senate, and in 1891, Minister of Public Instruction. During the time Villari knew the Brownings, when he was doing research for his work on Savonarola in Florence, he came to the Casa Guidi frequently to talk politics. He was primarily Elizabeth's friend, and corresponded with her about political events. Browning saw Villari at Elizabeth's funeral, and when he heard that he was in London in the summer of 1862, invited him to Warwick Crescent for lunch.[10]

In general, however, Browning never overcame the barrier that existed between Italians and the English residents in Italy, and never became intimate with an Italian. His knowledge of Italy, when it is not that of the historian or art lover, is that of the spectator, like the poet described in "How it Strikes a Contemporary," who learns about the people by watching the life of the streets.

Browning could not miss the effects which the spirit of 1848 was having on Tuscany. The Grand Duke, Leopold II, an Austrian of moderate abilities as a ruler, had the difficult task of reconciling the demands for liberty that were abroad in Italy with the firm control he was expected to exercise over his generally placid and easy-going subjects. During their first few years in Florence, the Brownings witnessed genuine advances toward self-government. A civil guard was established, a constitution was granted, a Tuscan Parliament met, and the press began to enjoy a degree of freedom. But nothing could really be accomplished unless Austrian power was overturned by force, and as even their most ardent supporters came to realize, the Florentines were simply too soft and undisciplined to face this task. Nevertheless, things went so far in 1849 that the Grand Duke was unseated for a period with the help of foreign troops, there was fighting in the streets, and Browning was apparently in some personal danger on one occasion.

Even before the failure of the revolts attempted in the Italian provinces in 1849, Elizabeth, who had been profoundly moved by what she thought was the approach of Italy's independence, had lost faith in liberation. Her disillusionment is recorded in *Casa Guidi Windows*, whose first part is ardent and militant, but whose second part is melancholy and resigned. Browning, always less fervent about the Italian cause, nevertheless expressed his hope some years later in "Old Pictures in Florence" that the Austrians might be expelled and Italy allowed to resume her greatness. T.A. Trollope reported that the political pressure that one felt in Florence after 1849 was mild, and the good behavior of the Austrian troops helped to prevent serious disturbances. The reason a revolution could not be expected is illustrated in an anecdote Trollope tells. During a demonstration, the Florentines went through the streets crying, "Death to the Austrians!" But when one of the Austrian soldiers fell from his horse, the demonstrators gathered round him with sympathetic words, and helped him to remount. Then they continued to shout, "Death to the Austrians!"[11]

If revolution did not seem imminent, there was, it had to be admitted, no desperate need for it. As the Brownings observed, classes mingled democratically in the Florence streets, food was abundant, agriculture proceeded in an orderly manner, and the beggars and prostitutes that infested other Italian cities were absent from Florence. (They were relegated by law to the suburbs.) Mary Shelley in *Rambles in Germany and Italy* (1844), described the townspeople as complacent, free to pursue their pleasures, and better off, on the whole, than their English counterparts.

There is also a tradition of opposition to Florence, one best represented, perhaps, by Ruskin. His complaints often concerned the Florentines themselves, whom he considered mercenary and unimaginative—"Leghorn bonnetmakers," idle, vain, and interfering. "The square is full of listless, chattering, smoking vagabonds, who are always moving every way at once, just fast enough to make it disagreeable, and inevitable, to run against them."[12] He complained about bad manners, laziness, the disrespectful way in which works of art were treated, and "pale, effeminate, animal eyed, listless sensualists, that have no thought, or care, or occupation, or knowledge, or energy. . . ."[13]

Browning, as we know, had reservations about contemporary Italians, but he did not share Ruskin's open hostility. The contrasting reactions Italy evoked from these two men of similar origins and tastes is beautifully illustrated by their attitudes toward Italian crowds. Ruskin, approaching San Marco in Venice, was repelled by the crowds of hawkers in the piazza outside, and made a detour to avoid them on his way to the sacred calm of the interior. Browning, confronted with a similar scene outside San Lorenzo in Florence, as he tells it in *The Ring and the Book*, delightedly surveyed the animated market, scanned its secondhand goods item by shoddy item, and bought the worn volume that gave him the story of his poem, completely ignoring the church.

In spite of their protests that they led a quiet life, the Brownings often left Florence for extended holidays that opened new regions of Italy to them. When the weather became oppressively hot in August of 1847, they went to the monastery of Vallombrosa, planning to spend a month in the cool hills. However, ladies were not welcome in the celibate community, and they had to return after a few days, but not before Browning had had a chance to play on the organ reputedly played by Milton when he visited the monastery. The following summer they sought relief from the heat at Fano and Ancona on the Adriatic, passed through Arezzo, so that Browning had his first sight of the setting of *The Ring and the Book,* and on their way home went to Rimini and Ravenna, where they visited Dante's tomb.

In Fano they saw two paintings that impressed them, a *David* by Domenichino and Guercino's *Angelo Custode,* which became the subject of the only poem Browning wrote during these years except *Christmas-Eve and Easter-Day.* "The Guardian Angel," though a minor lyric, is of some interest because it is personal rather than dramatic, takes an Italian painting for its subject, and illustrates Browning's approach to art. Though their tastes were to change, the Brownings at this time had no reservations about the opulent style of the Bolognese school.[14] Years later, when the Browning Society, in an excess of zeal, had a print of the painting distributed to its members, Browning admitted that he had not been able to make it out clearly, but had seen it in a *"favorable* darkness."

That was nearly irrelevant, however, for the painting interested him as a fragment of biography, his own, as well as the painter's. Guercino was sometimes at fault as a painter, and the poem is offered as compensation for that: "since I care / For dear Guercino's fame . . . I took one thought his picture struck from me, / And spread it out. . . ." The "thought" however, is in the observer's mind rather than the painter's. He feels that the angel who shelters the child will also shelter him. The poet's need and the sense of security offered by the painting meet at a point, like intersecting lines: "Guercino drew this angel . . . / And he was left at Fano by the beach. / We were at Fano. . . ." Physical and emotional positions become metaphorically interchangeable, suggesting that the poet can place himself emotionally with relation to *his* angel, Elizabeth, who is present, and his absent friend, Alfred Domett, just as he can place himself physically with relation to his setting. The par-

allels are developed in deceptively casual sentences that might be
scribbled on a postcard. The poet's attention moves from the paint-
ing to the natural scene, "This is Ancona, yonder is the sea," in the
same way as it moves from the painting to the personal emotion he
thinks it is the painting's function to evoke.

In 1849, after Pen was born, the Brownings solved the problem
of a summer refuge by taking a villa at Bagni di Lucca. Browning
had been reluctant to consider this small spa, high in the Tuscan
hills, because it was the popular summering place for the English
from Florence, and was overrun with an English population bent
on gambling, dancing, bathing, gossiping, and flirting. A fascinat-
ing place in its own way, it had a casino with gaming tables and as-
sembly rooms that was open to both sexes, an English church, and
an English cemetery. It was intersected by many small paths that
led over the hills to little villages and good sites for picnics. A stout
old lady named Mrs. Clotilda Elizabeth Stisted presided over pub-
lic entertainments as Queen of the Baths. She played the harp—
without, however, making any sound—and sent her crimson chair
ahead when she visited.[15] The Duke of Lucca spent his summers
there, and the English enjoyed taking part in the relaxed, but spirit-
ed entertainments offered by his court.

Bagni was not the sort of place to which the Brownings would or-
dinarily be drawn, but in 1849 the English had been kept away by
the uncertainties of the political situation, and the town was made
attractive by its cheapness and "the absence of our countrymen,"
as Elizabeth put it. Shelley had lived there in 1818, in a house lo-
cated not far from the casino, and had ridden with Mary to Prato
Fiorito, an excursion the Brownings repeated. The Brownings took
a secluded house, high on the hill over the town, and deep in the
woods. It was in this house that Elizabeth first showed Browning
Sonnets from the Portuguese. There were attractive walks and views
and unspoiled recesses of Italian countryside nearby. Not long af-
ter the death of his mother, Browning turned to this source for con-
solation; he took a long walk into the hills, came to a nearly des-
erted village and found there an old woman to whom he talked for
awhile.

Browning wrote little in the 1847–51 period except *Christmas-Eve
and Easter-Day,* a poem stemming from sources outside Italy, but it
would be a mistake to think that his powers were not in use. The
most important indication of his state of mind at this time is found

in a letter to Fanny Haworth, written about two months after he had come to Florence, in which he says that he has not given up his work, in spite of discouragement:

> I should not altogether wonder if I do something notable one of these days, all through a desperate virtue which determines out of gratitude. . . . So I mean to do my best whatever comes of it— meantime (not a stone's cast from the housetop under which I write) sleep, watch, and muse those surpassing statues of Michael Angelo. . . .[16]

The masterpieces of art he saw about him, and whose presence he felt when he did not see them, were keeping his sense of artistic responsibility alive. In spite of his report, in the same letter, that "We go about, sit on the bridge and see people pass, or take an ice inside Doney's after the vulgarest fashion," he was drawing latent powers from the spectacle of Florence, observing, thinking, and restoring energies depleted by his discouraging experiences in England.

He must have felt considerable satisfaction when, in 1849, a second edition of his poems appeared and *A Blot in the 'Scutcheon* was revived in far-off London. He was, of course, delighted when Elizabeth overcame her propensity for miscarriages in March of that year and gave birth to their son, Pen. But soon after news came of Mrs. Browning's death, and this conjunction of birth and death was, as Elizabeth wrote, too much for him. He fell into a long depression. After describing the beauties of Bagni di Lucca in a letter to his sister, he said that it was all useless, because "I am wholly tired of opening my eyes on the world now. . . ."[17] Just a year later, at the time Elizabeth had her most difficult miscarriage, he wrote to John Kenyon that he had had enough of Rome and Naples himself, but wanted Elizabeth to see them. Reactions of this kind should be read, not as disillusionments, but as indications that Italy was no longer a novelty. It was something more serious: a setting for life, death, and poetry.

"There is nothing *Italian* in the book," said Elizabeth, describing *Christmas-Eve and Easter-Day* in a letter to Mrs. Jameson.[18] It is not, in fact, the poem one might have looked for when Browning settled down to the first substantial work he did in Italy. He was writing in the study of Casa Guidi, whose windows faced the wall of his beloved San Felice church and admitted the street sounds of

Florence, but what he dealt with were religious issues that bedeviled English intellectual life. At this time, and throughout his residence in Italy, Browning remained an Englishman, a liberal, and a Non-Conformist. In this poem, cut off by miles and years from England, he annihilated the separation at a stroke, and wrote as if he had never left Camberwell.

When Browning read *In Memoriam* in December of 1850, about nine months after writing *Christmas-Eve and Easter-Day*, he might have been struck by the coincidence that he and Tennyson had confronted similar problems and reached similar conclusions. The two poems, published in the same year, fall together as Anglican and Non-Conformist defenses of Christianity. Both take the occasion of a bereavement as a test of faith, both examine reason as a basis for belief, reject it, and turn to intuition. Tennyson's answer to all doubts, "I have felt," also serves Browning. These parallels support Elizabeth's statement about Browning's poem, showing that it was in touch with issues that were occupying English minds.

Nevertheless, it is penetrated, here and there, by Browning's consciousness of Italy. There is a savage slash at Papal government, and an argument that even the greatest of artists cannot satisfy his spiritual needs by earthly satisfactions is supported by a memorable passage about Michelangelo, "Titanically infantine." *Christmas-Eve* symbolizes three forms of Christianity by a dissenting chapel, a rationalist theologian's lecture room and the basilica of St. Peter's. The description of St. Peter's is a brilliant "reading" of its architecture and design; the colonnade makes an embracing gesture, the wealth of the decoration is a dream materialized and made permanent, and the whole structure aspires to become heaven, a feeling expressed in the spirals of the baroque pillars supporting the canopy over the altar, which seem to lift it toward the sky. The building's energies are embodied in a vision of crowds swarming over it in excited expectation of a spiritual deliverance, and clustering about the portentous climax of the mass, when:

> *Earth breaks up, time drops away,*
> *In flows heaven with its new day*
> *Of endless life, when He who trod,*
> *Very man and very God,*
> *This earth in weakness, shame and pain,*

Dying the death whose signs remain
Up yonder on the accursed tree,—
Shall come again. . . .

Acknowledging that there is some truth in Rome, and that God accepts this form of worship as He does others, the speaker recalls that Christian love once rejected the artistic manifestations of Greece and Rome, and contented itself with the simple language of the gospels and primitive graphics, "true Christian art." But since love, the essential element, is also reflected in the offering of artistic and worldly beauty to God by Catholic congregations, the enlightened latter-day observer need not reject this beauty: "I will, on the whole, be rather proud of it. . . ." This position is a model of Browning's attitude toward Italy; he participated in it imaginatively, but directed his spiritual commitments elsewhere.

In the spring of 1851, with Pen growing up and Elizabeth in good health, it was time to think of visiting England. They made it a leisurely journey, seeing more of Italy on the way. Accompanied by Mr. and Mrs. David Ogilvy, their neighbors from an upper apartment of Casa Guidi, they left for Venice in May. They toured diligently, and Elizabeth made it a point to see Venice as she had expected to, sitting under the moonlight in the cafés on the Piazza San Marco. After a month, they traveled to Padua, where they made an excursion to see Petrarch's house and tomb at Arqua, and through Verona to Milan, where Elizabeth performed the very creditable feat, for a woman supposed to be physically weak, of climbing to the roof of the Duomo. From Milan they went to Como, and crossed Lago Maggiore, leaving Italy by way of Lugano. They were not to return for sixteen months, until the fall of 1852.

There was, in fact, some question as to whether they would return at all. The eight months they spent in Paris in the winter and spring of 1851–52, were stimulating and exciting. When Louis Napoleon and his troops passed under the windows of their apartment on the Champs-Elysées and they heard the firing of cannon during the *coup d'état* of early December 1851, they felt that they were at the center of historic events. Browning, who had done comparatively little work in Italy, took himself in hand in Paris, wrote the "Essay on Shelley," and, after opening the new year with a determination to write a poem a day, persisted for three days with excellent results, producing "Women and Roses,"

"Childe Roland to the Dark Tower Came," and "Love Among the Ruins." They visited George Sand, and Browning met Lamartine and Joseph Milsand, a critic who had praised his work, and who became a life-long friend.

It became obvious that Florence, compared with Paris or London, was a sleepy, superficial, slightly ridiculous suburb of nineteenth-century life, far from the centers of intellectual activity, and that if the Brownings took their position as writers seriously, they owed it to themselves and their public to remain in the world. Family considerations also arose. Pen's aunts and uncles wanted to see him, and with Mrs. Browning dead, Robert's father needed company and care. London's climate was too harsh, and its associations were unpleasant for Elizabeth. As a result, they began to think of Paris as a possible home.

But Florence prevailed. After Paris they spent the summer and autumn of 1852 in London, then returned to Casa Guidi early in November. Elizabeth was delighted to get back to the restful, familiar scene, but Florence was too quiet for Browning after Paris. Reporting this to Sarianna, Elizabeth wrote, "Oh, of course it *is* very dead in comparison! but it's a beautiful death. . . ."[19] Browning, writing to John Kenyon, said that they were happy to be back, and to see old and new friends, and added: "We don't go out, however, but live our old life."[20] The following spring, Elizabeth wrote to Mrs. Jameson that Robert was thinking of "that blaze of life in Paris." They intended to return, for Paris was for living; meanwhile, "Here, one sleeps. . . ."[21]

So they returned to what Elizabeth called "our old traditions." Now began what might be called the classical period of the Brownings' residence in Florence. They thought of Casa Guidi as their home, though they often left it for long absences in England, Bagni di Lucca, and Siena, and pursued a quiet, steady routine of writing, reading, and educating Pen, meanwhile developing relationships with a circle of friends among the more serious members of the Anglo-American community. These included not only Isa Blagden, Seymour Kirkup, Powers, and Story, but some new English friends, including Frederick Tennyson, Alfred's older brother, Robert Lytton, the son of the novelist, Sir Edward Bulwer-Lytton, Thomas Adolphus Trollope, and the American, James Jackson Jarves.

Tennyson, who had been the enigmatic third contributor to the *Poems by Two Brothers* in which the more famous Alfred's first published poems had appeared, had migrated to the Mediterranean region in 1833, when he came into family property. He married the daughter of a Siena magistrate and eventually settled in Florence. He was forty-six years of age in 1853, when he came to know the Brownings. They liked Tennyson and the poetry he wrote, and his friendship with them encouraged him both to publish some volumes of verse and to become active as a spiritualist. He left Italy in 1857, to spend the rest of his life in Jersey. Lytton, who was in his early twenties, had come to Florence as a member of the British legation. He was to have a long diplomatic career, to be Viceroy of India, and to become an author under the pseudonym of "Owen Meredith." The Brownings found him a charming and congenial companion; he spent much time with them, and gained their approval for the verses he was just beginning to publish.

Thomas Adolphus Trollope first came to Florence in 1843 with his mother, and married in 1848. His wife, Theodosia, had lived in Torquay as a child, where she and Elizabeth Barrett had been acquaintances. The family lived in the Villino Trollope, an elegant palazzo where they entertained frequently, making their house an active center of Anglo-Florentine social life. At the Trollopes', English and Italians could meet to exchange views, a rarity in Florence or anywhere in Italy. The lively and brilliant parties that took place there were, understandably, even more popular with visitors from England and America than the hour or so of serious conversation available at Casa Guidi.

Trollope, throughout his long career in Italy, was extremely active as a journalist, popular historian, novelist, and writer of personal reminiscences about Italy. Although Italy was not his sole subject, he was an invaluable interpreter of past and current events in Italy; he brought to them the insights of a liberal mind thoroughly informed by close observation of Italian affairs and intercourse with numerous Italians. (Browning, we must remember, had very little practical knowledge of this kind about Italy.)

Jarves, a Bostonian born in 1818, was the most assiduous of the Florentine art collectors. He settled in Florence in 1852, was the author of some books on art, and worked as a journalist, sending articles to *Harper's Magazine.* Intending to build up a sequence of works which would illustrate the development of Italian art from the tenth to the sixteenth centuries, and to install it in Boston, he pursued paintings with pathological intensity, borrowing money, denying his family necessities, credulously accepting false attributions, and searching everywhere. Browning knew him well, and seems to have been influenced by his mania for art, but as a spiritualist, Jarves was much more intimate with Elizabeth, and failed to win Browning's confidence.[22]

For Browning, life in Florence included long walks through the city and its outskirts, and communion with churches, galleries, *palazzi*, streets, and squares, illuminated by studies in Vasari and other sources. Elizabeth had said that "Here one sleeps," but it was actually a time of imaginative awakening, for before they returned to England, both did some of their best work; during this period, Browning wrote *Men and Women* and Elizabeth wrote a large part of *Aurora Leigh*.

Bagni di Lucca was becoming an essential part of their Italy. From July to October 1853, they lived in the Casa Tolomei, a house on the main street of the central part of the town called Alla Villa, not far from the river, between the casino and the bridge. It was a particularly satisfying summer. Story and his wife were there for the entire season, and the Brownings invited Robert Lytton to stay with them for a fortnight. There were dinners under the trees, conversations beside the noisy river, and long walks in the woods. Elizabeth reported that Browning was working busily—he wrote "In a Balcony" at this time—and that they often exchanged visits with the Storys. The atmosphere of this time is captured in a letter from Story to James Russell Lowell:

> . . . we are leading the most *dolce far niente* of lives. The place is beautiful. All about us tower the mountains, terraced with vines and noble groups of chestnuts, and through the valley below sings our mountain-brook river as it sweeps under its one-arched bridges, turns picturesque mills, and goes winding along through its rocky bed to the Mediterranean. Every evening we drive along the richly-wooded banks of the wild, roaring Lima, or else beside the rushing Serchio, where Shelley used to push his little boat, to the Devil's Bridge. . . . Of society there is none we care to meet but the Brownings, who are living here. With them we have constant and delightful intercourse, interchanging long evenings together two or three

times a week, and driving and walking whenever we can meet. We like them very much—they are so simple, unaffected and sympathetic. . . . B. says he is full of poetry.[23]

The Brownings' stay in Rome during the winter of 1853–54 seemed to confirm their attachment to Florence. They lived on the third floor of a house at 43 Bocca di Leone, in the neighborhood of the Piazza di Spagna, and not far from the Roman scenes of *The Ring and the Book*. They were welcomed by the Storys, who had preceded them, and had as a neighbor on the floor below the American artist, William Page, who was to paint a portrait of Browning in December. In spite of this promising outlook, the visit began with tragedy. On the day after their arrival, November 24, the Storys' little boy, Joe, caught gastric fever and died, and his sister, Edith, fell ill at the Brownings' house, was put to bed in Page's apartment, and did not recover for six weeks. Joe Story was buried in the Protestant cemetery Browning had seen on his first visit to Rome, just across the footpath from Shelley's grave.

Browning and Elizabeth met many new English and American friends during this winter in Rome, and went on excursions to such places as Frascati, Ostia, and the Campagna with them. Elizabeth presided over séances in their apartment, while Browning sought diversion at dinner parties and other engagements in the English-speaking colony. But Rome was not a success. A month after they had arrived, Browning complained that he was bored and would return to Florence if he could afford it. Elizabeth preferred Paris. Both were happy to go back to Florence in the spring. Elizabeth reported that, after an evening with Anglo-Florentine company at Lytton's villa, "We walked home to the song of nightingales by starlight and firefly-light. Florence looks to us more beautiful than ever after Rome. I love the very stones of it, to say nothing of the cypresses and river."[24]

Up to this time, Browning had done little work in Italy. His only sustained effort, *Christmas-Eve and Easter-Day*, was derived from past memories. But during this comparatively silent interlude, Italy was rooting itself in his feelings, and taking its place among his imaginative resources. Elizabeth reports that at a time when she was concerned about the reception of a performance of *Colombe's Birthday* in London, Browning tried to distract her by "calling me to admire this bright light across the mountains—that black shadow on an old wall."[25] His life in Italy was enfolded in simple sensory impressions of this kind, with their direct power to evoke emotion, so that the letters written after he left Florence often speak of the pain of recalling beloved details of the place. When Isa Blagden identified the new villa she had taken, he wrote:

> I fancy exactly how you feel and see how you live. . . . I well remember the fine view from the Kinney's upper-room—that looking *down* the steep hill, by the side of which runs the road you describe: that path was always my preferred walk, for its shortness (abruptness) and the fine old wall to *your* left (*from* the Villa) which is overgrown with weeds and wild flowers—violets and ground-ivy, I remember. Oh, me—to find myself there, some late sunshiny Sunday afternoon, with my face turned to Florence. . . . I think I should fairly end it all on the spot.[26]

Henry James, arguing that no other writer had succeeded in conveying so intimate a sense of Italy as Browning, attributed his power to a thorough assimilation of "the elements for which the name of Italy stands," and observed that this influence was permanent: "The Rome and Tuscany of the early 'fifties had become for him so at once a medium, a bath of the senses and perceptions, into which he could sink, in which he could unlimitedly soak, that wherever he might be touched afterwards he gave out some effect of that immersion."[27]

True as this is, it does not go far enough. Italy had become more than a bath of sensation and perception for Browning. The sights and sounds of the years at Casa Guidi had become involved with his most intimate feelings, and merged with his poetic motivations. An exceptionally emotional letter which Browning wrote to Isa Blagden after Elizabeth's death and his return to England suggests that Italy had penetrated to the center of his emotional life. He said that he had mixed feelings about visiting Italy again, and continued:

> The general impression of the past is as if it had been pain. I would not live it over again, not one day of it. Yet all that seems my real *life*, —and before and after, nothing at all: I look back on all my life, when I look *there*: and life is painful. I always think of this when I read the Odyssey—Homer makes the surviving Greeks, whenever they refer to Troy, just say of it "At Troy, where the Greeks suffered so." Yet all their life was in that ten years at Troy.[28]

Elizabeth's illness and death are, of course, major components of these memories. But Browning is also saying that his Italian years, painful as they seemed in retrospect, were the most authentic part of his life, the *only* authentic part: "before and after, nothing at all."

SIX

Old Pictures and Browning

Most of the poems in *Men and Women* were apparently written at Casa Guidi, but only about a third of them deal with Italy or Italian themes. Of these, the one that gives the most direct insight into Browning's thoughts about Italy, showing that he greatly enjoyed the period in his life that he recollected afterward with such pain, is "Old Pictures in Florence," a jocular, rambling, conversational celebration of the pleasure he took in living in Florence, sharing its political aspirations, learning its past, and studying its art. As one of his occupations, he wandered about the city, searching for pictures that he hoped would turn out to be neglected masterpieces. This had long been a common pursuit among Anglo-Italians. Walter Savage Landor collected actively between 1825 and 1828, and his pictures (now in the possession of Christ Church, Oxford) include a number of graceful and curious primitives. Browning must have penetrated into many corners of Florentine life on these forays. In the spring of 1850, for example, after rummaging through "a corn shop a mile from Florence," and looking behind the bed in an upstairs room, he found five pictures which he bought and took home to Casa Guidi. Browning called Kirkup, who optimistically assigned them to such figures as Cimabue, Ghirlandaio, and Giottino.

"Old Pictures in Florence" refers to these expeditions. James Jackson Jarves, who was far more deeply committed to collecting paintings than Browning, gives an idea of what searches of this kind led to:

> They involved an inquisition into the intricacies of numberless villas, palaces, convents, churches and household *dens* all over this portion of Italy, the employment of many agents to scout out my prey; many fatiguing journeyings, miles upon miles of wearisome staircases, dusty explorations of dark retreats, dirt, disappointment, fraud, lies and moneys often fruitlessly spent. . . . On one occasion to get nine pictures I was obliged to purchase a gallery of upwards of 200. . . . On another having discovered a fine old Pollajuolo . . . the owner would not let me have it unless I bought all in the room (44 in all). . . .[1]

Such investigations, even on a modest scale, were bound to bring Browning close to realities that lay below the surface of Italian life, to the old art and the experiences of the old painters, although his interpretation of what he saw was likely to be controlled by judgments he read in Vasari.

"Old Pictures in Florence" harbors an irony that nearly misfires. After reading it, Dante Gabriel Rossetti wrote: "What a jolly thing is *Old Pictures at* (sic) *Florence*! It seems all the pictures desired by the poet are in his possession *in fact*!"[2] This was not quite as true as Browning thought it was. The poet complains that, in spite of his persistent searches, he has not found any works of the artists he mentions, but the painting of the Casa Guidi drawing room he commissioned after Elizabeth's death shows that he actually owned pictures he attributed to them, and in two cases the attributions are correct. The "muscular Christ" he deceptively pleads to be allowed to find is an allusion to the genuine Pollaiuolo, *Christ at the Column*, which is seen on the left wall of the drawing room. (It was sold in 1913 for £500.) Also genuine was the Ghirlandaio altarpiece over the fireplace which represents the Eternal Father flanked by two angels; the angels were found separately and joined to the central portion. Browning believed that the four panels showing saints were by Margheritone, who is asked in the poem for "a poor glimmering Crucifixion," and that his *St. Jerome* was a Taddeo Gaddi ("But are you too fine, Taddeo Gaddi, / To grant me a taste of your intonaco"), but these cannot be included in the joke, for the attributions are probably wrong.

The poem begins with an address to Giotto, who is taken as the embodiment of Italy; it was originally titled "Opus Magistri Jocti," or "The Work of Master Giotto," as the proof sheets in the Huntington Library show. Browning ruefully complains that, in spite of his diligence as a searcher, someone else had been allowed to discover "a certain precious little tablet" by the master, and turns again to speak to Giotto at the end of the poem, claiming to be the first to predict the completion of the campanile he designed and the liberation of Italy, "that glory of Giotto / And Florence together."

The "tablet" is identified in a letter to John Kenyon.[3] It was a *Death of the Virgin*, or *Dormition*, which Vasari describes in his life of Giotto as a work praised by Michelangelo, adding that while it was extant in 1550, at the time of the first edition of his book, it had disappeared by 1568, the year of the second edition. When Browning complains that his efforts have been futile, "I, that have haunted the dim San Spirito, / Or was it rather the Ognissanti?" his second guess is the right one, for the painting had originally been seen in the Church of the Ognissanti.

In spite of the opening description of a spring morning in the suburbs of Florence and the allusions to contemporary politics, there is a special weight in the poem's assertion that Browning's "business" is with "empty cells of the human hive," the lonely spaces in churches and cloisters where paintings are to be found. His Italian materials lay in the past, for the most part. In the poem he acknowledges that his searches have enabled him to envision the ghosts of the old painters moving through the busy streets of Florence—imaginings that undoubtedly have much to do with the great artist monologues of *Men and Women*.

As Leonee Ormond has observed, it is often hard to tell whether Browning speaks from his own knowledge of the painters mentioned in "Old Pictures in Florence," or simply relies on Vasari.[4] The idiom of the poem is what Sordello called "brother's speech," an elliptical, allusive language meaningful to those who share the poet's range of knowledge, but likely to be enigmatic to others. When he visited the Louvre with Browning, Dante Gabriel Rossetti discovered that Browning's knowledge of early Italian art was superior to that of anyone he had ever met, including Ruskin. The reader of "Old Pictures in Florence," however, will find the key to its idiom, not in a general knowledge of art, but in *The Lives of the Painters:* nearly everything Browning expects the reader to know is to be found in Vasari.

In addressing his poem to Giotto, and adopting Nicola Pisano and Cimabue as his own, Browning singled out three figures whom Vasari identified as leaders in the rebellion against the stiff Byzantine style of medieval paintings. But he could also speak directly about them, because he had had some opportunities to see their work, though he undoubtedly saw them through Vasari's eyes. He had examined Nicola's pulpits in Pisa and Siena, and had very likely sought out his bas-relief of the Deposition in the porch of San Martino in Lucca which Vasari praises as an example of the early progress of sculpture. The Brownings had visited Padua in June 1851 on a journey to Paris, and stopped in Assisi in November 1853 on the way to Rome; both cities contain major sets of frescoes by Giotto where Browning could have seen, among other elements, convincing realistic effects clearly drawn from life, or possibly from the drama.[5]

The works of Giotto that survive in Florence, where Browning could have seen them repeatedly, are not extensive. The major remains (apart from the campanile built to his design) are the frescoes in the Bargello and the two sets of frescoes in the Peruzzi and Bardi Chapels of Santa Croce. Much of this work has undergone restoration and is in poor condition today, so it is difficult to say how much Browning might have made of these paintings; but they contain some striking individual figures and scenes of intense, subdued emotion. As for Cimabue, his masterpiece, the *Madonna and Child Enthroned,* ventures only a little distance from the Byzantine tradition, but Browning, prompted by Vasari who regarded Cimabue as a forerunner of the Renaissance, might have seen some signs of realism in the sense of depth with which the throne is treated, and in the individualized portraiture in the faces of the sages and angels. Vasari attributed the *Rucellai Madonna* in the Church of Santa Maria Novella to Cimabue, and Elizabeth, taking it as his work, wrote a moving description of it in *Casa Guidi Windows.* Browning also accepted this attribution, of course, but the picture is now assigned to the Sienese painter, Duccio di Buoninsegna, partly on the basis of a contract between Duccio and the church officials.

Up to about the time of the Brownings' residence in Italy the paintings of the fifteenth and sixteenth centuries had obscured the work of earlier painters, who were considered childlike, crude,

and, in short, "primitive." Some eighteenth-century English art-
ists, such as Reynolds, Romney, and Flaxman, had been sensitive
to the work of Giotto and his contemporaries, and after the Napo-
leonic wars, English people traveling in Italy began to make the
public aware of the neglected painters of the earlier period. There
was a new perception of their works in Germany, where a Protes-
tant religious sensibility not always comfortable with the Catholic
art it admired, turned to a general interest in medievalism, and to
an appreciation of the spiritual qualities of the primitive painters.[6]
This approach eventually led to the appearance of the Nazarene
school of painters in Germany, and the Pre-Raphaelite movement
in England. Its first exponent in England was a Frenchman, Ale-
xandre Rio, whose work *De la poésie chrétienne* (1836) took the view
that art should be judged according to the spiritual qualities exhib-
ited by the artist, and the moral influence it exerts. Mrs. Jameson
knew Rio, and assimilated his views into her popular studies of
Italian art. The chapter in her *Memoirs of the Early Italian Painters*
which contrasts Fra Angelico, as an "Idealist" or "Mystic" with Fra
Lippo Lippi as a "Naturalist" gives an estimate of Lippi's position
which corresponds closely with the one found in Browning's dra-
matic monologue. Ruskin read Rio's book, adopted his emphasis
on the spiritual aspects of art, and was enormously influential in
promoting the new taste for primitive paintings.

Lord Lindsay's *Sketches of the History of Christian Art* (1847) point-
ed out the importance of the early painters, urging readers not to
limit their studies to the perfection of Raphael and Michelangelo,
but to begin with such painters as Duccio, Giotto, Masaccio, and
Perugino, who were capable of evoking deep feelings in spite of
their faults. Vasari had praised the primitives for their craftsman-
ship and naturalism, but they were now admired for projecting a
strong, simple faith while ignoring problems of perspective, anato-
my, lighting, and other representational elements. The religious
approach to primitive paintings became very powerful in England,
leading not only to the founding of the Pre-Raphaelite Brotherhood
in 1848, but to Ruskin's praise of Gothic art, and a change in the
policy of the National Gallery, which, after rejecting the Woodburn
Collection of early paintings in 1847, began to admit them in the
following year.

By that time the new taste was well established, and large num-
bers of obscure pictures had already been bought up and formed

into private collections. In 1847, the *Tuscan Athenaeum*, the little weekly journal published for the Florentine English community, observed that early religious paintings had replaced baroque pagan subjects in popularity:

> The possessors of a Giotto or Gaddi or Beato Angelico little thought some fifty or sixty years ago, as they carelessly tossed into the hands of the *revenditore* these now precious relics of antiquity . . . that, in a few years, these selfsame despised tavole or "boards" as they were called, would in their turn completely upset the heathen Gods and Godesses, taking their places and driving the latter to pass the remainder of their days in the utmost neglect and destitution. . . .[7]

The Brownings were not in the forefront of this illumination. Henry James looks back with ironic condescension to this period when serious, but ill-equipped American (and English) lovers of art were purposefully developing their consciousness of Europe:

> I think of them all, the artless seekers of knowledge, would-be haunters of the fountainhead. . . . their simplicities become sacred to us and their very mistakes acquire a charm.[8]

Among those he smilingly tolerates are the Brownings: "Robert Browning and his illustrious wife burnt incense, for instance, to Domenichino." The charge is true, for the Brownings admired the Domenichino *David* at Fano in the summer of 1848, and wondered why the "graduate of Oxford" who had written *Modern Painters* had been critical of him. As James acknowledges, they were simply following the old-fashioned, but still current dispensation, which venerated the fifteenth and sixteenth centuries. A conversion took place before 1851, however, for in *Casa Guidi Windows* Elizabeth anticipates Browning by praising the *Rucellai Madonna*, Margheritone, and Giotto, while recognizing their archaic qualities, and two years later, in "Old Pictures in Florence," Browning himself dismisses the argument over "Old Master This and Early the Other" with the decision that "Old and New are fellows."[9]

The new taste for works from the Quattrocento and earlier periods embodied two attitudes that correspond to ideas about poetry that were emerging in Browning's thoughts. The motive that led art lovers to search for paintings parallels the idea expounded in *The Ring and the Book* that poetry is a process of regeneration or rehabilitation. And the conviction that naive works marred by technical faults nevertheless deserve respect resembles the love for imperfection expressed in "Old Pictures in Florence." The new preference for "primitive" paintings of this kind supported Browning's view that the aim of art should be, not to depict ideals far removed from the human condition, as classical Greek sculpture does, but to expose the inwardness of man as he actually exists. Accordingly, the best art is not that which is most accomplished technically, but that which discloses spiritual striving through its faults and irregularities, as the work of the early Renaissance artists did. In this "revolution," as he calls it, Browning sees a counterpart of the life of the soul after death, an instance of the rebirth which poetry itself brings about.

As much as he depended on Vasari, Browning differed with him on one subject. Vasari admired the art of classical antiquity, but Browning shared the Romantic and Victorian preference for art that follows the laws of its own nature into whatever excesses and irregularities its expressive aims require. Greek statuary, says "Old Pictures in Florence," functioned as an ideal; such powerful forms as the Elgin marbles impress the observer with his own weakness and teach submission. But then (presumably with the early Renaissance) "Growth came" in the form of an awareness of human potentialities, and the painters declared that it was their mission to "paint man, man, whatever the issue!" This sounds like Vasari's humanism, but as David J. DeLaura has pointed out, such an interpretation is inconsistent with the injunction that follows:

> To bring the invisible into full play!
> Let the visible go to the dogs. . . .

These lines emphasize a point neglected by Vasari: the primitives he praised were Christian artists, whose work had a specifically religious quality.[10]

In comparing the art of the early painters with Greek sculpture, Browning maintains that classical works lack the vitality and potential for growth that are found in the naive, deficient, and irregular. Hence, "What comes to perfection perishes." This doctrine is associated with the Christian belief that whatever is done in this life, including the creation of works of art, should not aim at completion, but should be a preparation for another state.

Browning's typically Victorian defense of the early painters follows the spirit of Romantic esthetic theory. It is descended from Coleridge's organicism, which regarded the work of art as a growth rooted in the artist's feelings and motives, and formed by processes originating with them. This is joined by an emphasis on the Christian virtues of humility and simplicity, traceable to Rio, which came on the scene most dramatically through the Pre-Raphaelites, but had been felt earlier. The central Victorian expression of this esthetic principle, Ruskin's chapter, "The Nature of Gothic" from *The Stones of Venice*, a book nearly contemporaneous with "Old Pictures in Florence," links the taste for imperfection to social conditions. Ruskin felt that the irregularities of Gothic church ornament reflected the freedom permitted to the workmen who made them, while finished, uniform art could only be achieved through deadening routine labor imposed by some authority.

Mingled with the good-natured complaint of "Old Pictures in Florence" is a much less sanguine note of objection to the indifference shown to the painters by their contemporaries, and especially by a posterity which allowed their works to fall into decay—"oh, this world and the wrong it does!" Here Browning is both expressing his own interest in keeping the past alive and reflecting a contemporary concern with the preservation of works of art. Many of the frescoes had been painted in cloisters or other places open to the weather, and were deteriorating from natural causes. But there was also much human neglect and active destruction of the kind Ruskin had seen in the Campo Santo in Pisa. Walls containing important pictures were often covered with whitewash. The refectory of Santa Croce, which had frescoes by Giotto and Taddeo Gaddi, had been rented out as a carpet factory, so that the looms blocked out the sight of the pictures.[11] The Bargello chapel, decorated with frescoes by Giotto showing scenes from *Inferno* and *Paradiso*, had been divided horizontally to make two rooms, the walls were whitewashed, and the upper portion was used as a prison. The paintings were discovered when a prisoner rubbed off some of the whitewash, exposing a spot of red drapery.[12] Browning's friend, Kirkup, led the campaign to obtain funds for restoration of this site, making a tracing of the portrait of Dante included among the figures in order to demonstrate its importance.[13]

Fra Lippo's church, Santa Maria del Carmine, seems to have been especially indifferent to its art treasures. The *Tuscan Athenae-*

um reported that the authorities planned to form a side entrance into the Brancacci chapel by cutting through the Masaccio frescoes, and Ruskin noted that two lamps had been nailed into the frescoes at the Carmine, splitting the wall. In an influential "Postscriptum" added to later editions of *Sketches of the History of Christian Art,* Lord Lindsay called attention to the general situation, and framed an appeal to the rulers of Italy "on behalf of the grand, old frescoes which are either perishing unheeded before their eyes, or that lie entombed beneath the whitewash of barbarism, longing for resuscitation. . . ."[14] Browning echoes this sentiment when he describes the ghosts of the old painters standing before pictures suffering from decay or desecration as

> . . . *wishful each scrap should clutch the brick,*
>   *Each tinge not wholly escape the plaster,*
> —*A lion who dies of an ass's kick,*
>   *The wronged great soul of an ancient Master.*

The virtue of "resuscitation" so strongly impressed him that it became an element of his poetic theory. The urge to redeem the past, already visible in the poems he had written on historical subjects, was confirmed by the spectacle of what was happening to the frescoes of Florence. He was so deeply convinced of the worth of this effort that he devoted his most ambitious poems to the task of making forgotten figures and events come to life again in the imagination of his readers. His explanation of his methods in *The Ring and the Book* identifies poetry itself as an act of "resuscitation."

SEVEN

Men and Women

Some of the shorter lyrics in *Men and Women* may have been written earlier, but the most substantial part of the two-volume work was probably composed after the Brownings had returned from England in 1852. Browning wrote at the stand-up desk in the small room off the dining room in Casa Guidi, where he could hear the noises of the Via Mazzetta and the Piazza San Felice. He was within walking distance of many of the settings used in the poems, and was surrounded by the works of the artists mentioned in them.

It is not easy to write in the presence of the subject. Ordinarily, immediate impressions are hypnotic, freezing the creative processes until memory can rework them, after Proust's fashion. Italy, with its many seductive appeals, certainly was capable of this effect. Henry James warned that "while subjects float by in Italy, as the fish in the sea," the writer is easily betrayed by "the golden air," and may not be able to establish a vital relationship with them while he is in their presence. Browning, he noticed, was an exception; he was energized rather than lulled by the abundance of Italy. In *Men and Women*, said James, which was

> . . . produced on the spot and face to face with the sources of his inspiration, his ten years of Florence and Rome may claim a full participation. . . . the writer's "relation to his subject," which I have so freely made the golden air responsible for undermining, was, in Browning, constitutionally stout and single. That weight of the whole mind which we have also speculatively invoked was a pressure that he easily enough, at any point, that he in fact almost extravagantly, brought to bear.[1]

The self-effacing, objective poetic mode Browning deploys with such perfect security in *Men and Women* had its roots in the moment of the *Sordello* digression. Having been developed, in *Pippa Passes*

and the early monologues, into the dramatic revelation of charac-
ter, it now became a medium of intense psychological penetration,
supported by a rich sense of environment. As James noted, Brown-
ing was strengthened by the ability to visualize such figures as Fra
Lippo Lippi and Andrea del Sarto against a backdrop of the houses
where they had lived, the streets they had walked, and the paint-
ings they had left behind. But this knowledge also formed his
poetry on a more radical level, for it enabled him to enter into the
lives and thoughts of people unlike himself, and to speak for them,
not subjectively, as an advocate, but objectively, as an artist. Sub-
jects that were both Italian and historical gave him an opportunity
to achieve Nietzsche's "deliverance from the self," and to deal with
what Browning called in *Sordello* "the veritable business of
mankind." His relation to these subjects corresponds to the spirit
that Saul Bellow identifies with the novel. "Novels," he said, "are
about others. They lack everything if they lack this sympathetic de-
votion to something else." In a letter written at this time to his
French friend, Milsand, the inconspicuous phrase Browning had
often used now emerged, not only as the title of his new book, but
as a disclosure of his real theme. "My poems go under the distinc-
tive title of 'Men and Women'—they being really dramatic attempts
and not a collection of miscellanies."[2]

The two great artist monologues of *Men and Women*, "Fra Lippo
Lippi" and "Andrea del Sarto," deal with the fundamentals of hu-
man nature, not with national characteristics, but in each of them
historical detail establishes an enveloping sense of place and time.
W.J. Fox, in one of his *Monthly Repository* articles, said that poetry
must "become incarnate in . . . forms which bear the peculiar fea-
tures of age, class or country," demanding a realism which seems
more appropriate to the novel than to poetry. Browning expressed
a similar view in the "Essay on Shelley," where he acknowledged
the importance of idealization, but insisted that poetry also had to
present things as they were generally perceived, and argued that
the contribution of the objective poet cannot be ignored.

> . . . it is with this world, as starting point and basis alike, that we
> shall always have to concern ourselves; the world is not to be learn-
> ed and thrown aside, but reverted to and relearned. The spiritual
> comprehension may be infinitely subtilized, but the raw material it
> operates upon must remain.[3]

In regarding Venice as "a type of life" as he did in the *Sordello* inset, Browning, we recall, took Italian settings and Italy itself as surrogates for "this world," as particulars embodying universal truths. In the artist monologues, Italian history and painting continued to function in this way, as "raw material" that is both "starting point and basis" of a general moral vision.

"Fra Lippo Lippi" exhibits a mind caught in a conflict between its own convictions and the commands of authority, a counterpart of the tension between religious purpose and the expression of individuality that is felt in much Renaissance art. Most of what Browning knew about Fra Lippo came from Vasari, whose account furnished the incidents within which the poem is placed. According to Vasari, Fra Lippo escaped from a window of the Medici-Riccardi palace by means of a rope made by cutting up a sheet in order to get away for a few days of revelry. He also gives details of Fra Lippo's later life, including his connection with Lucrezia Buti, a young woman he met at a convent where he was painting, and the amorous intrigues in which he became involved. Browning's painter, however, has erred through weakness rather than passion. His guilty pleasures are seen as perversions of his robust love of life, and he demonstrates a capacity for remorse and repentance, as well as a sturdy natural piety. None of this is found in Vasari or in the historical records. It is Browning's creation of a new character, an extrapolation from his reaction to the work of the painter.

Browning's Fra Lippo is militantly opposed to art that ignores esthetic possibilities for the sake of inculcating a spiritual message, for he believes that beauty calls forth a sense of gratitude to God. His essential belief is that the illuminating power of art depends upon an accurate representation of "God's works"—"Art was given for that"—and Browning presents him as a figure whose passionate love of the physical world carried forward the Renaissance tendency to turn for its models to immediate reality: "—paint these / Just as they are, careless what comes of it." Lippo's paintings— many of them on display in Florence and familiar to Browning—do not make an overwhelming case for this view of his esthetic philosophy. They do contain strongly representational passages, including some charming genre details, but these are far less prominent than the emphasis on design and technical effects, or the piety and fantasy that appear in certain works.

Browning's attribution of a realistic philosophy to Fra Lippo is an error based on his belief that Fra Lippo was the master of Masaccio, and that he had taught his supposed disciple a naturalistic style which represented an important departure from tradition.[4] In the poem, Fra Lippo expresses the hope that his student, Hulking Tom —Browning's inaccurate rendering of "Masaccio," a perversion of Tomasso Guidi's Christian name which would be more accurately translated as "slovenly" or "clumsy" Tom—will carry on his style. Actually, it was Masaccio, who, though not much older than Lippi, originated the representational style that influenced Lippi and other Renaissance painters. He came to Florence in 1425 to complete the frescoes depicting the life of St. Peter and other Biblical scenes in the Brancacci Chapel of the church of Santa Maria del Carmine that had been begun by Masolino (and were to be completed by Lippo's son, Filippino). At that time Lippi was nineteen, and had been living in the community adjoining the Carmine for three years. Vasari is undoubtedly right to say that the young priest saw Masaccio at work, and was strongly influenced by the frescoes, as were the many famous artists, including Michelangelo and Raphael, who came to study them.

The Carmine is not far from Casa Guidi, and since Browning said that he had been interested in the Brancacci Chapel, and in the relation between Lippi and Masaccio for a long time (though he never got it right), we can be sure that he, too, studied these frescoes and considered what Vasari said about them. Their main technical advance is a skillful and unobtrusive foreshortening, which gives the figures a rounded, sculptural quality and three-dimensional appearance. There are also individualized portraits and strikingly posed figures, such as the shivering man in the picture of *St. Peter Baptizing the Neophytes* mentioned by Vasari, and the massive nude male figures kneeling before St. Peter that strongly impressed later artists. Vasari emphasizes Masaccio's realism. Describing the *Sagra*, or *Consecration*, a lost fresco showing the ceremony of the church's consecration painted by Masaccio, he reports that it contained the portraits of many notables and crowds of diversified figures painted "with such excellence that they would not look otherwise in real life." The views of Browning's Fra Lippo correspond exactly with Vasari's explanation of Masaccio's reasoning: "as painting is nothing more than an imitation of all natural living

Masaccio, *St. Peter Baptizing the Neophytes*, Brancacci Chapel, Florence
(Archivi Alinari)

"A kind of break in the progression of the art" — Mrs. Jameson

things, with similar design and coloring, so he who should follow
Nature most closely would come nearest to perfection."[5] In her
Memoirs of the Early Italian Painters, Mrs. Jameson repeats this view
of Masaccio's contribution, saying, "He excelled . . . in the expres-
sion and imitation of natural actions and feelings," and observing
that he made so great an advance "that there seems a kind of break
in the progression of the art."[6]

Bernard Berenson greatly admired the Brancacci Chapel fres-
coes, for the very reason that Browning's Fra Lippo gives as the
purpose of art. Berenson judged art by its "tactile values," and
considered Masaccio's frescoes supreme in this respect: "I feel that
I could touch every figure, that it would yield a definite resistance
to my touch, that I should have to expend thus much effort to dis-
place it, that I could walk around it. In short, I could scarcely real-
ize it more, and in real life I should scarcely realize it so well,"[7] a
reaction that corresponds closely to Fra Lippo's "we love / First
when we see them painted, things we have passed / Perhaps a
hundred times, nor cared to see."

Though Browning was interested in the man described by Va-
sari, the naturalism he attributes to Lippi's art appeared on the
walls of the Brancacci chapel rather than in Lippi's paintings, and
was in reality the invention of Masaccio. One detail suggests that
the Brancacci chapel was in his mind as he wrote the poem. Fra
Lippo calls upon his listeners to be thankful for "yonder river's
line, / The mountain round it and the sky above. . . ." Idealized
landscapes corresponding to this description appear in some of
Lippi's backgrounds, but it is possible that what Browning had in
mind was rather the accurate rendering of the Arno and its neigh-
boring mountains in Masaccio's *Tribute Money*.

The authenticity of Browning's character is supported by a crowd
of vivid humanity that swarms into his monologue: the men of the
watch seen in torchlight; the people discussing pictures in church;
the fugitive admired by children, threatened by his victim's son,
and visited secretly by his sweetheart who brings bread and jewel-
ry. These were details of the kind Browning loved to observe in
paintings. He was critical of Mary Shelley's comments on Fra An-
gelico because she had missed "the divine *bon-bourgeoisie* of his pic-
tures; the dear common folk of his crowds, those who sit and listen
(spectacle at nose and bent into a comfortable heap to hear better)

Masaccio, *The Tribute Money*, Brancacci Chapel, Florence (Archivi Alinari)

"Do you feel thankful, ay or no,
For . . . yonder river's line,
The mountains round it and the sky above . . ."

at the sermon of the Saint—and the children, and women,—divinely pure they all are, but fresh from the streets and market place. . . ."[8]

David J. DeLaura has placed the poem as a rejoinder to Alexis Rio's advocacy of religious painting, and has derived the Prior's insistence that Fra Lippo paint souls rather than flesh from Rio's doctrines.[9] The Prior's floundering efforts to tell how this should be done are based on actual examples. The departure of the soul from the mouth at death in the form of a child is depicted in the great *Triumph of Death* in the Campo Santo at Pisa, a painting Browning undoubtedly saw. There are many similar examples, for the idea which earns Fra Lippo's contempt, the notion that the unseen soul could be shown in painting, was commonplace.

Before closing with a description of Lippi's *Incoronazione di Maria* as a work the monk intends to paint, the monologue refers to a number of Lippi's other paintings. In framing the Prior's objection to "Herodias" (an error for Salome), Browning seems to have had in mind the *Banchetto di Erode* or *Feast of Herod* in the cathedral of Prato, which has a graceful dancing figure at its center. Charles Thomas Flint associates Lippi's intention to use one of the watch as a model for "the slave that holds / John Baptist's head a-dangle by the hair" with Lippi's *Decapitation of John the Baptist*, also at Prato, and "Jerome knocking at his poor old breast" with a figure in his *Nativity with St. Hilarion, St. Jerome and Mary Magdalen*, the altarpiece he was painting for the Medici chapel at the time of the poem. However, Flint maintains that the St. Lawrence in Prato which Lippi says has been defaced by religious zealots is not by Lippi, and is not defaced.[10]

The painting most fully described is the *Incoronazione di Maria* or *Coronation of the Virgin* (Uffizi Gallery, No. 8352), which Fra Lippo promises to paint for the nuns of St. Ambrogio, and which he says will be a pretty thing rather than a realistic one. This does not do full justice to the painting, which has many striking individualized faces (including actual portraits of Lucrezia Buti, the "donor" of the painting, Canon Maringhi, and Lippi himself), as well as a colorful and opulent display of fabrics, flowers, angelic presences, and ornamental woodwork. Browning must have described it from memory, for Lippi's plans are not fully implemented in the picture. St. John, St. Ambrose, and Job (with his name inscribed on his shoul-

Filippo Lippi, *Coronation of the Virgin*, Uffizi Gallery, Florence (Archivi Alinari)

der strap) are there, but the Madonna is without her child, the por-
traits of Lippi and Maringhi have been confused, and neither corre-
sponds to the description.

Nevertheless, *The Coronation of the Virgin* contains a single re-
markable feature that connects it firmly with Browning's poem.
Vasari reports that a churchman had been critical of some of Fra
Lippo's paintings, and that afterward the painter was careful to
provide his figures with drapery. In the monologue, the objection
to indecency takes the form of the Prior's command that Fra Lippo
must stop painting bodies and concentrate on souls. The issue, as
we have seen, is widened into the great historic contest between
the medieval emphasis on order and the supernatural, and the
Renaissance passion for naturalism and individuality. An example
of what the Church objected to is seen in the female figure, proba-
bly an allegorical representation of Florence, who stands in the
midst of an assemblage of supernatural beings and pious person-
ages, unaccountably lifting her skirt to the very top of her thigh, re-
vealing the length of her leg, only lightly veiled.

The incursion of this detail into a pious picture reflects Fra Lip-
po's notorious irresponsibility. Browning shows a full appreciation
of this trait, but also turns it into a strength, when he has the paint-
er say, after he has been forced to realize his inferiority to Fra An-
gelico and Lorenzo Monaco, that in spite of his efforts to follow the
Church's commands, "there's pretty sure to come / A turn . . . A
laugh, a cry, the business of the world." His vision of life's abun-
dance will tempt him to new dissipations. The admission leads to
his marvelous defense of the real world as the justification both of
his moral weakness and his realistic painting style.

In the end, Fra Lippo regrets this speech, and promises to do
penance by painting *The Coronation of the Virgin*. But he persists in
believing that his feelings of desire and love of physical reality are
the true things after all, and he imagines that the St. Lucy of his
painting will introduce him to the holy company represented in it,
saying, "He made you and devised you, after all / Though he's
none of you!" and will join him in an earthy, confidential friend-
ship, separate from the rest. Thus, Browning uses *The Coronation of
the Virgin* as an emblem of his divided Lippi, who is willing to paint
attractive pictures to please the pious, but is also possessed by an
unrepentant appetite for life.

The character and situation of the speaker in "Andrea del Sarto" are so different from those of "Fra Lippo Lippi," that the traditional coupling of these two masterly poems does an injustice to both. Andrea, unlike Fra Lippo, is profoundly uncertain of his aims, and is tormented by an insoluble, if repressed inner conflict quite different from Fra Lippo's arguments with the authorities. The central issue of "Fra Lippo" is a segment of the conflict between medieval and Renaissance world views; in "Andrea del Sarto" it is a choice between life and art, an entirely personal, and therefore more universal question.

Yet Browning's sense of his artist's time leads him to endow Andrea with habits of mind related to both old and new eras. As an artist, Andrea is committed to a Renaissance scheme of values; yet his behavior sets him outside of it. Implicit in the poem is the Renaissance conviction that human greatness can be fully manifested in art, that the "light of God" burns in great artists, that their works display it, and that they themselves go to join Him after death. Andrea's ignobility lies in the fact that he possesses this potential divinity, but is willing to forgo it.

The rewards he hopes for, not through conviction, but through lack of conviction, are oddly pious and medieval: not praise, but forgiveness, not public recognition, but the monklike seclusion of a "weak-eyed bat." His situation might be read as that of a Renaissance man, endowed with Renaissance gifts, and committed to Renaissance modes of thought, whose temperament belongs to an earlier era. Two facts, however, prevent Andrea from deserving the sympathy appropriate to Pictor Ignotus, another weak, failed artist who actually took refuge in monasticism: his spineless submission to his wife, and the weak pride with which he defends his neglect of his parents. His parents, Andrea tells us, died in poverty, yet he promises Lucrezia money for her lover. Under these circumstances, his "Some good son / Paint my two hundred pictures—let him try!" makes it impossible to spare him ultimate condemnation.

"Andrea del Sarto" is less rich in local and human detail than "Fra Lippo Lippi" and its allusions to painting, while significant, are fewer and more general. The basic motive of the poem, the purpose of showing a painter who is deficient as an artist because he is deficient as a man, seems to have been suggested by Vasari's statement, in his introduction to the third part of his *Lives of the Painters*, that Andrea might be said to be a rare artist "because his works are faultless"—"perche l'opere sue son senza errori." This contradicted Browning's idea that great art exhibits the imperfections of the human condition, and he undertook to relate Del Sarto's faultlessness to both his weakness of character and his artistic sterility. Here he was following Vasari, whose hostile account of Del Sarto characterized his work as hesitant, mediocre, and without spiritual force, while conceding its technical excellence.

Browning also borrowed and gave much currency to the well-known tradition, launched by Vasari, and quite inconsistent with any known facts, that in marrying Lucrezia del Fede Andrea made himself the victim of a loose, designing beauty who came from a social class lower than his own. According to Vasari, Lucrezia mistreated Andrea's students (Vasari himself was one of them for a short time), made incessant money demands on him, caused him to leave the service of Francis I, and deliberately kept away from his deathbed for fear of catching the disease he died of. These statements are all falsehoods or distortions.[11]

Del Sarto was a pious, dutiful son of the church whose works in the church of Santissima Annunziata testify to his devotion as well as his talent. He was a vigorously creative draughtsman, colorist, and maker of compositions, and a superb portraitist who captured the interiority of his subjects with great sensitivity in such works as the *Madonna of the Harpies* (Uffizi, No. 46) and *Portrait of a Man* (National Gallery, London, No. 47). Browning's reliance on Vasari, and possibly on Mrs. Jameson's sketch of Del Sarto in *Memoirs of the Early Italian Painters*, which is very close to Browning's conception, produced a very different figure. Although he had easy access to many of Del Sarto's paintings in Florence, he never uses a specific picture to support his poem's premise that the moral character of the artist is reflected in his art.

However, the paintings he saw may have contributed to his conception of *Lucrezia*, who is vividly characterized though she never says a word in the poem. Lucrezia is portrayed over and over again in Del Sarto's paintings. Mrs. Jameson says that he used her as the model for all of his female figures, and that he was so obsessed with her that he used her face for that of every "Virgin, or saint, or goddess."[12] Some time after Del Sarto's death, Jacopo da Empoli, an admirer of his works, was copying the fresco of the *Birth of the Virgin* in the porch of the church of Santissima Annunziata, the

Andrea del Sarto, *Birth of the Virgin*, Santissima Annunziata, Florence
(Archivi Alinari)

Chiostro dei Voti, when an old woman who had come to pray stopped and told him that she had modeled for the painting. It was Lucrezia. According to Baldinucci, who is the source of this anecdote, she spoke tearfully of the time, place, and circumstances of her marriage. She was apparently the model for three of the women in the *Birth of the Virgin*, one seated, the other two standing side by side in the foreground, wearing dresses identical in cut, but not in color.

The face that Browning saw in this painting, the *Madonna del Sacco* in the cloister of the same church, and the numerous Madonnas in the Pitti Gallery is not reassuring. It is not conventionally pretty, but nevertheless conforms to what was apparently the fashionable manner of the time in its cool, expressionless dignity. The hair is generally auburn, the nose long and prominent with a straight bridge, the eyes deep and rather close together, and made to appear small by the broad cheeks and general fleshiness of the face and figure. The forehead is wide and of moderate height, the eyebrows scanty, the mouth straight and small, and the chin juts stubbornly, sometimes appearing as if it were a lump of clay attached to the jaw. Browning could easily have read this face as an image of selfishness and sensuality.

The plausible suggestion has been made that the uneasy relationship between Andrea and his wife is based on the family situation of William Page, the American painter whom Browning knew both in Florence and Rome.[13] Page occupied a flat on the floor below the Brownings in the Via Bocca di Leone in the winter and spring of 1853–54, and Browning sat to him for a portrait at the very time that Mrs. Page was carrying on a flirtation with an Italian. Vasari does not say that Lucrezia was unfaithful to Andrea, or demanded money from him, but Sarah Page was guilty of both these actions, so that Browning seems to have added some episodes drawn from life to his historical materials.

In spite of its expansive discussion of painting and painters, which serves, as usual, to illuminate character and attitudes, no specific picture is mentioned in "Andrea del Sarto." When Andrea says that he could easily correct the drawing in a copy of a Raphael work that stands nearby, Browning seems to be making use of a detail from Vasari. According to Vasari, the Duke of Mantua had asked for Raphael's *Leo X and Two Cardinals*, which was the proper-

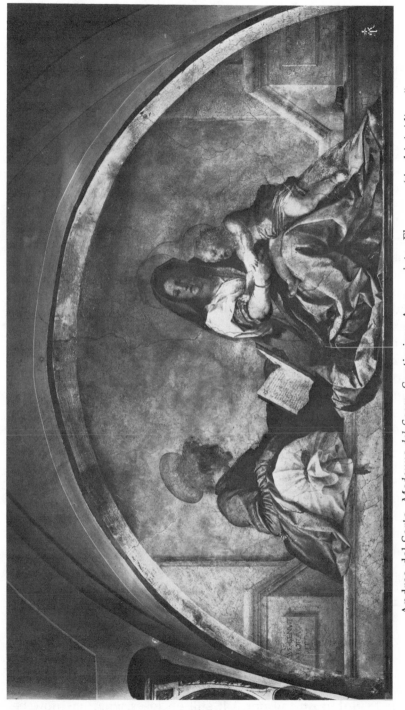

Andrea del Sarto, *Madonna del Sacco*, Santissima Annunziata, Florence (Archivi Alinari)

" 'the other's Virgin was his wife' "

121

ty of Florence. Pope Leo was a Medici, and the Medici who ruled the city were unwilling to part with the picture. They had Andrea secretly paint a duplicate, which was sent to Mantua, and remained a successful counterfeit for many years. Vasari was in a position to know these facts, for he had seen the copying in progress when he was a student in Andrea's studio.

However, instead of following the bad drawing of the original, Andrea improved on it, making some of its forms more distinct, and achieving, as John Shearman has put it in his *Andrea del Sarto*, a criticism of Raphael. The result was as Browning would have predicted; the emotional values were lost. "In Sarto's picture," says Shearman, "the prismatic clarity of each figure makes them too isolated to transmit Raphael's study in cross-purposes, and emotionally nothing happens."[14] As Browning's Andrea admits, "But all the play, the insight and the stretch— / Out of me, out of me!"

Andrea is one of the least Italianate of Browning's Italians. His national characteristics are overshadowed by his human ones, and this universality is one aspect of the poem's greatness. But it is nevertheless firmly embedded in its place and time by allusions to contemporary figures and to Morello, the nearby mountain, and by the incomparable rendering of the "twilight piece," the scene Andrea sees from his window. This quarter of Florence seems to have established a claim on Browning's imagination, much as the piazzetta in Asolo did. The house Andrea built with King Francis's money, and whose bricks he describes as mortared with the king's gold, stands at the corner of the Via Gino Capponi and Via Guiseppe Giusti, facing the side of the Santissima Annunziata, which contains some of Andrea's best paintings. Andrea and Lucrezia are imagined sitting in an upper room, with a view of the hills and Fiesole not far away. Andrea's evocative description is also accurate.

> *That length of convent-wall across the way*
> *Holds the trees safer, huddled more inside;*
> *The last monk leaves the garden; days decrease,*
> *And autumn grows, autumn in everything.*

The wall and garden are still there. The wall is now partly replaced by a chemistry building connected with the University of Florence built in 1878, but on the north it still encloses what has now become the University's botanical garden. Just down the Via Gino Capponi is the Piazza Santissima Annunziata, surrounded by imposing Renaissance facades. One of them is that of the Annunziata church, within whose cloisterlike porch are to be seen a number of Del Sarto frescoes and a memorial bust of the artist. This is the spot where Lucrezia spoke to Jacopo da Empoli about her marriage. Browning might well have felt that the neighborhood was steeped in associations with Andrea.

Elizabeth used the Piazza Santissima Annunziata as the setting where Aurora Leigh's English father first saw her Florentine mother, walking in a religious procession. It is also the setting of "The Statue and the Bust." The traditional tale Browning tells in this poem is based on the equestrian statue of Grand Duke Ferdinand I in the middle of the piazza, and on the Palazzo Riccardi-Manelli which faces it. The poem is an indiscriminate mixture of fact, distortion of fact, and pure fancy, which exhibits Browning's immersion in Florentine lore and reflects genuinely Italian themes and social conditions. The theme of the imprisoned bride stems from the Mediterranean custom of female seclusion and the sudden irresistible passion of the lovers is a phenomenon perfectly at home in the land of Paolo and Francesca, and for that matter, of Dante and Petrarch. The motive of display that leads the Duke to erect the statue was one of the most powerful forces in the hearts of Renaissance Florentines. The bride's resignation and the Duke's procrastination harmonize both with the Italian self-image and the notions of foreigners. But Browning's familiar concluding comment, assigning sin to those who reject fulfillment, combines an impetuous hedonism he might well have encountered in Italy with crisp English pragmatism.

There is no record, or even likelihood, that the Grand Duke ever became infatuated with another man's wife, or that he hesitated to do anything he wanted to do. He succeeded to the Grand Duchy of Tuscany at the age of thirty-eight, after spending his early life in Rome as an extremely youthful cardinal. He was a vigorous and enlightened ruler who achieved progress in trade and commerce as well as in the arts. Florence still exhibits many signs of his reign. He removed the butchers' and tanners' shops that occupied the Ponte Vecchio, and installed the goldsmiths and jewelers who have been there ever since. He built the Tribune, made other improvements in the Palazzo Uffizi, improved the Medici Chapel, and is buried in one of the grandiose marble sarcophagi there. His statue shows him as a bearded, curly-haired man, dressed in armor, but bareheaded, with one extended hand holding a rodlike object whose end rests on his thigh. He is a regal, imperious, unlover-like figure.

Many of the details in the poem are atmospheric rather than accurate, and Browning failed to clarify them when he was challenged. The palazzo in which the lady was confined was not completed until about 100 years after the time of Browning's story. There is, of course, no bust by Della Robbia, and the lady could not have ordered one, since the last of the line of famous sculptors, Giovanni, died in 1529, fifty years before the time of the story. The small world of the piazza the bride looked out on had, as its eastern boundary, the facade of the Spedale degli Innocenti, which is decorated with medallions by Andrea della Robbia, and this may have suggested the bust to Browning. However, the medallions do not exhibit portraits, but babies wrapped in swaddling clothes.

"The Statue and the Bust" is a poem that originated in a street scene, and the same is true of "Up at a Villa—Down in the City," which is in an entirely different key, and is connected with a generalized, rather than a specific locale. The grasp of local color is, of course, impressive. Browning's novelistic gift for seizing upon detail and making it reflect character is in evidence. After he had left Florence, he implored Isa Blagden to write to him about it, saying: "Do be minute—tell me trifles—no trifles to me!"[15] The vivid assemblage of specifics, repellent ones from the country on one side, and lively, colorful ones from the city on the other, set in the bouncing meter of the poem, convey an ironic judgment about the speaker, who loves the diversions which the noise and bustle of the city streets offer to a thoroughly empty mind. But he is not condemned; the poet obviously shares his pleasure, and the reader is made to share it too.

In two of the poems in *Men and Women*, "By the Fire-Side" and "Two in the Campagna," Italian landscapes become involved in the psychological processes of lovers. "By the Fire-Side" is spoken by an Englishman—or at least a foreigner—who visits the village of Prato Fiorito with the woman he loves, just as Browning did. The village is high in the mountains, five miles from Bagni di Lucca, a place with fine scenery and the small church, bridge, and stream described in the poem, a favorite goal for excursions. Shelley and Mary had gone there in the summer of 1818, while they were staying at Bagni di Lucca. Browning and Elizabeth made a first visit in the summer of 1849, accompanied by Pen, Wilson, and some guides.

But the trip on which "By the Fire-Side" is mainly based took place in the middle of September 1853, in company with the Storys, Lytton, and another couple. Browning describes the hillside, the small bridge, and the derelict chapel of Prato Fiorito, but is so indifferent to questions of accuracy that he gives his scene the name of an Alpine village, Pella. The poem seems to merge his two visits, for there are two descriptions, one fairly neutral, the second emphasizing the decrepitude and poverty of the place. The setting plays its part by preparing the lovers for their moment of spiritual recognition, and then, by withdrawing its influence, committing them to each other. We must turn to each other, says the speaker, for this place that has brought us together—and by implication all of the external world—is, in the final analysis, inaccessible.

The poem begins with the speaker as an old man reminiscing about the event at Prato Fiorito. In the elusive image of the hazel trees that he employs, the arch under the spreading branches of the trees leads him to thoughts of the scene he is about to describe, so that "we slope to Italy by degrees." But he thinks of it as "woman country, wooed, not wed," in contrast to Leonor whom he did win, a reflection of Browning's feeling that Italy, for all its familiarity, escaped him in essence. In the moment of their love, the lovers were left to their merely human relationship as the woods "relapsed to their ancient mood." The two will come, ultimately, to their communion by the fireside, while the village and its people carry on in their own separate way. Among the feelings it expresses, "By the Fire-Side" records Browning's lasting sense of Italy's remoteness.

Laurence Lerner has called "Two in the Campagna" "one of the central poems of its age" on the ground that its acknowledgement of the pain involved in what is really a happy love relationship leads to the recognition that suffering is inherent in the human condition.[16] This universalization is powerfully augmented by the setting in which Browning has placed his speaker.

The Roman Campagna had long been notorious as a picturesque wasteland, a place where man had come only to ravage the beauties of nature. It had been part of the thriving land of Etruria in pre-Roman times, and excavations revealed that the ruins of such great cities as Tarquinia and Veii, whose very locations had been lost, lay beneath the plain.[17] "Dead generations lie under your feet wherever you tread," wrote Browning's friend, Story, in *Roba di Roma*. "The place is haunted by ghosts that outnumber the myriads of the living. . . ."[18] The Roman civilization that came after that of the lost cities had left behind extensive underground quarries and catacombs, and precious relics were constantly being found in the soil of the Campagna's poor farms.

History persistently prevented the Campagna from recovering its past prosperity. Always an agricultural area, it was poor in antiquity, and it remained poor, even for Italy, throughout the nineteenth century. The paradoxical barrenness of the countryside near Rome struck many nineteenth-century visitors. Samuel Rogers asked, in his poem, *Italy*:

> *Have none appeared as tillers of the ground,*
> *None since They went—as though it still were theirs,*
> *And they might come and claim their own again?*
> *Was the last plough a Roman's?*

Murray's Guide for 1850 spoke of "the desolate Campagna" (p. 286), and said that the road from Siena to Rome passed over "one of the most dreary and barren districts in the whole of Italy" (p. 217). In spite of its natural beauty, the Campagna had the aspect of a bare, treeless expanse, wild and neglected, dotted here and there with poor hovels and primitive efforts at cultivation. Two of Browning's friends, George Stillman Hillard and Story, discuss it at length in their writings on Italy, and explain its puzzling lack of development. It suffered from a system of absentee landlords, hired holdings, and exorbitant taxation. Short leases discouraged improvements; low wages impoverished the tenant farmers who could not spare money for fertilizer or labor-saving devices. The people suffered from malaria, which even then was understood to be due to the proximity of the Pontine marshes. Laborers were forced to leave their homes to work for a pittance under conditions so miserable that they often led to death. Hillard observed that if foreign travelers understood these conditions, they would be more sympathetic with the beggars who besieged their carriages.

The speaker of "Two in the Campagna" is indifferent to, if not unconscious of, the dead civilizations of the past and the poverty of the present in the landscape he is observing. He is occupied with his own contradictory desires, for he wants freedom from the woman he loves, but knows that the loss will be painful. Before this thought is formulated, however, its configurations are projected through imagery drawn from the landscape. Because it recurs, it is like the gossamer that repeatedly crosses the path of the lovers. The thread winds among the weeds and ruined masonry of the desolate countryside; it goes everywhere, and is hard to trace, suggesting that the thought, too, is all-enveloping and elusive. Another part of the scene discloses tall grass, fresh air, and flowers, the joyful energies of nature renewing the life of the countryside in contrast with the Roman buildings that have fallen into ruins. Only after this description of the freedom of nature is the thought that has been troubling the speaker brought forward: he wants his devotion to be an ideal one, to last forever, but knows that it is already passing.

The new spring growth suggests the promise of another love, but the weeds and ruins, and the image of the thistle-ball blown over the desolate landscape embody the pain of losing this one. In the last stanza, the spider thread returns to represent the psychological situation again; it has lost its anchoring point, and cannot be traced. In the same way, the speaker has passed through the felicity of "the good minute" of communication with his lover, and now feels only the anguish of one who wants to love forever but cannot.

Browning places the speaker's discovery in a setting where many others before him have discovered that happiness is fragile and that life is pain. It is true that his suffering is hardly commensurate with theirs; it is private, individual, perhaps even somewhat superficial, while the other is a great tragedy of humanity, involving many generations. Yet the Campagna, the scene of both, has endured to link the present with the past, and to relate them to each other. The lover's feelings are only an insignificant fraction of the sufferings caused by the crushing momentum of time manifested in the barren plain. But they are respected as an instance of the universal condition of the "finite hearts" whose silent presence is felt among the weeds and ruins of the scene.

" 'De Gustibus—' " consists of two independent descriptive lyr-
ics, one envisioning an English landscape, the other an Italian one,
and only the title suggests that a comparison is called for. The
speaker imagines that the English scene will be witnessed by some-
one else's romantic ghost. It is a fertile, harmonious pastoral, with
moonlit lovers but, like the lovers, it will pass away. Italy, on the
other hand, is a place that he himself wants to see again, if, as he
realistically says, he can recover his health and his will to travel.
The Italian scenes he calls to mind are not obviously attractive.
His descriptions of a distant castle perched in a "gash" of "wind-
grieved" mountains and of a sun-baked, forbidding southern
shoreline with a house whose walls are crumbling, tell us that he
loves Italy, not for its beauties, but for itself. The scorpion from
"The Englishman in Italy" reappears, together with other details
from the region of the early poem. The barefoot girl—always a per-
sonification of Italy in Browning—impertinently tumbles her mel-
ons to the ground as she reports an attempted assassination of the
Emperor. All the speaker can say is "Italy, my Italy!" The poem's
title admits that this devotion is illogical, but we know that it is
based on the pleasure Browning derived from the common sights
the poem celebrates.

Two of the dramatic monologues in *Men and Women*, "A Toccata
of Galuppi's" and "Bishop Blougram's Apology" are spoken by
Englishmen who are, in different degrees, concerned with Italy. "A
Toccata of Galuppi's" has no direct connection with the composer,
or, apparently, with a specific piece of music. Browning said that
he had once owned "two huge manuscript volumes" of music that
contained "Toccata pieces" by Galuppi, and the poem seems to be
based on his general memory of these.[19] The seriousness Brown-
ing heard below the sprightly surface of Galuppi's keyboard pieces
seems to have suggested a situation often presented by Italian his-
tory, the spectacle of an intense moral consciousness forced to sur-
vey a scene of license. It was the position of Dante, Savonarola,
and, for that matter, of Browning's Pope. Galuppi, however, is
hardly a suitable figure for this role. A prolific composer of light
operas and pasticcios as well as vocal and instrumental music,
he spent his life producing entertainments for the citizens of
eighteenth-century Venice, and gave no sign that he disapproved
of their revels.

It was the music itself, then, that suggested to Browning, and to the naive, scientific-minded Englishman who speaks in the poem, a vision of the superficial, pleasure-loving life of Venice. The conversation of the lovers in the poem, if it amounts to anything at all, records the resumption of an affair that has been temporarily suspended. It is tempting to assign the last question, "Did *I* stop them, when a million seemed so few?" to the composer, who realizes the folly of the young people as he sits in the room playing for them, reluctant to interfere. Arthur Domett asked Browning about this sentence in later years, but the poet insisted that "the words were the lover's" spoken while the music was being played. In that case, Domett said, "Must" would have been better; Browning disagreed, and left Domett dissatisfied, feeling that the past tense of "Did *I* stop them" was inappropriate.[20] He might also have mentioned the tense of "seemed" and the italicized *I* as indications that the line was spoken by someone else.

The poem is a masterly performance, creating both a credible character and a lively vision of eighteenth-century Venice as he imagines it, and bringing them together in an experience that approaches a religious conversion. The English speaker sketches himself, in skillful touches, as naive, untraveled, science-minded, complacent. Yet he is capable of so sensitive and thoughtful a reaction to the cheerful music that he turns it into a moral lesson. His first reactions to the toccata are vague and banal. He has heard of the custom of wedding the sea with rings, of San Marco, the canals, and the Rialto, identified as "Shylock's bridge." He has to imagine all this, "I was never out of England—it's as if I saw it all." But then the music brings before him an intimately felt picture of Venetian life, vital young people deaf to the lesson in Galuppi's music, wasting their beauty and vigor in frivolity, "lives that came to nothing." He feels the sadness of this instead of condemning it, and the music warns him ironically that he is not exempt from their fate. It has the effect of making him feel a kinship with people whose lives were entirely unlike his own, with its serious scientific pursuits, so that he can even share their values to some extent: "Dear dead women, with such hair, too—what's become of all the gold / Used to hang and brush their bosoms?" There is no answer, but instead a sense of his own mortality: "I feel chilly and grown old." The manner in which the speaker sympathizes with the otherness of Italy without surrendering to it, and makes use of it in his own spiritual quest, is an excellent reflection of Browning's own position.

In "Bishop Blougram's Apology" Browning created an Englishman who has been sufficiently reshaped by Italian values to believe that religious devotion and sensuous pleasures are capable, not only of coexisting, but of supporting each other. The Bishop's world is "Rome or London." His double vision is natural for an Englishman, reputedly born in Rome, who is a Catholic and a prince of the Church. As Browning makes us see, it corresponds perfectly with his character. His discourse, undertaken to "see truth dawn" says little about metaphysical truths. Instead, he is concerned with how imperfect human nature can maintain self-respect in a world where faith is difficult. "We speak of what is; not of what might be," he specifies. It is striking that so much of "what is," so many things that are both tests of faith and illustrations justifying it, should be located in his experiences of Italy.

One of his arguments involves the point that he has had advantages Shakespeare never knew. His list of them includes Italian sights: "the Vatican . . . Venetian paintings, Roman walls . . . Terni's fall, Naples' bay." Another rests on the wisdom of accepting what is possible, expressed through the great simile of the overambitious voyager on the sea of life who takes nothing with him, in contrast to another who has his comforts because he is satisfied with little. Among the impediments too large for the ship's cabin in this fanciful excursus is "Parma's pride, the Jerome" by Correggio. This work, the *Madonna and Child with Sts. Jerome and Mary Magdalen*, is appropriate to the image. It is large and sumptuous, showing sinuous draperies and majestic figures. The treatment is warm and sentimental; there is an angel modeled after a smiling girl of fifteen, and Mary Magdalen nuzzles her cheek against the Christ child's bare thigh in an apparently irresistible wave of affection. The painting was praised by Vasari, and Browning may have made a point of seeing it when he and Elizabeth were in Parma in 1851. (However, there is a copy by Federigo Baracci in the Sala d'Iliade of the Pitti Palace.)

The Bishop's inference that Shakespeare acquired "Giulio Romano's pictures" during his prosperous later days is based on the passage in *The Winter's Tale*, act 5, scene 2, where the Third Gentleman identifies the statue of Hermione which her husband and daughter have been invited to see as a work of "that rare Italian master." Since Romano (actually, Giulio Pippi), the mannerist and student of Raphael, was a painter and architectural designer known for his erotic works, who did no sculpture, Shakespeare's knowledge of him seems to be based on hearsay.

In acknowledging that his faith is not perfect, the Bishop refers, with some irony, to such Italian survivals as the Naples liquefaction and the argument that true belief is to be found among "King Bomba's lazzaroni." The coagulated blood of St. Januarius, kept in a small glass tube in the Cathedral of Naples, is seen to liquify and form bubbles eighteen times each year, and it is believed that the failure of this miracle would be an ominous portent for the city. The lazzaroni were picturesque street men of Naples who enjoyed the protection of Ferdinand II, called "King Bomba" because he had attacked Messina by bombarding it. Hillard described them as penniless beggars who slept in the streets, and "were rich if they could call a shirt, a pair of trousers, and a red cap their own."[21] He reported that they became extinct as Naples was modernized, so that the argument for the survival of the faith the Bishop attributes to them has been growing obsolete.

The Bishop's arguments cut both ways; duplicity is his instrument. Yet what he knows Gigadibs will interpret as hypocrisy is a style of thinking natural in a country where the reasons given for any action have to satisfy both Church and state, both national conscience and the requirements of an occupying power.

This poem and "Holy-Cross Day" bear closely on the question of Browning's attitude toward Catholicism and the part it played in his idea of Italy. Santayana, in his attack on Browning in "The Poetry of Barbarism," declared that Browning's failure to understand Italy's religion limited his understanding of Italy, and put an understanding of Dante, Michelangelo, and the idealization of love outside his range. More recently, Barbara Melchiori has argued that in spite of a surface tolerance, Browning often exhibits intense prejudice against the Church.[22] Browning undoubtedly shared much of the casual anticlericalism common to Englishmen of Dissenting origins, and was, in addition, consciously opposed to the main body of Catholic doctrine, yet his feelings about Italian Catholicism are mixed, and not easily characterized. If there is a key to them, it is his tendency to adhere to the human dimension. He tended to reject, and to hold in contempt, claims that transcended human powers, including miracles and the special authority and infallibility of the Church. He thought of it as an organization of men sufficiently prone to such failings as pride, corruption, casuistry, sensuality, and indifference to duty. But he also felt that it provided an arena within which men could work out their moral destinies, as Caponsacchi and the Pope do in *The Ring and the Book*. More specifically, he seems to have learned from his Italian experiences that there was no inconsistency between devotion to an imperfect Church and genuine goodness. In *The Ring and the Book*, Caponsacchi and Pompilia have to deal with evil clerical officials, but this only deepens their commitment to the Church itself.

In spite of his distrust of Church doctrine and apparatus, his impatience with a Pope who refused to fight the Austrians, and his many other objections to Catholicism as a creed and a reigning power, Browning understood that their religion was an immense spiritual resource to ordinary Italians. In *Christmas-Eve* he wrote of the Church, "I see the error; but above / The scope of error, see the love. . . ." The people attending mass, he says, seem to have the word "lover" inscribed on their foreheads. He himself enjoyed the Church's art and ritual for their esthetic qualities, dissociating them from their religious values, as most English people did; but he also saw that they brought grandeur and spirituality into narrow lives. What is at issue in his poetry is not an objective judgment of Catholicism (though it cannot be denied that his opposition to it is often near the surface), but the question of its meaning within individual lives. Browning is less interested in the Church itself than in the believer's way of responding to the religion which is part of his character.

Bishop Blougram is a strong and independent personality who finds it perfectly natural to accept the authority of the Church. His arguments showing that religious commitment and the enjoyment of life's pleasures can coexist, which are so convincing that Browning had to add a passage of comment to discredit them, belong of course to the Italian view of these things, or, perhaps, to the English notion of that view. His freedom from Puritanism, his acceptance of man's imperfections and the impossibility of pure faith spring from a milieu in which religion is too familiar and secure in its relation to daily life to sustain a high idealism. Elizabeth, at her first Italian church service in Pisa at Christmas 1846, was irritated by the lack of respect displayed by the people, who walked about and conversed, falling silent only at the moment when the priest lifted the host over his head. Browning observed that a dog who sat with his eyes fixed on the altar seemed to be the most attentive member of the congregation. After witnessing this behavior, Elizabeth could not understand how English people could favor the return to ritual favored by the Tractarians.[23] By the time he wrote "Bishop Blougram," however, Browning had learned that this informality showed, not lack of respect, but the deep penetration of religion into the lives of the people.

"Holy-Cross Day," on the other hand, subjects Catholics and their Church to ridicule. As Barbara Melchiori has shown, the diary entry of the Bishop's secretary that forms its epigraph is subtly sown with Biblical texts which ironically undermine the claim that the custom of compelling Jews to hear Christian sermons was motivated by good intentions.[24]

There is no doubt that Browning earnestly deplored the aspect of Italy and its Catholicism to which "Holy-Cross Day" refers. After the Reformation, the treatment of Jews, which had had a checkered history, took a particularly severe turn, and in 1555 Pope Paul IV issued a bull imposing certain disabilities upon them. They were confined to ghettos, excluded from most professions, forbidden to own land, forced to wear an identifying badge, and subjected to special taxes. The requirement to attend conversion sermons of the kind described in "Holy-Cross Day" was instituted by Pope Gregory XIII in 1584, so that it had been in force for only sixteen years by the date Browning uses in his poem. The custom was not confined to Rome, though the Papal States were particularly diligent in implementing anti-Jewish laws, and it was not abolished, as Browning observed, until the nineteenth century. Browning seems to have been under the impression that the sermon was an annual event, occurring on September 14, but Story says that it took place *every Sunday*, and that a certain number were required to attend. His description of the scene is vivid: "Every Sunday came the *sbirri* (police) into the Ghetto, and drove the wretched inhabitants with the crack of their whips, like veritable overseers of a slave plantation, into the precincts of the church. Guards stood at the door to make sure that the appointed number were there; and the *sbirri* within, if they caught a poor devil of a Jew asleep or inattentive, brought him to his bearings at once by a lash of the whip over his shoulders."[25]

Browning's treatment of Jews in "Holy-Cross Day" and elsewhere illustrates the way in which his reaction toward the persecuted and oppressed entered his art, and parallels his approach to Italian materials. He was a life-long student of Hebrew (as was Elizabeth), quotes the original language of the Book of Job in "The Melon-Seller," and sympathized with contemporary Jews; but when he wrote about Jews, he adopted a mode of totally uncompromising realism. Instead of pitying or sentimentalizing them, he entered imaginatively into their condition of life and state of mind, making them the subjects of a vivid dramatic poem in which their virtues and defects come together to create an impression of real life.

The Jews in "Holy-Cross Day" are far from attractive; they provided Walter Bagehot with one of his best examples of Browning's grotesquerie—a mode Bagehot describes as that which "makes you see the perfect type by painting the opposite deviation." But they are palpably and inescapably human, and never more so than when comparing themselves to "Rats in a hamper, swine in a stye." They react to their ordeal with hatred, cynicism, and contempt; it appears that the Christians have been taken in by some of the thieves and beggars among them who claimed to be converted in order to improve their lot. Story describes the gorgeous annual ceremony at San Giovanni in Laterano in which a converted Jew was baptized, but suggests, with a quotation from Browning's poem, that the same convert appeared from year to year.

The speaker of the poem wickedly plans to tell the Bishop that he has been so reformed by a passage of the sermon that he will no longer lend him money for his amorous pursuits, and expresses bitter resentment that "Men I helped to their sins, help me to their God." He recalls that the persecutions began with the Corso races instituted by Papal law in 1468, in which elderly Jews were forced to race with animals, stripped, except for loincloths, and with ropes around their necks.[26] They ran the full length of the Corso to the Piazza di Venezia, providing a spectacle that afforded mirthful entertainment to members of the nobility and princes of the Church. The custom was abolished in 1668, on condition of the payment of a tax, which seems to be what Browning's character is thinking of when he complains that "the hand indeed / Which gutted my purse, would throttle my creed."

The large group of love poems in *Men and Women* gives the title of the collection special point. Like some of the other poems that do not refer to Italy, they contain reflections of Browning's life there. Italy seems to make subtle contributions to the exceptionally fine studies of feminine psychology in such poems as "A Woman's Last Word" and "A Lover's Quarrel," which might be read, on the basis of the situation in "Two in the Campagna," as if they had Italian settings. "Cleon," the superb monologue dramatizing the plight of a noble mind cut off from Christianity, is set in antiquity, but the artist who enjoys the unquestioning support of a generous patron and excels in many arts is a Renaissance figure. He admits that he does not have the gifts of the great artists of old times, but maintains that latter-day men may achieve progress by synthesizing the contributions of their forerunners. These are less the ideas of a first-century Greek than the Victorian conception of the Renaissance consciousness declaring itself. There is no real counterpart of Browning's successful, yet spiritually restive Cleon among figures of the ancient world; but the Renaissance offers many, including Michelangelo and Da Vinci.

Although the final poem of *Men and Women*, "One Word More," was written in London, it shows that Italy had become an integral part of Browning's poetic consciousness. Its manuscript is dated September 22, 1855, showing that it was written after the rest of *Men and Women* was already in the press. The poem is a personal statement, a dedication of *Men and Women* to Elizabeth. It confronts the unfortunate fact, illustrated, Browning says, in his own volume of poems, that the artist's work absorbs all of his personal ardor into "art that's turned his nature," and precludes self-expression. The works of Raphael and Dante are mere public properties, "Seen by us and all the world in circle," spoiled by their popularity. In order to express his feelings directly, the natural man inside the artist sometimes employs another medium than his own, "Using nature that's an art to others," as Browning proposes to do in his poem. Those who want to gain a sense of intimacy with great men ought to turn to their amateur efforts of this kind. He illustrates his point through anecdotes taken from the lives of Raphael and Dante.

Raphael's true feelings, Browning speculates, appeared in the sonnets written for a woman he loved, who is imagined keeping the volume that contains them until her death, and letting it fall beside her on the pillow where Raphael's cheek once lay. Browning had learned of this volume of a hundred sonnets from Baldinucci's *Notizie de' Professori del Disegno* which reported that the painter, Guido Reni, had left behind at his death "il famoso libro de' cento sonetti di mani di Raffaello" which he had bought in Rome. The volume is no longer extant, but five authentic love sonnets by Raphael do survive, together with an apocryphal sixth. Three of these are written in Raphael's hand on pages containing sketches for the great fresco of the *Disputa* in the Vatican. They are obscure, labored, and conventional, and if "artisticamente considerati," says the editor of a volume of documents pertaining to Raphael, "privi di valore."[27] If he had read them, Browning might have been forced to revise his notion that they echo "the bosom-beats of Rafael."

He might also have had to alter his idealized view of the relationship they celebrated. He seems to believe that they were addressed to La Fornarina, the black-haired model who appears in the *Madonna of San Sisto,* which is mentioned in "One Word More." This was Margherita Luti, the daughter of a Sienese baker; there is a record that in 1520 she entered a Conservatorio for fallen women who wished to leave the world and do penance.[28]

The anecdote about Dante drawing an angel is from the *Vita Nuova*, though Browning, as usual, has seriously altered his original. The picture was drawn, not to please Beatrice, but to commemorate the first anniversary of her death. Dante does not say that the "people of importance" who interrupted him appeared in the *Inferno;* and, instead of dropping his drawing, he continued it when the visitors were gone. Still, Dante's angel, together with Raphael's volume of sonnets, serves to illustrate Browning's point that artists sometimes employ other skills than their own to express their feelings directly.

The passage treating Moses as an analogue of the artist who faces a suspicious and unappreciative public is, of course, connected with Browning's feelings about his failure to achieve recognition. But its insistence that the artist is one who serves mankind, "who smites the rock and spreads the water, / Bidding drink and live a crowd beneath him," reminds us of the humanitarian roots of the poetic role he had decided to adopt. It is true that as late as 1845 Browning was agreeing with Elizabeth that he ought to turn from his dramatic style to attempt a "First Poem," a revelation, in the

Romantic manner, of the secrets of his soul. But the issue had already been decided, and he remained primarily a dramatic poet who employed external materials. His knowledge of such artists as Raphael and Dante confirmed him in his view that the artist must sacrifice the display of his feelings and a close personal relation with his public, for, as the incisive trochaics of "One Word More" assert, "Heaven's gift takes earth's abatement!" and "Never dares the man put off the prophet."

In the end these sacrifices overcome the division between man and artist; committing all one's feeling to one's work becomes a way of satisfying the claims made upon them by humanity, by one's beloved, and by one's ego. Reminding Elizabeth that he will never adopt a self-expressive mode, even in another medium, Browning nevertheless says that he can offer her the tribute of his art: "I stand on my attainment." His true self is in his work, and if he wants to speak directly, it is best to let it speak for him:

> Let me speak this once in my true person. . . .
> Though the fruit of speech be just this sentence:
> Pray you, look on these my men and women . . .
> Where my heart lies, let my brain lie also!
> Poor the speech; be how I speak, for all things.

Nevertheless, the artist does have a private emotional life, a point developed through the parable of the moon that closes the poem and the volume. A contrast between Italy and England is suggested in the difference between the glorious full moon seen in Florence and the pale, diminished orb that hangs over London. If the moon were to love a mortal, fantasizes Browning, she would disclose a reverse side of limitless beauty, but no one will ever see it, and London and Florence are alike in suffering this deprivation. Yet every person has such a hidden side, and Browning feels that, in sharing Elizabeth's private emotions, he enjoys a privilege comparable to the one offered by the sonnets of Raphael and the drawing by Dante. In this way, he deftly connects his love for Elizabeth with the loves of the great Italian artists, arguing that he shares a common experience with them, that of the man who survives within the artist.

In Chapter 38 of Henry James's *The Princess Casamassima*, the Princess asks Hyacinth Robinson to read to her from *Men and*

Women. The scene occurs at a time of dissension, for Hyacinth is learning to value culture, while the Princess, in her revolutionary ardor, has become convinced that civilization must be sacrificed if social injustices are to be rectified. It is just possible that James introduced this allusion to Browning's book because it is related to both interests, and was therefore a potential medium of reconciliation between his characters. It illuminates the world of art and knowledge that has aroused Hyacinth's enthusiasm, but it also deals with individual figures whose troubles would have engaged the Princess's humanitarianism. Hyacinth reads, but the Princess pays no attention. If she had, Browning's poems might have offered the estranged friends common ground, and led to an understanding between them.

EIGHT

Pauses of the Pen

When the Brownings went to England in July 1855, they brought their publisher, Chapman, about eight thousand lines of verse apiece, consisting of all of *Men and Women* (except "One Word More"), and most of *Aurora Leigh*. Elizabeth had been reluctant to leave the comfort and distinction of Casa Guidi, and found it difficult to turn her back on Florence. She sympathized with Penini, who, when he heard that they were to visit England, protested, "Sono Italiano, voglio essere Italiano."

There was a brisk initial demand when *Men and Women* appeared in two volumes on November 17, but then sales fell. This change may well be attributable to the effect of the reviews. Browning, who had moved to Paris after completing the proofreading, hunted out the notices in the reading room at Galignani's there, and found them to be, with few exceptions, not only hostile, but positively indignant. "Energy wasted and power misspent," declared the *Athenaeum* (17 November 1855). The *Saturday Review,* alluding to "madness and mysticism" and "false teaching," said: "It is really high time that this sort of thing should, if possible, be stopped" (24 November 1855). *Fraser's Magazine* solemnly announced that Browning's book displayed "genius unfaithful to its trust" (January 1856). On the other hand, George Eliot, writing in the *Westminster Review,* observed that while the reader would have to exert himself to understand *Men and Women,* the effort would be rewarded, and said, "we would rather have 'Fra Lippo Lippi' than an essay on Realism in Art . . ." (January 1856). Browning did his best work in *Men and Women,* and hoped that it would bring him recognition, but five years later Elizabeth reported that he was so little known in England that an acquaintance of hers did not realize that her husband was English or a poet.[1]

139

Browning said that he was undeterred by the hostile criticism. To Carlyle, who praised his work, he wrote that a poet must continue to improve, and said, "I shall begin again and again as often as you set me right."[2] And he answered a critical letter from Ruskin with a defiant defense of his methods. Ruskin and Browning, as we have noted, reacted differently to Italy. Ruskin loved the art and despised the people, while Browning admired the art mainly as a revelation of the human scene. In spite of their differences, the two can be paired as the most prominent interpreters of Italy to their generation. They had first met at the home of Coventry Patmore in September 1852. Some visits were exchanged, and when *Men and Women* was published, Chapman was directed to send a copy to Ruskin, who found the poems "a mass of conundrums." Dante Gabriel Rossetti, the foremost Browning enthusiast of the time, spent an evening explaining the poems to him; next morning, Rossetti had the satisfaction of forwarding a letter from Ruskin to the poet which, Rossetti hoped, acknowledged Browning to be "the greatest man since Shakespeare."[3] Actually the letter, after some praise, complains of obscurities, and goes through "Popularity" in detail, asking for explanations and questioning ellipses and metrical lapses.[4] Browning's well-known reply of December 10 is perfectly unrepentant, calling on Ruskin to drop his timidity, and leap with the poet from ledge to ledge of thought.

Ruskin seems to have been won over, for in January 1856 he wrote to say that he would refer to *Men and Women* in the next, or fourth, volume of *Modern Painters*. He also asked what "onion-stone," a word that occurs in "The Bishop Orders His Tomb," might be a translation of, and Browning replied that it represented the Italian *cipollino*. The passage Ruskin devoted to Browning is generous, but not quite coherent. It praises Browning's sureness of touch in dealing with the Middle Ages, but then quotes fifty lines of "The Bishop Orders His Tomb" as a reflection of the *Renaissance* spirit. These passages are divided by a discussion in which Ruskin says that Browning, "being much in Italy," appreciated the Italian love of stone for buildings, as Shakespeare could not. A footnote is devoted to *cipollino* and its appropriateness as a designation for stone that tends to peel off in layers.[5] Browning did not see this book for some time, but Rossetti sent him the relevant quotation in April 1856, providing a ray of encouragement at a time when it was badly needed.

From the publication of *Men and Women* until the death of Elizabeth in 1861 Browning wrote very little. In spite of this apparent inactivity he was, no doubt, continuing to absorb impressions, especially in Rome. *The Ring and the Book*, written a few years later, shows that Elizabeth was right to say, in reference to his long silence, that "the brain stratifies and matures creatively, even in the pauses of the pen."[6]

Nevertheless, Elizabeth feared that Browning might be losing his sense of direction during the Paris winter of 1856. The whole question of how he would occupy himself now began to trouble her, for he did not write, and his silence continued through the nearly incessant traveling of the next few years. Elizabeth herself was toiling at *Aurora Leigh* when they returned to John Kenyon's house in London in the summer of 1856, visited the Isle of Wight to see Elizabeth's relations and the ailing Kenyon himself, and went to Taunton to spend some time with her sister, Henrietta. She completed her poem before they left England, and it was published in 1856.

The Italy of *Aurora Leigh* differs from the one that is seen in Browning's work. Elizabeth's heroine is born in Florence, of a Florentine mother whose English husband first sees her in a religious procession in the Piazza Santissima Annunziata, and is raised by the widowed father in the Tuscan countryside. At her father's death the reluctant child is taken from her Italian nurse and educated in England where she comes to accept the tame, intimate countryside so different from the mountains she had known with the view that "Italy / Is one thing, England one."

Browning's sense of social responsibility, as we have seen, was identified specifically with Italy. Elizabeth, on the other hand, responded to English social conditions, and expressed her sorrow and indignation about them with open vehemence in such poems as "The Cry of the Children," and in the substantial part of *Aurora Leigh* devoted to the poor English girl, Marian Erle. Italy reappears in the story as Aurora, now a successful poet who has suffered disappointment in her love for her cousin, Romney Leigh, returns to the land of her birth, where her parents are buried,—"Thou piercing silence of ecstatic graves"—and moves into a villa in Bellosguardo overlooking Florence and the Arno. Elizabeth's account of her futile effort to recover a sense of her Italian past involves some excellent descriptions of the town, the people, and the nearby countryside, and echoes Browning's sense that something vital about Italy remained elusive. Like Browning, Elizabeth found Italian women especially significant, though in a different way; the women who appear in the sequence of vignettes in Book 7 are not as beautiful as Browning's *Sordello* girl, and do not represent social injustice, but rather personal experiences of defeat, uncertainty, and unfulfilled love.

The long climactic scene of the poem, in which Romney Leigh appears to restate his responsibility for Marian Erle, and ultimately to unite with Aurora, takes place on the terrace of her villa with its view of Florence, so that the city becomes a witness of their reconciliation and of Romney's acceptance of Aurora's attitude toward social injustice. Romney feels that "this moon-bathed promontory of earth" has played a part in leading him to share Aurora's view that

> . . . *men who work can only work for men,*
> *And, not to work in vain, must comprehend*
> *Humanity, and so work humanly,*
> *And raise men's bodies still by raising souls.*

This creed parallels Browning's belief that Italy had taught him how to value humanity. When he called Italy the "land of souls" in a letter to Isa Blagden written on August 7, 1866, he was quoting from the passage in *Aurora Leigh* where the heroine, approaching Italy, says, "I felt the wind soft from the land of souls."

After they returned to Casa Guidi in November 1856, Browning began to spend three or four evenings a week with the group of Anglo-Florentines who gathered at Isa Blagden's Villa Brichieri in Bellosguardo. Conditions in Florence were such that Isa, who had only a modest income, could occupy a spacious hilltop villa of fourteen rooms staffed by two servants, and usually shared with a woman friend. Isa conducted something of a salon there, entertaining members of the English community in the evenings and at Saturday teas on her terrace overlooking the town. Her coterie included a number of minor writers who were related to well-known literary figures: T.A. Trollope, the brother of Anthony, Frederick Tennyson, the brother of Alfred, and Robert Lytton, the son of Edward Bulwer-Lytton. Oddly, Browning seemed to fit into this group, for he was considered a satellite of Elizabeth. Frances Power

Cobbe, who was sharing Isa's villa at this time, later wrote: "I do not think any one, certainly no one of the society which surrounded him, thought of Mr. Browning as a great poet, or as an equal one to his wife. . . ."[7]

The winter and spring of 1856–7 were punctuated by reports of death from England. In December 1856 John Kenyon died, leaving the Brownings individual legacies which amounted to eleven thousand pounds. When the money actually became available to them a year later, the Brownings invested it in Tuscan government securities which brought an income of £550 a year. In March Elizabeth heard of the death of Miss Mary Tripsack, her grandmother's old companion, who had remained a family friend.

Florence retained its old charm for Elizabeth. During the carnival in February of 1857, all three Brownings put on masks and dominoes and mingled with the populace in the streets. Although they had now spent nearly ten years in Italy, Elizabeth's comment was that of a new arrival: "I like to see these characteristic things."[8] Describing the coming of spring in a letter to Mrs. Jameson, she said, "Oh, I do hope nothing will drive us out of our Paradise this summer."[9] But evil news invaded Casa Guidi soon afterward, when Elizabeth learned that her father had died. It is not surprising, considering the intensity and ambivalence of her feelings about him, that she had to remain in seclusion for a month afterward.

In the summer of 1857, the heat forced them to go to Bagni di Lucca for the third and last time. They took a house called Casa Betti in the part of the town known as Alla Villa, not far from their former Casa Tolomei. It was a difficult summer, marred by illnesses, full of "blots, vexations, anxieties," as Elizabeth later wrote to Miss Haworth."[10] An especially terrifying event occurred during an excursion into the countryside which the Brownings undertook in the company of Sophia and David Eckley, a wealthy couple from Boston who had become attached to them. While the two men were making a side-trip on horseback, the ground gave way beneath Browning, and his horse fell sixty feet, while Browning saved himself by catching at a rock.[11] In spite of these troubles and the season's oppressive heat, Browning went riding morning and evening, and bathed in the cool streams, as Shelley had done many years before.

On the evening of October 5, just before he was to leave Bagni, Mrs. Stisted showed Browning a faded manuscript. She had no idea what it was, but Browning could tell her that it was the auto-graph of Shelley's "Indian Serenade" that had been found on the poet's body after his drowning, along with a copy of Sophocles, and a volume of Keats's poetry lent to him by Leigh Hunt. The manuscript had evidently been taken away by Trelawny and given to his friend, Captain Daniel Roberts, who had passed it on to Mrs. Stisted. Browning examined the indistinct writing carefully with a magnifying glass, detected a number of variants, and sent them to Hunt. They are now included in the standard version of the poem.[12]

Throughout the winter of 1857–58, the coldest Florence had seen in many years, and the following spring, Browning gave Pen piano lessons, frequented the studios of Hiram Powers and Giorgio Mignaty, spent many evenings at Isa's villa, and studied homeopathy. Visitors, many of them American, continued to call. Nathaniel Hawthorne, accompanied by his wife and William Cullen Bryant, came on June 9, 1858, and made a record of the visit. He found Elizabeth "elfin" and only "remotely akin" to the rest of humanity. But Browning surprised him; he was struck, as many others were, by the difference between Browning's talk and his poetry. In conversation, the poet was clear and cogent, lively, agreeable, and concerned with small talk rather than philosophic or literary topics. He assured Hawthorne that Italians would not cheat visitors if they were trusted and treated generously.[13]

Hawthorne heard that their child's nickname, "Penini," was a jocular diminutive of "Appenino," a colossal statue by Giovanni da Bologna at Pratolino. Elizabeth maintained that the name arose from the boy's attempt to pronounce his Christian name—Wiedemann—and Browning, later in life, told Alfred Domett that Hawthorne's information had "not the slightest foundation in fact."[14] A final and no doubt authoritative explanation came from the mature Pen himself. He said that his stammering effort to say "Nini," the Italian term of endearment for a child, came out as "P-n-n-n-nini," and was picked up by English visitors.[15]

The Brownings went to the Channel coast of France for their holiday in the summer of 1858 because the doctor recommended sea bathing for Elizabeth. Her health was very much improved, but the holiday was not a success in other ways. The town was ugly, relations from both sides of the family joined them, and Browning, who had apparently planned to write, accomplished nothing.

The French holiday ended in October, and after a few weeks in Florence, the Brownings went to spend the winter of 1858–59 in Rome accompanied by the Eckleys, who gave them free use of their spare carriage for the journey. They went through Arezzo, Perugia, and Terni, following the route taken by Pompilia and Caponsacchi on their flight in *The Ring and the Book*. After a trip of seven days, made notable by threats of robbers, and a fight between ox drivers in which Browning intervened and got his trousers torn, they arrived at their old flat at 43 Bocca di Leone on November 24.

Rome was full of English and American visitors, and Browning spent the winter in social activities. Elizabeth wrote that he sometimes went to several parties in one evening, and had "plenty of distraction, and no Men and Women. Men and women from without instead!"[16] She said that the city was a scene of "reckless dissipation" with incessant dancing and crowds, but that Browning liked it, and she feared he might find Florence stagnant after the clamor and brilliance of Rome.[17] His social engagements reached a sort of climax on February 25, when he was invited to dine with the young Prince of Wales, who was visiting Italy. By the spring, Browning wrote that he was looking forward to quiet summer evenings in Florence.[18] This winter's activities were not totally irrelevant to his future writing; he was learning the streets of Rome by wandering about for an hour before breakfast each morning with Mr. Eckley, and the two explored many byways and obscure corners.

"I missed the revolution in Tuscany," wrote Elizabeth to Mr. Browning after her return to Florence in May.[19] A turning point in the history of Florence had taken place on April 27. On that day there was a mass demonstration in the streets, the Grand Duke left the city for the last time, and Tuscany was governed by Baron Ricasoli until union with Piedmont was carried out, after a year of political maneuvering. This event was part of a larger pattern. Victor Emanuel, King of Piedmont, and his gifted minister, Cavour, had joined with Louis Napoleon of France in a secret plan to provoke an attack by Austria which would justify the French in intervening and lead to the liberation of some part of northern Italy. As part of this scheme, Cavour had been in touch with revolutionary elements in Florence, and had urged them to press the Grand Duke to offer his subjects a constitution and to support Piedmont in its fight to resist Austrian control over Italy. The demonstration of April 27, which had not been intended to unseat Leopold, was followed two days later by the outbreak of war between Austria on the one hand and Piedmont and France on the other. The allies won victories in June at Magenta and Solferino, and the war was ultimately to lead to the unification of all Italy.

However, this outcome was delayed by the notorious peace of Villafranca. On July 11 Louis Napoleon unexpectedly made peace with the Austrians after gaining the concurrence of Victor Emanuel, who was allowed to annex most of Lombardy. But the peace terms were disappointing, Louis Napoleon was regarded as a traitor to Italy, the movement toward independence was interrupted, and Cavour resigned.

Elizabeth was possessed by an intense enthusiasm for the Italian cause in the months preceding the outbreak of the war in April. "Just now," she wrote to Isa in March 1859, "I am scarcely of sane mind about Italy."[20] The Italians regarded her as an important advocate of liberation, for in the same month the prime minister of Piedmont, Massimo d'Azeglio, visited her in the Brownings' flat in Rome. He praised Louis Napoleon and criticized the attitude of the British government, which remained unwilling to see hostilities break out, or to see France gain the upper hand over Austria. Elizabeth's *Poems Before Congress,* a book of verse devoted to Italian politics, opens with an extravagant ode to Louis Napoleon—"He came to deliver Italy"—but also contains "A Tale Told in Villafranca," recording her intense disappointment at Napoleon's failure to pursue liberation, which ends with the question, "in this low world, where great deeds die, / What matter if we live?"

It is hardly an exaggeration to say that the peace of Villafranca prostrated her. The Brownings had had great hopes for Italian liberty when they returned to Florence in May 1859. The city was calm and cheerful, and the air was filled with the confident expectation that the approaching war would advance the Italian cause. Pen said he would fight for Italy if he were of age, and Browning pledged ten *scudi* a month to the war effort. The French troops who had been sent to protect the city from Austrian attack (and also to prevent the republicans from gaining power) were seen everywhere. According to a scene described in Elizabeth's poem, "The Dance," they danced with the Italian ladies in the Cascine, and accepted embraces from their men in a grave ritual of brotherhood that "might have been a Mass and not a dance."

When Louis Napoleon faltered in his pursuit of Italian independence, the shock was too much for Elizabeth. Coughing and chest pains sent her to bed, and she dreamt of Italy as a masked woman who walked on the mountains of the moon. Still worshiping Louis Napoleon, Elizabeth managed to think of him as a victim of circumstances. Later, she even acknowledged that the peace had produced good results by forcing the Italians to act independently, and in the following year she was optimistic about the future of Tuscany, reporting that she felt that a nation was about to be born.

Like most Liberals, Browning wanted to see freedom of speech and the rule of law established in the Italian provinces, where the press was either under state control or nonexistent, and which were governed autocratically, without constitutions. And like most English observers, he favored independence for the provinces, and disapproved of the British government's failure to take their part against Austrian domination, as France had. But he did not trust Louis Napoleon, and did not seem to believe that Italy, or any large part of it, could be formed into a national entity in the near future. Nevertheless, the stirring events of 1859 and 1860 nearly awoke his poetic faculties, after a long silence. He apparently began a poem about Louis Napoleon in Rome in 1860, but destroyed it, and kept only some prose notes which eventually became "Prince Hohenstiel-Schwangau, Saviour of Society," written twelve years later.[21]

Elizabeth's dangerous condition forced the Brownings to flee the summer heat of Florence, so they went to Siena, where the Storys and Landor were already established. They arrived on August 1, 1859, at the Villa Alberti, a plain, rough old house two miles from the center of the city, which was cooled by welcome breezes. Browning apparently did not have enough freedom to visit Siena's great artistic and architectural treasures, but limited himself to enjoying the countryside near his villa. "I do nothing," he wrote to Isa on September 9, "but walk up and down one lane, and feel how good it is to be in Italy."[22] In actuality, however, he was burdened by a number of concerns during this summer. Elizabeth's condition required constant attention, and Pen had to be given his lessons. In addition, Browning now became responsible for the aged, cantankerous, and still vigorous Walter Savage Landor.

Landor had lived in Italy between 1815 and 1835, then left his uncongenial wife in their villa at Fiesole to return to England.

Forced to leave England by legal difficulties, he returned in 1858 to Fiesole and to open warfare with his family. In the spring of 1859, angered by some changes being made in the garden, the poet, now aged eighty-four, left home, walked the very considerable distance to take a room at a hotel on the Arno, and then continued to Casa Guidi, meeting Browning on the way.

On July 18, Browning took Landor to Siena to deposit him with the Storys, where he stayed three weeks instead of the one day they had agreed to keep him. When Browning arrived in Siena on August 1, he brought a bag containing some of Landor's clothes and Latin books, articles surrendered by Mrs. Landor, and soon after, Landor was established nearby where Browning could see him from time to time. He was often brought to take tea with the Brownings and Storys on a lawn near their villas, a daily ceremonial of the peaceful Siena summer.

The Brownings returned to Casa Guidi in October, intending to move on and to spend the winter in Rome. The summer had been beneficial, both for Elizabeth and for Landor, and nothing kept them from joining the Storys in Rome but the need for seeing the old poet set up in his house on the Via Nunziatina (now Via della Chiesa) with Wilson and a servant girl to care for him. He was now fully dependent on Browning, who walked about with him, cheered him by quoting from his works, and listened patiently to his interminable complaints.

In November Elizabeth read a book dedicated to her, a novel about Italian revolutionaries called *Roccabella* by Henry Fothergill Chorley. Chorley was a versatile man of letters; as an *Athenaeum* critic, he had always praised Elizabeth's work, and in 1850 had even proposed her as Poet Laureate to succeed Wordsworth. He published *Roccabella* under the pseudonym "Paul Bell" and, by dedicating it to "the author of 'Aurora Leigh'," emphasized its treatment of Italian nationalism, a subject in which Elizabeth was known to take a fervent interest.

Chorley's forgotten novel depicts Italian revolutionaries as grubby, grasping, quarrelsome, and meretricious, if faithful to their cause. It reflects the suspicion with which they were viewed by most English people, and reminds us that the sympathy demonstrated by the Brownings was exceptional. After reading it, Browning told Elizabeth that he thought he detected some sarcasm in the dedication to her, for Chorley's treatment of the revolutionaries was entirely hostile. He had described the type of Italian patriot found among Mazzini's conspiratorial republicans, and the original of his hero, Roccabella, may have been Felice Orsini, who attempted to assassinate Louis Napoleon in January 1858. Elizabeth was severe with Chorley, telling him in a letter that he had overlooked the justice of the Italian cause and made the mistake of thinking that only Englishmen could be generous and noble. She urged him to write another novel dealing with honorable Italian leaders like Massimo d'Azeglio and Cavour.[23] Browning told Chorley that he had chosen the worst examples of those who were working in a good cause, and assured him that he would see the other side of things if he were an Italian. He cited instances of oppression in the Papal States, and said that resistance to them would have to be called "Roccabellaism"—if Chorley's character were not an inferior imitation of a real revolutionary. He added that agitation had the desirable effect of keeping things stirred up.[24]

The Storys were in Rome to welcome the Brownings when they arrived in the winter of 1859, but Browning had no crowded social calendar this year, for the war and the atmosphere of crisis in Italy's affairs had driven most of the English and American visitors home. Pius IX, who had created an impression of liberalism when he came to the papacy in June of 1846 by declaring an amnesty for prisoners and allowing his people a measure of self-government, was opposed to the nationalist effort, and his regime continued the oppressive political tradition of the Papal States. Browning felt this directly in small ways. When the jeweller Castellani displayed some ornamental swords presented by the Romans to the two leaders of Italian unity, Louis Napoleon and Victor Emanuel, the exhibition was condemned as treasonous, and the Brownings had to rush to see it at five in the evening before it was closed. Some of the books and periodicals Browning wanted were forbidden, and he had to ask Isa to have them forwarded to him through the privileged diplomatic channel that went to the foreign minister, Odo Russell. When the police noticed that Russell was receiving two copies of the *Nazione*, they confiscated one. Browning had to adopt a different tactic, and asked the bookshop in Florence that sent the newspaper to address it directly to him, but to wrap it so that its name could not be seen.[25]

The enthusiasm for Italian nationalism expressed in Elizabeth's *Poems Before Congress* hardly corresponded with English opinion, and the volume was received with hostility by the reviewers. At about the time it was published, in March 1860, a plebiscite in Tuscany approved fusion with Piedmont. Once again the Brownings were away from Florence at a significant historical moment. Elected assemblies in Tuscany, Emilia, and Romagna had demanded annexation by Piedmont, plebiscites took place, annexation followed, and the final unification of Italy was under way.

It was unusual for Browning to have time on his hands in Rome, as he did in the season of 1859–60. He worked at sculpture in Story's studio, and went riding with Pen, who had a new pony bought for him in Siena. He also made casual evening excursions among the young artists of Rome, and to working-class restaurants where patriotic songs were sung and the police sometimes appeared to survey the scene. Perhaps because he had few diversions, his Muse, quiescent for at least five years now, reappeared and he began to write a little poetry.

Of the two poems presumably written or in process in the spring of 1860, one, "Mr. Sludge, the Medium," has little to do with Italy and everything to do with Daniel Home, and with Elizabeth's new discovery that Mrs. Eckley, who claimed mediumistic powers, was an impostor. The other, "Youth and Art," is spoken by a lady who recalls a Bohemian youth and a mild flirtation in a setting that may replicate the scenes Browning encountered while visiting young artists in Rome at about this time. She was an aspiring singer, the neighboring young man a sculptor. She meant to rival Grisi, the famous soprano; he intended to surpass John Gibson, the English sculptor who was a permanent resident of Rome, and one of Browning's friends. The poem suggests that these two young people were enjoying a freedom they could not have at home. An improvised blind was enough to protect her privacy; he adopted an artist's casual clothing and demeanor. Silent intentions passed between them, but each concentrated on his art, and nothing was ever said. Now they are both successful, wealthy, presumably back in England, and emotionally unfulfilled.

While Elizabeth sent long letters from Rome to her friends explaining the political situation, Italy was putting itself together around her. The north had been united under the leadership of Piedmont and Cavour, and in May Garibaldi landed in Sicily to begin the campaign that would soon put the Papal States inside the nutcracker of a liberated north and south. Three weeks later, the Brownings left for Florence to spend a month there before taking refuge again in Siena in July.

During this interval occurred a quiet event that opened to Browning's imagination the forgotten episode of Italian history which he was to turn into his greatest poem. On June 15, 1860, he bought the old volume that was to become the main source of *The Ring and the Book*. As he tells the story in the first book of his poem, he was walking through the colorful market that still occupies the Piazza San Lorenzo, and found the book among the tattered secondhand wares a vendor had spread over a "palace step." After paying a sum equivalent to eightpence, he walked home to Casa Guidi, his nose buried in the volume he called the Old Yellow Book, a collection of legal papers and letters, some in print, some in script, and in this way first learned the facts of Guido Franceschini's crime and trial.

The Siena summer of 1860, Elizabeth's last, was made painful by the illness of her sister, Henrietta, who died the following November, and by the still unsettled state of Italian political affairs. The friends of the previous summer were around them: the Storys, Landor, this time under the care of Wilson, and Isa Blagden. Pen and Browning went riding together, and Elizabeth enjoyed the absolute silence of the Villa Alberti. In November they returned to Rome, stopping for only a week at Casa Guidi. The atmosphere of the city was far more sociable than it had been the previous winter; the omnipresent French soldiers created an air of security, and the triumphal entry into Naples of Garibaldi and Victor Emanuel on November 7 was a climactic event in the developing unification of Italy. But Elizabeth was clearly losing ground, and the news of Henrietta's death, which reached her in December, reduced her strength even further. She did not go out, and had few visitors. Browning, on the other hand, was as gregarious as usual, spending his days sculpturing in Story's studio, and making bachelor excursions in the evenings.

During this time, Browning made inquiries in Rome about the Franceschini case, but learned nothing, partly because the records of events that had occurred in 1697 and 1698 were said to have been destroyed, and partly because he was suspected of anticlerical intentions. Actually, Browning seems to have been motivated by the curiosity he always felt about actions involving exceptional violence or passion. He did not, at this time, intend to use the story himself.

On June 6, a few days after the Brownings returned to Florence, Cavour, who was only fifty, died suddenly. His work of unifying Italy had, in effect, been accomplished, and a first Italian Parliament had met in Turin on February 18, but the news of his death was a blow for Elizabeth, who was very weak. Her last illness began late in June when she caught a chill. An English doctor attended her, Pen was sent to stay with Isa, who paid numerous anxious visits, and Browning tended her carefully, often staying awake through the night. She died at 4:30 in the morning of June 29.

With Elizabeth's death, Browning realized that his life in Italy was over. "I go away from Italy at once," he wrote Sarianna, "having no longer any business there."[26] When Story arrived, he found the newly bereaved Browning in the drawing room at Casa Guidi, and he listened as the poet told him how every corner of the apartment exuded memories of Elizabeth; "the cycle was completed for us here," Browning said, "and where the beginning was is the end." Two powerful and complementary motives are perceptible in the speech recorded by Story: Browning wanted to close the Italian phase, with its inescapable memories of Elizabeth's decline, and to begin a vigorous new one in England, to "go to England and live and work and write."[27]

The reverence the Italians felt for Elizabeth as an advocate of their cause became apparent at her funeral. The Florence newspapers carried articles about her, the shops near Casa Guidi were shut, and crowds gathered along the street where the hearse passed and at the Protestant cemetery in the Piazzale Donatello where whe was buried.

On July 12 an extraordinary event occurred, and Browning reacted to it in a significant way. Ubaldino Peruzzi, who was a member of an eminent Florentine family, a leader of the Risorgimento, and one of Cavour's ministers, came to Casa Guidi to ask Browning to remain in Florence and to raise Pen as "a Tuscan" so that he might take part in the glorious future envisioned for Italy. Browning declined. "Of course," he wrote to Forster, "Pen is and will be English as I am English and his Mother was pure English to the hatred of all un-English cowardice, vituperation, and lies. . . ."[28]

The Salon at Casa Guidi by George Mignaty.
Reproduced by permission of the Goewey Library, Mills College,
Oakland, California

The xenophobia released by the bereaved husband's resentment against the place where his wife had died is a genuine part, though only a part, of Browning's attitude. Peruzzi's request must have brought forward the sharp realization that he was excluded from the relationship to Italy shared by Elizabeth, the Italian patriot, and Pen, the native of Florence. His stance was different from theirs. He had never identified himself with Italy, or idealized it, but had observed it, from an affectionate distance, as an arena of moral and spiritual drama. His answer to Peruzzi was to take Pen away as quickly as he could, and to make him as English as possible. Years after Browning's death, an American visiting Pen in Florence observed that he must feel like an Italian after his long residence in Italy. "Oh, dear no," Pen quickly replied, "I'm an Englishman."[29] Nevertheless, he was never happy in England, and had to return to Italy to find appropriate channels for his energies.

Elizabeth's death was a turning point in Browning's relationship to Italy in two senses. It separated Elizabeth from Italy in his mind. In the long letter he wrote to Sarianna describing the circumstances of Elizabeth's death, he said, "I shall live in the presence of her, in every sense," following nearly immediately with, "I shall leave Italy at once. . . ."[30] And it marked the moment of division between the living Italy he had experienced directly and the imagined and remembered Italy of *The Ring and the Book*.

It was a month before Browning was able to leave Florence. During most of that time he slept at Isa's villa to escape the associations of Casa Guidi, but he had no intention of leaving its memories behind. He even arranged to have the drawing room photographed, and when that was unsuccessful, commissioned Giorgio Mignaty to execute the painting which shows the room where the Brownings spent much of their time in Florence.

On August 1, Browning, Pen, and Isa left for France, where Browning was to join his father and sister at St. Enogat on the Channel coast. Before long, he was to return to the Italy envisioned in *The Ring and the Book*, and in later years, he returned to Italy itself, but he never set foot in Florence again.

NINE

London and The Ring
and the Book

When they returned to London in October 1861, Browning and Pen lived in lodgings for a few months, and in the spring of 1862 moved into a rented house at 19 Warwick Crescent, not far from the home of Arabel Barrett. This house, where Sarianna joined him after the death of Mr. Browning in 1866, was to be Browning's home until two years before his death in 1887. His windows faced a scene that faintly recalled Italy, a spot on the Grand Union Canal called "Little Venice," where an island divided the canal into two waterways.

Many strands of Browning's Italian life followed him to London. He continued to hear from such friends in Italy as Isa, Landor, Kirkup, Trollope, and Story, and was eager to learn what was taking place in the English colony at Florence. Also, the designing and building of a monument for Elizabeth's grave dragged on with many difficulties until December of 1865, and he had to communicate with people in Florence about it frequently. In the summer of 1862, the books and heavy Italian furniture from Casa Guidi arrived; Browning wrote to Isa that he was not sure that he did not prefer them "at the bottom of the sea."[1] But he took them in, hung up the tapestries that had looked down upon his life with Elizabeth in Florence, and carried on among these reminders of the past.

He missed Italy and, to judge from his letters, would have soon returned if the need for attending to Pen's education did not keep him in England. In January 1862 he wrote to the Storys, still using mourning paper more than six months after Elizabeth's death:

And for me,—my end of life, and particular reward for myself will be,—one day—years hence—to just go back to Italy—to Rome—and die as I lived, when I used really to live. If you knew—but you *do* know, and can conceive how precious every mud-splash on the house walls of Rome is: how every minute of those last six months in Rome would *melt up* into gold enough for a year's use now, if I had it![2]

After he had been away for about a year, thoughts of Italy became nearly intolerable. He wrote to Isa:

. . . particular incidents in the Florence way of life recur as if I could not bear a repetition of them—to find myself walking among the hills, or turnings by the villas, certain doorways, old walls, points of sight, on a solitary bright summer Sunday afternoon—there, I think that would fairly choke me at once: on the other hand, beginning from another point of association, I have such yearnings to be there! Just now, at the approach of Autumn, I feel exactly like a swallow in a cage—as if I *must* go there, have no business anywhere else, with the year drawing in.—How thankful I am that all these foolish fancies never displace for a moment the solid fact that I can't go but have plain duty to do in London,—if there could be a doubt about that, I should drift about like a feather: at times (to give you a notion of what I might do if free to be foolish) I seem as if I should like, by a fascination, to try the worst at once,—go straight to the old rooms at Casa Guidi, and there live and die![3]

In asking Story for news from their old summer refuge, Siena, he wrote: "Remember . . . you cannot tell me the number of flies that buzz in your window without interesting me."[4]

Memories of Elizabeth made it impossible for him to think of living in Florence again, "But Italy,—Rome or Naples, I will go to the moment I can. . . ." He often told Isa that he *yearned* for Italy again. When she wrote of visiting a village inn where he had stopped for lunch sixteen years before, Browning replied that he remembered it well, and added, "Oh those days—I think of little else. . . ."[5]

After his return to England, Browning became productive again. For the first time since the publication of *Men and Women* in 1855, he did some vigorous and sustained writing, and in 1864 published his volume of verse, *Dramatis Personae*. A few of these poems date from the time before Elizabeth's death, but most of them, especial-

ly the five substantial monologues which rank among his best
work were (with the possible exception of "Mr. Sludge, the Medi-
um") probably written after he had returned to England.

There are only slight allusions to Italian materials in this volume.
Most of the longer poems deal with spiritual or doctrinal issues of
the kind that would naturally have occupied Browning on his re-
turn to England.

He had not at first intended to use the story from the volume he
called the Old Yellow Book himself, but offered it to a number of
other authors, including Anthony Trollope and Tennyson. He had
been curious enough about the case to take the volume to Rome
while making his inquiries there, and to consult town records in
Arezzo, where some of the events occurred. Elizabeth's death led
him to forget the matter for awhile, and he was probably separated
from the Old Yellow Book until it was sent to London with his
other books in July 1862. Soon afterward, his interest was revived.
In September, while on holiday in northern France, he wrote
to Isa and asked her to remind Mrs. Georgina Baker, a Bellos-
guardo neighbor, that she had promised to lend him her copy of a
seventeenth-century manuscript found in London that gave anoth-
er account of the case.[6] He used this document intensively, and it
has become known as the Secondary Source. It also seems to have
played a part in his decision to write the poem that became *The
Ring and the Book*, for in his next letter to Isa he thanks her for her
help in obtaining Mrs. Baker's manuscript, and adds: "I am going
to make a regular poem of it."[7] However, it appears that he did not
begin the actual writing for about two years, until *Dramatis Personae*
and the task of revising his poems for the three-volume edition of
1863 were out of the way.

Toward the end of 1863 his thoughts were turned to Italy by a fa-
vor he undertook to do for Story. Since 1848 Story had been pub-
lishing articles describing his impressions of Rome in the *Atlantic
Monthly,* and these were collected and published by Chapman in
two volumes in the early part of 1863 under the title *Roba di Roma*. A
second edition in one volume was planned, and Browning agreed
to do the work of cutting down the original text. *Roba di Roma* is a
series of leisurely, intimate studies of Roman life and customs
which display Story's gift for entering fully into the life of the peo-
ple and the atmosphere of places, as well as a thorough knowledge

of the city's history. Browning was immersed in this long, rich evo-
cation of Rome toward the end of 1863, and a number of its details
of Roman life found their way into *The Ring and the Book*.

He began to work on his poem as soon as he returned from his
French holiday, for on October 17, 1864, he asked Frederic Leigh-
ton in Rome to send the details about the church of San Lorenzo in
Lucina which he used in Book II. His first conception must have
been of a much shorter poem; in October 1864 he wrote to both
Julia Wedgwood and Isa that he expected to finish it in a matter of
months. Ultimately, he spent four years writing it. It was pub-
lished in four installments, in volumes published monthly begin-
ning in November 1868, an unusual method intended, as Brown-
ing told William Allingham, to prevent readers from turning
prematurely to the end.[8]

The Ring and the Book: The Frame

The poem begins, not with its historical characters in seventeenth-
century Rome and Arezzo, but the Browning himself as he moves
through the Florence of his own time. It opens by focusing on two
objects that Browning holds up before us, the Ring, a replica of an
Etruscan original found in the ruins of Chiusi, and the Book. This
time and place, this speaker, and these objects play no part in the
tale of forced marriage, flight, and murder that is about to unfold;
Browning introduces them to present an analysis of the process he
will use to shape his poem.

The Ring (or, more strictly, its original) and the Book have both
been buried in obscurity, but once discovered, are capable of gener-
ating vivid speculations about past times. They illustrate the poet's
power of bringing things that are moribund to life by projecting his
imagination into them. Presented as metaphors of the poetic proc-
ess, they also have a metaphoric relation with each other. Each
contains a valuable component that remains inert until another ele-
ment is added to it; alloy must be added to the gold in the ring, and
the book needs the poet's fancy to make its facts live. Both situa-
tions correspond to the way in which the poet's imagination regen-
erates the past and finds truth.

Browning's Italy attributed extraordinary importance to the re-
trieval of the past. Such terms as "Renaissance" and "Risorgimen-
to" embodied an idea of rebirth that was a central theme in the

consciousness of a country whose claims to freedom and digni-
ty rested largely on lost traditions. Many of the people around
Browning were occupied with the search for evidence of Italy's
former greatness, including historians like Villari and T.A. Trol-
lope, bibliophiles like Kirkup, and art historians like Jarves. Brown-
ing was, of course, fully prepared to enter into the spirit of this re-
vivalism, and in *The Ring and the Book* responded to its influence by
developing the theory that poetry itself is a process of recupera-
tion.

He introduces his theory with the report that he made inquiries
to learn what was known about the events narrated in the Old Yel-
low Book, and finding that they had been entirely forgotten, felt
that they must be told again. To forestall the charge that a poet's
"fictions" cannot tell truth, he pauses to explain and justify his
poetic method.

Man, he says, must create if he is to grow; yet he is paradoxically
denied a power reserved for God, and can only "Repeat God's
process in man's due degree." That is, while he cannot create new
things out of the void, he does have the power to project his imagi-
native vitality into dying things that originally took their life from
the divine source, and revive them: "The life in me abolished the
death of things." In an impressive illustrative passage, a hypothet-
ical "mage" shows the poet seeking out the lost and discarded
remnants he needs as the material for his work of renewal, and
breathing life into them. The Old Yellow Book is a remnant of this
kind. It was found among an assortment of worn and broken
household objects, "Some fragment of a whole, / Rags of flesh,
scrap of bone in dim disuse," nearly extinguished germs of life that
the poetic imagination has the power to rescue from oblivion. It is
not only Browning's source, and a physical link with the setting of
his poem, but a symbol of the power of renewal. "Give it me back!"
the poet says, after letting his listener hold the Book for a time,
"The thing's restorative / I' the touch and sight." Denying that the
poet's restorative power resembles Faust's black magic, Browning
prefers to identify it with the sacred power of Elisha, who revived a
dying boy; the passage from 2 Kings 4 is reproduced nearly *verba-
tim* in Book I, lines 761 to 771.

In this Bible-centered passage, Browning seems to have the Res-
urrection in mind as a prototype of poetic renewal. But the setting

of the Piazza San Lorenzo, where the Old Yellow Book is found, and the allusions to buildings and art works of the fifteenth and sixteenth centuries puts the theory within the context of the Renaissance and the metaphor of rebirth formulated by Vasari and elaborated by Victorian historiographers. Vasari presents both the idea that modern Italy had revived the culture of antiquity, one of the central tenets of Humanism, and the metaphor that expresses it, in his Preface to *Lives of the Painters*. He describes the great outburst of naturalism in the arts as a reversion to the vitality he saw in the ruins of Roman buildings and monuments, and calls it "the second birth" (*la rinascita*). The name could not have been adopted as a historical term until the fashion for historical periodization arose in the nineteenth century, but by that time the idea of the Renaissance was perfectly familiar. The English word came into use in Browning's time; the OED's earliest listing of it in this sense is dated 1840, from a book by Browning's friend, T.A. Trollope.

The word, the metaphor, and the idea that the Renaissance had been a vast project of cultural renewal carried out by Italian artists and Humanists soon became fixed in the minds of historians. Michelet called one volume of his history *La Renaissance*; Ruskin and Arnold treated the term as a familiar word. Jacob Burckhardt's *Civilization of the Renaissance in Italy* (1860) and John Addington Symonds's *Renaissance in Italy* (1875) synthesized the current ideas about the period into the definitive nineteenth-century view. The idea of renewal took so strong a hold on the nineteenth-century mind that the historians applied it to their own work. Michelet, Barthold, Niebuhr, Carlyle, and many others approached the writing of history as a process of restoration that brought the values and emotions of the past to life.

The developing field of classical archaeology supplied the theory of renewal with a convincing practical dimension. The discovery of the ruins of Pompeii and Herculaneum beneath the soil of Campania in the middle of the eighteenth century showed that it was possible to recover the actual physical remains of lost ages, and with them an intimate sense of the daily lives and thoughts of the ancients. The work of exhuming the relics of lost civilizations went on throughout the nineteenth century. Elaborate excavations were undertaken at such sites as the Roman Forum, and the peasants of the Campagna brought the fragments of worked stone and metal they found to the market in Rome, where they could be sold to antiquarians. The climactic archaeological episode of the century, Schliemann's discovery of the site of Troy, showed that even the most remote historical events could be authenticated and put into place as parts of the modern consciousness.

Browning had allowed the hero of *Sordello* to learn that the poet's task involves the reinterpretation of history, and "Old Pictures in Florence" connected future freedom with the greatness of the past by arguing that Italian liberation was related to the preservation of endangered frescoes and the completion of Giotto's campanile. Now, in *The Ring and the Book,* under the influence of contemporary historical and archaeological activities, he gave the concept of re-birth a central place in his poetic theory, identifying poetry itself with it. Within this context, the theory appears as one expression of a general spirit of historical recovery. By bringing the forgotten episodes of the Old Yellow Book to light again, and asserting that the poet could read their significance, Browning was taking both the Renaissance and the powerful archaeological energies of his time as analogues of the poetic process. Lord Lindsay had observed that the Italian frescoes hidden by whitewash longed for "resuscitation." His word and the idea it expresses became the germ of the discussion in Book I of Browning's poem, where the poet declares that man cannot originate, but can only revive what has been made by God; he "Creates, no, but resuscitates, perhaps." In this way, Browning transformed the historicizing thrust of the period into a theory of poetry.

If the Book provided the material for Browning's poem, the Ring corresponds to its form, a circle of observations enclosing a sequence of events. But it also illustrates the details of the poetic process; the gold of truth is mingled with the alloy of the poet's imagination, then restored to purity again after it has been shaped into poetic form. Like the Book, the original of the Ring was an actual fragment of the Italian past, which existed long before Browning did. Its replica passed into his possession for a time, survived him, and is now in the collection of the Balliol College Library. It was a gift from Isa Blagden that Browning wore on the little finger of his right hand until his death.[9] Apart from its symbolic value within the poem, the Ring is significant as a symbol of Browning's relation to Italy. The inscription on the plaque at Casa Guidi refers to Elizabeth's poems as "aureo anello fra Italia e Inghilterra," and Browning closes his work by merging this metaphor with his own, asking that the ring of his poem may parallel Elizabeth's works in linking England and Italy.

The Old Yellow Book is not a book at all in any strict sense, but rather an *objet-trouvé* such as Marcel Duchamp would have admired. It consists of eighteen pamphlets, some in "Latin cramp enough," some in Italian, and three manuscript letters bound into a vellum-covered volume by a private collector. It can be seen as the volume the poet holds propped up on his knee in the portrait of Browning by Pen which hangs in the Balliol College Library. In the seventeenth century, Browning tells us, attorneys submitted their arguments in writing; they were then printed for use by the judges in considering the case. Sixteen of the pamphlets in the Old Yellow Book are copies of these arguments, documents submitting evidence, or summaries; two are entirely different kinds of publications, narratives of the case printed for public sale or circulation. The three manuscript letters were written immediately after Guido was executed, and are addressed to a Florentine attorney named Francesco Cencini, which led Browning to believe that Cencini was the original compiler and owner of the volume.

Browning describes it as "print three-fifths, written supplement the rest"; in fact, only about a dozen of its 262 pages are in script, and these include the title page and the index (actually a list of the contents), which appears at the beginning, not at the end as Browning implies. The legal arguments are in Latin, the summaries in Italian; also in Italian are the statements of witnesses, the love letters introduced as evidence, the public pamphlets, and the letters written to Cencini. Before being bound, the sheaf of pamphlets had been folded vertically; Browning, referring to every physical detail of this talismanic object, mentions and explains the crease. The pamphlets for general circulation bound into the Old Yellow Book belong to a once-popular class of publications, narratives of sensational crimes. Researchers have discovered a number of other pamphlets bearing on the Franceschini case in Italian archives, showing that there was wide interest in it.[10]

It involved enough bloodshed and intrigue to enthrall the crime-loving public and to support the impression that Italy was a country where the passions were given free play. The bare facts of the story (as distinguished from Browning's recasting of them) appear to be about as follows: in the year 1680, Violante Comparini, a Roman matron of forty-eight, arranged to buy from one of the poor women of the city the child with which she was pregnant, and to have it accepted as her own, deceiving even her husband. Her reasons were mainly mercenary. Her husband had been left a fortune which would revert to him only if he had an heir, and the couple was childless. When the child, a girl, was born on July 16, 1860, an elaborate mock lying-in was staged; she was christened Francesca Pompilia, and raised as the child of the Comparini.

Late in 1693, when Francesca (Browning's Pompilia) was fourteen, she was married to Guido Franceschini, an impoverished thirty-six-year-old nobleman of Arezzo, who expected to profit financially from the marriage. The Comparini moved to Arezzo to live with the Franceschini, but the two families disagreed, and they moved back to Rome in the spring of 1694. Soon after, they revealed that Francesca was not really their daughter, and Franceschini's right to the dowry was disputed. The young wife was unhappy in her husband's household, and on April 28, 1697, after nearly three years of marriage, she fled in the company of a Canon of Arezzo, Giuseppe Caponsacchi. The husband pursued, caught up with the couple, and had them arrested. Francesca was confined in a convent, but being found to be pregnant, was sent to her parents' home. On January 2, 1698, Franceschini, with four peasant lads from his estate, appeared at the Comparini home and murdered Francesca and her parents. Francesca, however, survived long enough to identify her murderer. The bodies of the victims were displayed in the Church of San Lorenzo in Lucina, and this is the point where the narrative part of Browning's poem begins, in Book II. Franceschini and his men were apprehended in the environs of Rome, imprisoned, tried, and executed before a large crowd in the Piazza del Popolo on February 22, 1698.

Browning set out to transform this story into a spiritual drama transcending time and place, yet seventeenth-century Italy and its people are vital parts of the total impression made by his poem. This combination of the actual with the imagined reflects Browning's view of poetry. In his "Essay on Shelley" he had divided poets into two types: the objective poet, who exploits externals, seeing them more clearly and more fully than most men; and the subjective one, who presents idealizations drawn from his own mind. Ordinarily, these tendencies alternate with each other in the history of poetry, yet there is no reason, says Browning, "why these two modes of poetic faculty may not issue hereafter from the same poet in successive works. . . ."[11] Two apparently contradictory statements about *The Ring and the Book* show that he thought he had employed both modes in this one work. "Before I die," he wrote to Julia Wedgwood in defending his poem, "I hope to purely invent something,—here my pride was concerned to invent nothing. . . ."[12] Yet about fifteen years later he said, "There is nothing in any part of *The Ring and the Book* that, properly speaking, is not wholly mine,—that is, my imaginary deduction from certain naked *facts* recorded in the original collection of documents."[13]

The second claim seems much nearer to the truth. As we know from his conversation with Gosse, and from his usual practice, Browning often thought like a subjective poet, turning his *données* into universals by ingeniously displacing their facts so that they yielded unexpected depths of meaning that corresponded with his personal moral insight. The material of the Old Yellow Book underwent an extensive revision of this kind. Browning lets us see the process going on in the passage in Book I where he steps out on the terrace of Casa Guidi to look toward Rome and to recapitulate in imagination the events he had just read in the Old Yellow Book. His purpose, as I observed in Chapter 1, is not merely historical but also self-fulfilling: "I turned to free myself and find the world." The moment when the authentic self finds its authentic reality gives the poet the freedom to reshape his materials, "Letting me have my will again with these," with the assurance that, in the final analysis, "Fancy with fact is just one fact the more." Nevertheless, the "Essay on Shelley," after acknowledging that the powers of the subjective poet are "the ultimate requirement," immediately turns to its warning that

> the objective, in the strictest state, must still retain its original value. For it is with this world, as starting point and basis alike, that we shall always have to concern ourselves; the world is not to be learned and thrown aside, but reverted to and relearned.

The colorful, substantial world evoked in *The Ring and the Book* embodies this sober consciousness of the enduring claim of ordinary reality. This was a characteristic part of the Victorian view of poetry. In one of his articles in the *Monthly Repository*, for example, John Stuart Mill declared that, while it was the function of poetry to arouse feelings, not to represent externals, the feelings must nevertheless proceed from externals. Poetry, says Mill, originates in the observation of reality, and cannot succeed unless it is "taken from individual nature," and maintains its relation with it.[14] Browning's poem is a creation of the objective poet's "double faculty" that consists of first grasping externals and then fashioning them into a recognizable vision of the world in a work that "will of necessity be substantive, projected from himself and distinct."[15] Browning assured the sender of some accounts drawn from historical records that he might use them for poetry some day, and said, "These *petits faits vrais* are precious," using a phrase associated with fictional realism.[16] His devotion to actuality and the testimony of the senses makes the color, the atmosphere, or, as Henry James put it, the "temperature" of Italy an indispensable component of his poem.

In his circumstantial account of the discovery of the Old Yellow Book in the Piazza San Lorenzo, Browning anchors his poem in actuality, and anticipates one of his themes by showing a scene where past and present are thrown together. The spot is bracketed "Twixt palace and church—Riccardi where they lived . . . and San Lorenzo where they lie," that is, between the Medici-Riccardi Palace once inhabited by the Medici, and the church of San Lorenzo whose two sacristies contain their tombs. The market life circulates familiarly around these ancestral monuments but it is also interfused with the remains of a nearer past, the secondhand wares that are for sale.

The palace is perhaps more deeply rooted in the period of Florence's ascendancy than any other building in the city. Built by Cosimo de' Medici about 1430 as a combined residence and place of business, it was a notable architectural innovation, expressing the urban dignity appropriate to a bourgeois prince. It is "the house that caps the corner" which Fra Lippo mentions when he means to impress the watch with his patron's power, and also the palace in "The Statue and the Bust" which overshadows the Via Larga. Designed by Michelozzo, it had contained works of art by Lippi, Lucca della Robbia, Uccello, Gozzoli, and many others, most of which had been removed before Browning's time. Michelangelo had resided in it for four years, and had remodeled its exterior by piercing the wall of the ground floor with the windows supported by ornamental scrolls that have been called "kneeling windows." Browning says that he found the Old Yellow Book lying among the articles displayed on a "palace step." Actually, this was one of the broad ledges or benches at the base of the wall that runs along the Via Gori and was later extended from the palace to enclose its garden.

The glory of Florence's Medicean past is ostentatiously displayed in the interior of the church which stands diagonally across the piazza from the palace, in the splendor of the two chapels designed by Brunelleschi and Michelangelo where the remains of the Medici lie, and in the adjoining Laurentian Library. Fronting all this, however, is a reminder of the many eclipses the Medicean power suffered. The facade of the church was never completed, and still presents a bleak and ugly face of unfinished stone to the piazza where Browning's market pursues its busy life.

The stately palace and church are mentioned only briefly, but Browning pointedly devotes thirty lines to an exhaustive catalogue of the humble and disreputable artifacts that surround the Old Yellow Book in the stall where it is for sale. These chipped, broken, and discarded relics of obscure lives have nothing to do with the plot of the poem or the people in it, but they strike a significant keynote because, like the Old Yellow Book itself, they are traces that provide the poet with the material for his work of renewal.

The setting combines reminders of Florence's noble history with ephemeral events of the day. Having paid his eightpence for the Book, Browning tells us, he leaned on the rail surrounding "Baccio's marble" to examine his find. A few steps had taken him to the equestrian statue of Giovanni delle Bande Nere, a descendant of the junior branch of the Medici and the father of Cosimo, the first Grand Duke, who was called "John of the Black Bands" because he ordered his troops to substitute black insignia for their white ones as a sign of mourning at the death of Pope Leo X. The fountain Browning mentions is a part of the statue's marble base; the water comes out of a lion's mouth, and the pedestal is decorated with the ubiquitous shield and balls of the Medici *stemma* and the *fleur-de-lis* of Florence.

The juxtapositions of past and present continue as Browning tells us that he took in the contents of the Old Yellow Book while walking home. The route is carefully specified; he went down the Via Tornabuoni, past the pillar from the Baths of Caracalla brought to Florence by Cosimo I as a token of his victories, past the Strozzi Palace, home of a family hostile to the Medici, across the Santa

Trinità Bridge, and down the Via Maggio, absorbed in the book he had just bought. In the *salone* of the Casa Guidi he pondered what he had read, looked from the terrace down the street that leads to Arezzo and Rome, the scenes of the story, and relived its events in the intimate darkness of a summer night where the singing from the nearby church and the voices of people in the street toned his reactions to the old tale of murder. The remote and the familiar were brought together as he put the book down on "the cream-colored massive agate, broad / 'Neath the twin cherubs in the tarnished frame / O' the mirror," the mantel and mirror that appear in Mignaty's painting.

Chesterton has speculated on the poem Browning might have written if he had taken Parnell's trial as his subject, but it seems clear that there would have been no poem at all without an Italian subject. The Franceschini case is, as Ian Jack has said, "a very Italian story." It might perhaps better be described as Italianate, for its picture of Italy corresponds with the Machiavellian tradition reflected in Renaissance tragedy and the Gothic novel. As Browning admitted to Julia Wedgwood, he liked the study of wickedness, and felt drawn to "the curious depth below depth of depravity" revealed in the documents he had read.[17] The period of the story was a time of moral and religious decline; but Browning found this propitious, for it was a setting where, as he says in *Sordello*, "mere decay / Produces richer life."

There are many divergences between the bundle of papers Browning took as his main source and the finished poem. The Pope, whose monologue is the centerpiece of the poem, does not appear in the Old Yellow Book at all, and the major characters give only brief depositions. As Browning said in a letter to Furnivall, he knew only that Guido and Caponsacchi must have been examined, and "raised the structure of the speeches" by imagining what they might have said.[18] He uses the actual names of the lawyers in the case, but the personalities he attaches to them are entirely fictional. Many events and characters are changed, omitted, displaced, and, more seriously, altered to fit in with Browning's purposes. Carlyle, who had not read the source, realized that the girl and the priest had been lovers, and the documents that have come to light since Browning's discovery of the Old Yellow Book have added to the evidence that there are fundamental discrepancies between the historical events and Browning's version of them.

Browning creates a vivid impression of time and place by details drawn from his experience and written sources. Most of these are also functional; the smallest flecks of local color and grains of historical fact are used to characterize, motivate, or embody some feeling or idea. For example, he learned from the so-called Secondary Source that Guido had committed the murders with a Genoese dagger of triangular shape that had hooks along its edges intended to tear the wound in such a way as to make it incurable.[19] The dagger is mentioned by a bystander in San Lorenzo in Lucina in Book II, and Guido's lawyer, Arcangeli admits that it was illegal. But when the Pope mentions it, it is transformed into a symbol of Guido's vengeful intentions: "Cut, but tear too!"

Similarly, nearly every speaker in the poem refers to Molinism, a heretical doctrine mentioned only once in the Old Yellow Book that emphasized faith rather than works and denied the importance of ritual and the organized church. Miguel de Molinos, the Spanish priest who originated it, had been tried, condemned, and imprisoned ten years before the action of the poem, but one of the dates given for his execution puts it only a few days before the day of Guido's crime on January 2, 1698.[20] There is no sign that Browning was acquainted with the theological merits of Molinism, but he did realize that the recent execution of its founder would have revived public interest in it, and that it could be safely condemned in casual conversation. Like the dagger, it serves both historical and functional purposes. It helps to capture the atmosphere of a time that was deeply immersed in religious issues, and also reflects the character of each of the speakers who mention it.

The Characters

The characters in the poem represent extremes of good and evil. This polarized moral landscape does not appear in the Old Yellow Book, or in Browning's other sources, but expresses his own sense of the possibilities of Italian character. The most thoroughly evil of the major characters, Guido, is joined in his wickedness by some of the minor ones: his brother, Paolo, who arranged the marriage for mercenary reasons; his mother, Beatrice, who was motivated by greed and spite; the poor mother of Pompilia, who agreed to sell her unborn child; and her unnamed father, who took his pleasure and went his way long before the main events began to unfold. At the other end of the moral scale are the Pope, who regards his judgment in the case as a test of his own integrity, and Pompilia, whom he acknowledges to be more virtuous than himself. Pompilia and Guido fit securely into traditional Italianate patterns, the first being a vulnerable, innocent girl comparable to figures in Mrs. Radcliffe's Gothic romances, the second a fierce villain resembling Iago and the scoundrels of Webster's plays. Both have parallels in *The Cenci,* and Browning may have had Shelley's play in mind as a model, for he intended to call his poem *The Franceschini.*

Browning's heroine has little to do with the actual Francesca Pompilia of the Old Yellow Book. She is an idealized figure, embodying qualities that Browning felt to be characteristic of Italian women, a middle-class counterpart of Pippa and the street girl in *Sordello.* He wanted Pompilia to demonstrate that the innocence of the secluded Italian woman was not inconsistent with exceptional intelligence and moral courage. When Julia Wedgwood complained that parts of Pompilia's speech seemed too complicated for an illiterate girl, he replied, ". . . it is Italian ignorance, quite compatible with extraordinary insight and power of expression too. . . ." And he illustrated his point by one of his few allusions to personal experiences with Italians. No ordinary English servant, he felt, could have expressed herself as the maid, Annunziata, did at the time of Elizabeth's death. What she said about her mistress was: "She had a certain nobility of mind which, finding in itself nothing of the base and evil, could not credit their existence in others."[21]

Browning makes Pompilia's piety a vital part of her character, and roots many of her actions and feelings in religious sensibility. After the birth of her child, Pompilia identifies herself as a Madonna figure and says she hopes she resembles the broken clay image of the Virgin at her street corner; she is referring to one of the little shrines which, Story points out, are found in every street in Rome, each with a little light before it and a Latin inscription. Almost the first thing she says is that she is sorry her son was not baptized in the church where she herself was baptized, married, and hopes to be buried.

Browning employs Pompilia to make his usual distinction between the sincere individual Catholic and the corrupt Church. It is, of course, natural for her to consult clerical authorities about her marriage difficulties, but her religious nature is developed in an extraordinary way when she disobeys them, and acts according to conscience. As the Pope observes, she rises "from law to law" with an unfailing religious instinct. This is one of the best examples of Browning's ability to immerse himself in the Italian state of mind, for, as Shelley notes in his preface to *The Cenci*, Protestants find it hard to accept the direct apprehension of divine presence felt among Italian Catholics. For the latter, says Shelley, religion is "interwoven with the whole fabric of life. It is adoration, faith, submission, penitence, blind admiration; not a rule for moral conduct. It has no necessary connection with any one virtue. . . . Religion pervades intensely the whole frame of society, and is according to the temper of the mind which it inhabits, a passion, a persuasion, an excuse, a refuge; never a check."[22] Because Browning grasps this sense of personal relation to God, he is able to show Pompilia's defiance of clerical authority and desertion of her husband as aspects of her religious devotion.

Many of Guido's villainous characteristics can be traced to Machiavellian prototypes in English literature, but he is a distinct figure in his own right, a coward, a liar, and a proud and desperate man who is forced to fight for survival. In Book V, when he appears to plead his case before the court, he claims to be pious, eager to serve the community, zealous in defense of tradition, and confident that the law will exonerate him. The portrait he paints of himself has convincing touches and moments of unintentional self-exposure. He certainly accepts the tradition that the husband has absolute rights over his wife, and feels the traditional jealousy when he suspects Pompilia of loving Caponsacchi. He says that the shame he felt on returning to face his townsmen in Arezzo after his wife had left him was worse than the physical tortures he suffered, a reaction natural in Italy where, as Luigi Barzini says, "the fundamental trait" of national character is the desire to make one's life a spectacle of public admiration.

Having found that playing the role of a pillar of the community who killed his erring wife in order to defend the rights of husbands has not saved him, Guido, in his second monologue, spoken in his cell the night before his execution, unmasks himself and expresses his real feelings. He exhibits himself as a naked individualist who rejects all social ties, without exception. He has contempt for "Gospel and Law," the two institutions that are presuming to judge him, and dismisses "civilization and society" with irony. For him, life is a contest of one against all. Law, as he analyzes it, originated as a means of protecting men against each other's vicious qualities. He maintains that religious men who are faced with some practical need "laugh frankly in the face of faith / And take the natural course," such as leaving mass to turn off a tap of wine that has been left running.

This sounds as if Guido's individualism caused him to reject all convention, but Browning, in an interesting anticipation of Freud's analysis in *Civilization and Its Discontents*, took the view that the rejection was a cause, not a consequence, of the individualism. He wrote to Julia Wedgwood that

> gross wickedness can be effected by cultivated minds,—I believe, the grossest—all the more, by way of reaction from the enforced habit of self denial which is the condition of men's receiving culture. Guido tried the over-refined way for four years, and in his rage at its unsuccess let the natural man break out.[23]

This represents Browning's understanding of the relationship between the cultivation and the violence that have always been paradoxically associated with each other in the concept of Italy. He thinks of Guido's cynical realism as the result of a pattern often repeated in Italian life, often exhibited in major historical figures, and thoroughly characteristic. When Guido proudly declares, "I stand on solid earth, not empty air," he is saying that the needs and desires of "the natural man" transcend the intangible ideals imposed by church or custom.

Because he believes that it is wrong to pretend to know more than man can know, or to claim less than man desires, Guido is contemptuous of the myths of church, state, and social custom. But he maintains his right to profit from whatever benefits they may offer. He identifies Christianity as a new form of paganism with one advantage: it provides forgiveness for the pagan excesses that survive, in spite of its reforms. His attitude is beautifully embodied in his story of the Franceschini coat of arms. Inside the front cover of the Old Yellow Book is pasted a picture of this *stemma*, inscribed with a note from Seymour Kirkup saying he had copied it from an Aretine manuscript and sent it to Browning in July 1868. It is a watercolor in green, buff, and blue, showing a greyhound tethered to a palm tree atop a hill consisting of three gold balls. Whether

Browning knew this detail earlier, or introduced it into his poem after receiving Kirkup's copy is not clear, but he does use the *stemma* in *The Ring and the Book* as an effective characterizing stroke. The tree, says Guido, represents a sprig of furze the Emperor gave a Franceschini ancestor as a token of his promise to grant him a large estate. The *stemma* therefore means that symbols of reward must be accompanied by something substantial. He regards old-fashioned chivalric idealism as a disability that keeps the nobility helpless while more practical segments of society reach for wealth and power.

His attitude is an accurate reflection of the Italian aristocratic consciousness. Feudalism never gained as firm a grip in Italy as it did in northern Europe, and the incursions of such families as the Sforza, who were of peasant origin, and the Medici, who were middle class, put the nobility on warning that they could not ignore practical considerations. Guido says that he will not surrender his self-interest to a hollow ideal of nobility, but will overreach his meretricious enemies at their own game, and cheat the cheaters. He speaks of his marriage to Pompilia as a business transaction, insisting that he has the right to profit from it to the full, and drives home his mercantile approach to it by a mundane comparison. Pompilia, he says, belongs to him as if she were a bird he had bought at the Rotunda, the bird market near the Pantheon, a place described by Story in *Roba di Roma*. It is ironic, however, that the representatives of the middle class he fears should be the helpless Comparini, just as it is ironic that Guido himself should be no more than a bedraggled version of Castiglione's courtier.

His claim to self-determination is unqualified: "Life, without absolute use / Of the actual sweet therein, is death, not life." This results in a shocking distrust of everyone except himself. When he asks, "What are these / Called king, priest, father, mother, stranger, friend?" he is not only denying the ties imposed by social relationships, but implying that any of those named who stand between him and his ambitions may be put out of the way. The roots of this individualism are to be found in the later Middle Ages and Renaissance, when Italian history was characterized by the rise to power of gifted or unscrupulous men who succeeded through their personal abilities. Guido does not reject his class, his nationality, or his culture, but uses them as vessels of individuality. He greets the two clerics who have come to share his last hours as fellow Tuscans

whose sympathy he has a right to claim, looks to his native prov-
ince (where the courts have vindicated him) as the true seat of his
dignity, refers to episodes in the history of his noble house as pre-
cedents, and even reaches back to pre-Christian Italy to describe
himself as a "primitive religionist," a pagan. He prefers the bright
colors of Titian to the pale ones of Fra Angelico, and declares that
he should have had Lucrezia Borgia as his bride.

Caponsacchi is perhaps the most interesting character in *The
Ring and the Book*, but he is less Italian than any of the others. Nev-
ertheless, he is Italian enough to associate Pompilia with the Ma-
donna, especially with Raphael's representations, and to adopt an
attitude toward her that recalls Dante's worship of Beatrice. In ad-
dition, Browning has provided him with certain surface traits of na-
tionality. He is a Tuscan nobleman, like Guido, and claims to out-
rank him. His family, which originated in Fiesole, and was once
dominant in Arezzo, is so ancient that an ancestor, Caponsacco, is
mentioned in the *Paradiso* as one who migrated to Florence when
Fiesole was conquered in 1125.

He is at least as individualistic as Guido, but his independence of
mind follows a very different course. He is self-effacing, introspec-
tive, melancholy, romantic, and idealistic. His sensitivity of con-
science and his indifference to public opinion and self-interest do
not belong to any traditional understanding of Italian character. He
is conscious of the moral responsibilities imposed by his position as
a churchman, but this piety only generates guilt and discontent un-
til Pompilia's call enables him to accept the task of rescuing her as a
religious duty. When he is with Pompilia, he adopts a restrained
and uncommunicative manner, keeping his thoughts to himself,
the behavior of an English gentleman.

The current of ideas in the Pope's monologue is notoriously in-
appropriate to a Pope, or to any Catholic of religious temperament,
and it has little to do with Italy. But Browning's sense of Italy is
present in the Pope's approach to the problem of adjudicating the
case, and in his idea of human nature. It is odd that the Pope
should resemble Guido in both of these, sharing with him certain
national characteristics, even though the Pope is a Neapolitan of
humble birth and Guido a Tuscan aristocrat. Like Guido, the Pope
has a double nature, a public or official one, and a natural, private
one. He begins his deliberations by setting aside his papal identity,
and approaching the case as a man, not an oracle, one whose judg-

ment is limited and liable to error, acknowledging that all he can do will be characterized by its human qualities, "But be man's method for man's life at least!" The case moves him to bring forward, as it does with Guido, not the self he aspires to, but the less lofty, common self he actually possesses, "the mere old man o' the world." The monologue has been criticized because its emphasis on private conscience reflects a Protestant, rather than a Catholic orientation, but the Pope's application of common sense standards to moral problems is recognizable as the Italian intuition that life does not transcend the limits of man's understanding, that human actions must be understood through man's knowledge of himself.

From this perspective, the Pope takes a brutally realistic view of human nature, and it is surprising to find that he is hardly less cynical about it than Guido himself. "What does the world, told truth, but lie the more?" he asks, and he is especially depressed when he thinks of the four peasant lads who might have been expected to reflect the natural goodness of humanity by rejecting Guido's proposal, but "Not so at all, thou noble human heart!"—they agreed to take part in the murders for pay, and when they were not paid, planned to murder their master. "These are the world!" declares the Pope. He admits that he is "Heart-sick at having all his world to blame," and finds "dark, difficult enough / The human sphere" after he has considered the individual actors in the case. These convictions are the basis of his pessimism about the moral status of the church. The view of human nature Browning shared with Guido and the Pope is not unique; but *The Ring and the Book* enables us to trace it to at least one of its sources—his consciousness of Italian history and Italian social conditions.

Much of this pessimism about ordinary humanity is brought into the poem by the monologues of the minor characters, which link the spiritual conflicts at the poem's center to the background of a specific historical moment. "Half-Rome" is a sarcastic busybody who takes us directly into San Lorenzo in Lucina to view the bodies of the Comparini, complaining that the apse of the church is too small to accommodate the crowd. He says that he has often seen bodies displayed in this manner; but the custom seems to have been reserved for the funerals of children who died unexpectedly.[24] "The Other Half-Rome" is a sentimental idealist who gives us an intimate view of Pompilia's childhood and death. "Tertium Quid" leads his aristocratic listeners past a game of cards into a window seat to entertain them with his story. The Venetian whose letter appears in Book XII is a lover of spectacles who lingers on the details of Guido's execution, reporting that a lame beggar was cured by the condemned man's prayers.

The most vivid of these minor characters is perhaps the lawyer, Arcangeli. His monologue combines elements of jocularity, sentimentality, and cold sagacity into an intimate picture of an Italian *paterfamilias.* As he drives industriously ahead with the preparation of his brief, his mind strays to the recipes of the dishes being prepared for dinner, the numerous playful variants of his son's name which Italian makes possible, proud thoughts of the boy's progress in Latin, and anxious ones about his dressing for the cold weather. Dante Gabriel Rossetti told Browning that the monologue accurately recalled his own childhood in an Italian household. These characters and their varied concerns generate the dense solidity of atmosphere that James admired, but they also establish the nature of humanity, seen in its Italian manifestation, as one of the major themes of *The Ring and the Book.*

Images

Apart from certain first hand observations, the stories told by the three bystanders in Books II, III, and IV are reconstructions of what they have heard, and the details in them are hypothetical. When "Half-Rome" reports that Pietro, while his estate was dwindling,

> *Crawled all-fours with his baby pick-a-back,*
> *Sat at serene cats' cradle with his child,*

he is describing a father's typical behavior, not something he has actually seen. The movements of Abate Paolo during his visit to the Comparini are vividly described:

> *giving his great flap-hat a gloss*
> *With flat o' the hand between-whiles, soothing now*
> *The silk from out its creases o'er the calf,*
> *Setting the stocking clerical again. . . .*

The narrator was not present at this scene, and his vignette is a generalized representation, in spite of its details. Such images are fully as authentic as actual reports would be, but have, in addition,

a quasi-symbolic effect. As admittedly imaginary re-creations of ac-
tual events, they resemble the metaphors drawn from local life that
are often introduced throughout the poem. For example, "The
Other Half-Rome," in justifying Violante's ruse, gives a vivid snap-
shot of a crowd reaching out to catch a coin thrown into it; and
"Tertium Quid" invents a whole family of vinedressers who eat
porridge and keep their tinderbox in a goatskin pouch.

Some of these particulars can be traced to sources in Browning's
experience. For example, "Tertium Quid" describes the impover-
ishment of the Franceschini through some imagined vignettes from
the daily life of a servant:

> *Out of the vast door 'scutcheoned overhead,*
> *Creeps out a serving-man on Saturdays*
> *To cater for the week,—turns up anon*
> *I' the market, chaffering for the lamb's least leg,*
> *Or the quarter-fowl, less entrails, claws and comb:*
> *Then back again with prize,—a liver begged*
> *Into the bargain, gizzard overlooked.*
> *He's mincing these to give the beans a taste,*
> *When, at your knock, he leaves the simmering soup,*
> *Waits on the curious stranger-visitant,*
> *Napkin in half-wiped hand, to show the rooms,*
> *Point pictures out have hung their hundred years,*
> *"Priceless," he tells you,—puts in his place at once*
> *The man of money: yes, you're banker-king*
> *Or merchant-kaiser, wallow in your wealth*
> *While patron, the house-master, can't afford*
> *To stop our ceiling-hole that rain so rots:*
> *But he's the man of mark, and there's his shield,*
> *And yonder's the famed Rafael, first in kind,*
> *The painter painted for his grandfather,*
> *And you have paid to see.*

The first part of this sketch seems to have been suggested by—but
not copied from—the testimony in the Old Yellow Book by Angeli-
ca Battista, the Franceschini's servant, who gives specific informa-
tion about the niggardliness of the household's diet. The second is
no doubt based on scenes Browning encountered during his expe-
ditions in search of paintings.

The poem as a whole is a fabric of irrefutably authentic images
which create the effect described by Henry James as "that breath of

Browning's own particular matchless Italy which takes us full in the face and remains from the first the felt, rich, coloured air in which we live."[25] The decaying Franceschini palace on a side street in remote Arezzo houses starving nobility suffering anguish and dissension; in contrast, the warm, lively bourgeois household of the Comparini is full of playfulness and family affection; in his state chambers, the Pope receives ambassadors, and is dramatically interrupted by a conscience-stricken soldier of his guard, who asks to confess his sins. Only one candle was burning when Pompilia was secretly and shamefully married at the altar of San Lorenzo in Lucina, but fifty light up the scene when the bodies of the Comparini are displayed there. Guido is useless to the Cardinal he serves, and is dropped—like a plume decorating the head of a horse that draws the Cardinal's coach. The sequence of trials is like the squabbling of the puppets at the Piazza Navona. Beside the miserable flight of stairs leading to the room of the prostitute who is to become Pompilia's mother there is a rope instead of a banister. As a farmhouse burns, the past emerges in the form of the blackened Roman ruin around which it was constructed. A scared she-goat is made to stand on four vertical sticks as a form of street entertainment. A veteran gambler about to leave the casino destitute is urged to play again until he wins. A verger shows a priest the scorpion he has caught in the church writhing at the end of his prong. Browning seems to have access to an endless store of these impressions, scenes plucked out of the air, but an air which is unmistakably that of Italy.

Settings

The Ring and the Book is a poem of three cities: Rome, Arezzo, and Florence. Florence appears only in the story's outer frame, but it is the point of reference in present space and time the poet uses to place himself in relation to the crime and trial that speak to him after more than 150 years. His state of mind is shaped both by his thoughts of Guido, Pompilia, and the rest, and by the sights and sounds of Florence and Casa Guidi; the black spot at the foot of the stairs in Casa Guidi and the fly circling a white flower on the terrace are braided together with the old events to form a single impression.

If Florence brings the present into the poem, the remotest past with which it is concerned is represented by Arezzo. Browning knew Arezzo well. He spent a week there in July 1848 while on his way to Ancona, and stayed in it from November 19 to 24, 1853, while en route to Florence. After reading the Old Yellow Book, he apparently went to Arezzo again to look for further information connected with the story, for he says in the poem that he found a document in its archives showing that Franceschini's sister had asked for a testimonial of her brother's good reputation after his death.

Arezzo remains a treasury of medieval towers and churches and Renaissance palaces and fortifications. Its main streets and squares have not changed much since Guido's time, and Browning could have traced the action of his story through them, as is still possible today. It is not surprising that the Comparini, accustomed to the liveliness of the neighborhood of the Piazza di Spagna in Rome, should have been depressed by the narrow, gloomy streets, gently curving, in accordance with medieval taste, among the tall buildings, and by the old Franceschini palace, "Grimmest as that is of the gruesome town."

Arezzo's ancient main thoroughfare, the present Corso Italia, apparently aroused Browning's imagination, as the Piazzetta in Asolo and the Piazza Santissima Annunziata in Florence had done, for he uses many of its features in his poem. Its most conspicuous building is Caponsacchi's church, Santa Maria della Pieve. Sir Frederick Treves, in *The Country of the Ring and the Book*, locates the inn from which the lovers took flight in the house just across the narrow Corso Italia from the Pieve. The theater where Canon Conti threw comfits into Pompilia's lap, precipitating one of the crises of the story, was the Salone delle Commedie, which occupied the western end of the Logge Vasari, a few steps up the street.[26] Nearly opposite is the Palazzo Pretorio, the palace where Pompilia went to see the Governor. Also nearby is the palace of the Bishop, whose help she implored several times, only to be lectured and sent home in a carriage. The Duomo, or Cathedral, where Caponsacchi takes refuge from Arezzo's social life is a Gothic church, larger and later than the Pieve, somewhat further along and around a corner; Browning provides Caponsacchi with an offhand reference to its lancet windows, which are masterly works by the French stained-glass craftsman, Guillaume de Marcillat, who was Vasari's first teacher.

The age and beauty of the Pieve justify Browning in introducing it as a special object of his hero's devotion. Its facade is in the so-called Pisan style, with rows of small pillars supporting each level, the style of the churches in Lucca that first opened Ruskin's eyes to architectural beauty. The facade is a thirteenth-century work, and incorporates on its ground floor six Roman columns brought from another site that link the church to a remote, pre-Christian past. The interior of the church is spacious, simple and bold; it consists of a nave flanked on either side by four high, vigorous Romanesque arches, and a broad choir before the altar, with a railing. The architectural strength and simplicity of the Pieve is a part of Browning's poem; it embodies the religion Caponsacchi aspires to, in contrast to the superficial, time-serving church organization he has entered.

At one point in his monologue, Caponsacchi feels that Pompilia standing in the window with her lamp has

> *the same great, grave, griefful air*
> *As stands i' the dusk, on altar that I know,*
> *Left alone with one moonbeam in her cell,*
> *Our Lady of the Sorrows.*

W.H. Griffin's collection of photographs shows the statue in the crypt of the Pieve to which this passage apparently refers.[27] It is still there, a commonplace full-length figure of the Madonna with her blue robe over her head and her hands clasped, enclosed in a glass case. A nearby plaque identifies the piece as *B. M. V. Doloribus,* the work of Raynaldo Bartolini. The only illumination in the darkness of the crypt is a dim electric bulb inside the Madonna's case, which has no doubt replaced the lamp Browning called a moonbeam.

Arezzo's formidable wall, whose gates were locked at night, represented a serious obstacle to the lovers when they planned their escape. They planned to have Pompilia climb it at a spot near the bastion called the *Torrione,* where it was broken, and to meet Caponsacchi outside the San Clemente Gate nearby. Photographs of the bastion and the low spot in the wall appear in Treves's volume, and show how plausible this plan was. Afterwards, the lovers drove their carriage around the wall to the San Spirito Gate on the

Interior of Santa Maria della Pieve, Arezzo
Hall Griffin Photographs, British Museum

south, which faces the road to Rome. All of these places are today much as they were in Pompilia's time, and we can be sure that Browning had them in mind as he envisioned the action of his poem.

Old Arezzo comes to life in the poem as Browning describes glimpses of its social life. Calling, perhaps, on memories of Bagni di Lucca, he conjures up a charming evocation of a sprightly but shallow provincial scene, with its Carnival, theater, casino, and promenades, enlivened with gossip and flirtation. There are idle, fashionable parties infiltrated by Church intrigue, the glum, isolated Franceschini household, the squares, streets, and winehouses where Pietro loiters, and the noble churches with their works of art where some of the characters find spiritual solace.

Browning knew the route between Arezzo and Rome where some important parts of the poem's action take place, for the Brownings sometimes went between Florence and Rome by way of Arezzo (the alternate route went through Siena). He retraces it in his imagination in Book I until he thinks of Castelnuovo, where the fugitives stopped at an old inn called the Osteria. W.H. Griffin's photographs show some of the places along this route, many of them now demolished, and prove that even the small landmarks in Caponsacchi's account of the journey are authentic. He says his party stopped at a post house "and a hovel or two" for refreshment; one of Griffin's prints shows houses of this kind, huts with peaked roofs made of reeds or thatch, with one side open to the road. At the spot where Pompilia holds a child in her arms, a roadside shrine reminds her of a childhood episode in church. Griffin's picture of such a shrine near Castelnuovo shows a small structure with a brick front, stucco sides, and a round, arched doorway with a pediment above surmounted by a cross.

The real fugitives stopped at an inn at Castelnuovo where Guido overtook them, and this building survived long enough to be photographed both by Griffin and Treves. It is of double interest, because it was the scene of the actual events in the seventeenth century, and was also known to Browning. He refers to it as the "squalid inn," a description supported by the photographs. Exterior views show three arches supporting the first floor, a sign saying "Albergo e Ristorante della Posta," and the remains of a stable opposite. Browning imagined Caponsacchi as standing in this spot, urging the stablehands to hurry when Guido arrived. A few steps

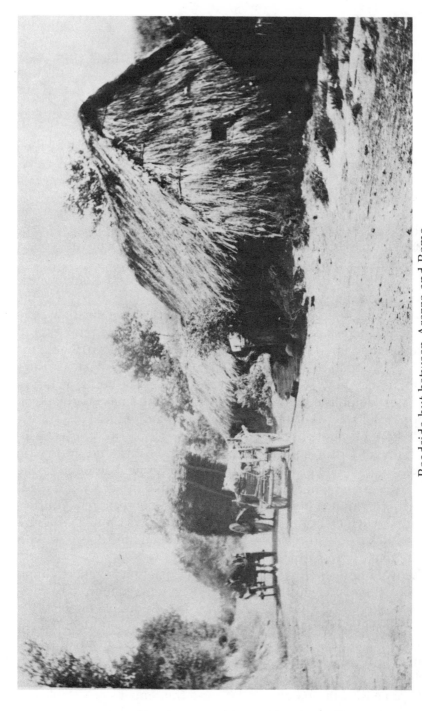

Roadside hut between Arezzo and Rome
Hall Griffin Photographs, British Museum

past the inn the dome of Saint Peter's can be seen sixteen miles away, marking Rome, the goal the lovers were traveling to.

The second half of the story takes place in Rome, and it is a coincidence that the neighborhood where the Comparini lived was that of Browning's flat in the Via Bocca di Leone. The Roman part of the story is embedded in particulars that would be familiar to readers who had visited Italy, and who could therefore visualize the actions in their settings. Browning establishes a sense of place early by assigning each of his three speakers to a more or less specific spot in Rome for his recital. "Half-Rome's" allusions show that he is at first in San Lorenzo in Lucina, and that he then strolls through the small piazza outside to the corner of the Corso occupied by the Palazzo Ruspoli. "The Other Half-Rome" stands in the market at the Piazza Barberini, at a spot where Bernini's Triton fountain can be seen. "Tertium Quid" speaks to the guests at a party in an aristocratic house not otherwise identified.

The Roman settings cover a wide range, from the prostitute's squalid room where Violante strikes her bargain for buying a child to the Pope's secluded study, where he muses over a history of the Papacy, and then turns to consider the case. Between these extremes lie the comfortable Comparini home near the Piazza di Spagna, their suburban villa, street scenes with crowds, women washing clothes at fountains, puppet shows in the Piazza Navona, Christmas festivals, the imposing palazzo where Guido comes to deliver a message, the wig shop where Paolo and Guido seek a bride, a convent, a hospital, a prison, and so on. For many of these Browning had identifiable locales in mind, while others are generalized.

The three main Roman settings are the Comparini home on the Via Vittoria and several adjacent places, the prison where Guido delivers his second monologue, and the Piazza del Popolo, the place of his execution. The court chambers where Guido's and Caponsacchi's testimony is given are not clearly identified, and the Pope's study, buried in the depths of the Vatican, is left to the reader's imagination. The country villa where Browning has the murders occur is fictional, the result of an error or a deliberate change.[28]

The Via Vittoria, where the Comparini lived, runs between the Corso and the Via del Babuino, two thoroughfares that converge on the Piazza del Popolo, the scene of the story's climax, the execu-

The Inn at Castelnuovo
Hall Griffin Photographs, British Museum

Interior of the Inn at Castelnuovo
Hall Griffin Photographs, British Museum

tion of Guido and his henchmen. Treves has described the quarter as it must have been in the time of the Comparini as a quiet, secluded spot, where children played in the street.[29] Browning imaginatively expands the life of the old couple and their child into an intimate domestic picture that uses various places in the neighborhood, many of them mentioned in his sources, to anchor his story to the reality of the locale. Pietro confides in his cronies at the boat fountain in the Piazza di Spagna, and Violante first observes Pompilia's mother at the cistern in the Piazza di Monte Citorio, where she pursues the two trades of washerwoman and prostitute. Browning brought these sites into the story himself, but the shop of the wigmaker near the Piazza Colonna where Paolo and Guido first hear about Pompilia is based on that of a hairdresser mentioned in his sources. Browning has Pompilia die in a "long white lazar-house"; actually, she died in her home on the Via Vittoria. Fra Celestino, the Augustinian who heard her confession, was from the nearby church of Gesù e Maria in the Corso. The Convent of Santa Maria Maddelena delle Convertite, the "Convertites" who later sued for Pompilia's property, was also on the Corso in the immediate neighborhood.

Browning did not connect the Church of San Lorenzo in Lucina with his poem until he had read, in the Secondary Source, that it was the scene both of Pompilia's wedding and of the display of the bodies of the Comparini nearly five years later. Struck by this ironic convergence, he added others, making the church something like the focal point of his story. It is presented as Pompilia's favorite church, where she usually attended mass, and Browning has her going to it from her home by a route which takes her past his flat in the Via Bocca di Leone. It is the scene of her baptism, the setting for the monologue of "Half-Rome," and the place where Fra Celestino delivers his sermon on Pompilia's death in Book XII. In witnessing so many varied actions, the church becomes a symbol that survives the extremes of human behavior. Browning was anxious to describe it accurately, and wrote to Frederic Leighton, asking him to send some details about it, which he used in "Half-Rome's" monologue. Hence, there are complaints about the confined space in the apse, and a vivid allusion to people crowding the organ loft that hangs over the altar. The crowd could not have broken "the wooden work / Painted like porphyry to deceive the eye," for the marble around the altar is all genuine, but Browning's point is not entirely astray, for some of the pillars at the rear are made of painted wood, a fact perhaps mentioned by Leighton.

Pompilia, in reviewing her attachment to the church, recalls as "an ominous sign" the marble figure of a lion eating a man which made her wonder when she was a child. The marble lion is one of a pair of worn and ancient pieces that flank the door. However, it is not eating the small human figure laid across its paws, but allowing itself to be stroked, and wears, as Treves describes it, "a singularly benevolent and even fatuous expression."[30] Treves speculates that Leighton may have misinformed Browning about some of the details of the church, for the poet transposed the positions of the two lions, and gave the church an aisle it did not have. But Browning was entirely capable of going to much trouble to learn small facts of this kind and then altering them to suit the needs of his poem. Here the child's misinterpretation of what is meant to be a symbol of the church's benevolence is an accurate prediction of the sorrows she is to suffer.

The place where Guido was imprisoned, and where he delivers his second monologue, was a new facility of the Roman penal system, the Carceri Nuove on the Via Giulia which had been built in 1655. Browning makes use of this fact in Book V, where Guido feeds his bitterness about the ascendancy of the lower classes by recalling (or imagining) that one of the prison officials, a man who had served his father, had him transferred to this superior prison as a favor—"anything for an old friend!" The building is in a perfect state of preservation, and Treves (who was under the mistaken impression that Pompilia and Caponsacchi were also confined there) devotes a chapter to it. As Treves points out, Browning's description of Guido suffering in an airless underground cell is inaccurate, for the cells in the Carceri Nuove were large, high-ceilinged and airy; furthermore, the real Guido was housed in one of the death cells on the roof of the building, not underground.[31]

The last important Roman setting of the poem is the scene of the execution, the Piazza del Popolo. Browning asserts that the usual place for these procedures was a spot near the Castel Sant'Angelo, but that the Pope chose the Piazza del Popolo on this occasion in order to give a warning to the nobility who frequented that part of the city. This is fictional; Treves says that in the seventeenth century the Piazza was a rough, unfinished place frequented by peasants bringing crops and livestock into the city, and so was truly

The New Prisons, Via Giulia, Rome
Hall Griffin Photographs, British Museum

188

"del popolo," and not a haunt of the aristocracy as Browning's Pope suggests.

In his second monologue, Guido contends that the "laughter-loving people" of Rome will be dismayed if he is put to death. But Browning casts an ironic light on this by showing, on the basis of firm historical evidence, that the spectators thoroughly enjoyed the executions. The Venetian who is the author of the letter in Book XIII says that executions provided a climax for Carnival. Stands were built for spectators, windows overlooking the square were rented, and an atmosphere of gaiety and confusion prevailed. These facts are drawn from the Secondary Source, and are corroborated by an independent account of Franceschini's trial and death, which reports that a crowd numbering forty thousand had begun to gather in the Piazza the night before, that the roofs were covered with spectators, and that windows were rented for as much as eight scudi.[32]

In his account of a nineteenth-century execution in the Piazza del Popolo in *The Count of Monte Cristo,* Dumas describes women in the crowd holding their children on their heads to give them the best view. Browning did not miss this aspect of the event. In *The Ring and the Book,* Arcangeli takes his beloved son, Giacinto, to view the hacked bodies of the Comparini, and then to witness the execution of the client he failed to defend properly, having promised him this on his birthday. Father and son share their point of vantage with a lady who tells the boy when to watch for the fall of the blade, and Giacinto explains that his father lost the case deliberately in order to avoid displeasing the Pope.

At the close of his second monologue, Guido asks, "Who are these you have let descend my stair? / Ha, their accursed psalm!" Browning had read in some of his sources that Guido was accompanied from the prison to the Piazza del Popolo by "the Company of Death and Pity," whom he describes as waiting for the condemned men

> Crow-wise, the frightful Brotherhood of Death.
> Black-hatted and black-hooded huddle they,
> Black rosaries a-dangling from each waist;
> So take they their grim station at the door,
> Torches lit, skull-and-cross-bones-banner spread,
> And that gigantic Christ with open arms,
> Grounded. . . .

This group was from the *Arciconfraternita della morte e del'orazione*, whose church was in the Via Giulia near the prison, and whose primary function was that of burying the dead bodies of the poor; however, they also appeared at executions. T.A. Trollope explains that the parallel Florentine institution, the Misericordia, originated during the plague when those who came to bury the dead concealed their identities under black robes and cowls.[33] The Roman counterpart consisted of respectable men who could be called to bury unclaimed bodies, and Story's description of it is clearly related to Browning's Brotherhood:

> The messenger informs the brethren when their services are needed, and towards evening, dressed in their black sacks, their heads and faces covered, and with only two holes cut in the *capuccio* to look through, they may be seen passing through the street, bearing the body on their bier to the church, preceded by a long, narrow standard of black, on which are worked a cross, skull and bones, bearing torches and chanting the *Miserere* and other psalms.[34]

Browning must have seen such a procession from the windows of the Collegio Ferdinando in Pisa in 1847, on the occasion when he told Elizabeth he could not turn away because "it *draws* me."

Two gallows were erected for the peasant boys, but Guido, in consideration of his rank, was executed on the guillotine which Browning refers to by the unfamiliar, chilling term, *mannaia*. The word means "blade," and, by synecdoche, the instrument as a whole. It recurs incessantly throughout the poem, gathering symbolic force. Browning introduces the device early by having Guido come across it accidentally near the church of Santa Maria in Cosmedin, an out-of-the-way spot where it has been stored.

Guido describes the guillotine in his second monologue, connecting it both with his grievances about his social position and his own final meeting with it. It had just been used to execute a peasant who had struck a Duke for abducting his sister, and Guido considers this a proper assertion of the fast-disappearing power of the nobility. Now that he is condemned to die under its blade, however, *mannaia* has a very different meaning for him, and he gives a long, circumstantial description of the instrument and its mode of operation. In the Criminological Museum of Rome there is a "Ghigliottine già in uso a Roma" which corresponds fairly well with this

A member of the "Brotherhood of Death"
Hall Griffin Photographs, British Museum

191

description. Can it be the one—the very one—which was used to execute the historical Guido? Did Browning see it in the Castel Sant'Angelo where it was kept in his time, and call on his memory of it when he wrote Guido's monologue?

The circuitous route by which the prisoners were taken to the Piazza del Popolo is described in detail in the Secondary Source, and introduced in Book XII of the poem. The map shows that it passed close to some of the most important scenes of the story that led up to the execution. It went through the Piazza della Colonna, which adjoins the Piazza di Monte Citorio, where Violante first saw Pompilia's mother, and where the wig shop in which Guido first learned about Pompilia was located, then up the Corso, not far from San Lorenzo in Lucina on the left, and the Comparini house in Via Vittoria on the right. Thus, it has the odd effect, somewhat like that of the viceregal cavalcade in the Wandering Rocks chapter of Joyce's *Ulysses*, of linking several places connected with different events in the poem into a single retrospective chain.

Art and Artists

Numerous allusions in *The Ring and the Book* suggest that the people of seventeenth-century Italy were familiar with art and artists. Even the fatuous Bottini turns to art for an elaborate comparison that goes on for 150 lines before he realizes that it will not serve his purpose. In a rhetorically sophisticated passage that has been described as a parody of the passage about the creative process in Book I, he gives a creditable account of the way in which a painter prepares preliminary sketches, and then, when ready to produce his picture, sets them aside and relies on his general impressions.[35] He even identifies the figures in the painting with Pietro and Pompilia, but then gives up the parallel bit by bit as untenable.

Raphael, who is mentioned more often than any other artist, comes into the poem as a representative of purity and holy splendor. While no specific painting of his is ever named, many of the religious images seem to be connected with him. Most significantly, Raphael is used to identify the attitude of pious chivalry which Caponsacchi adopts toward Pompilia. The canon compares his first sight of her to the time when a Raphael—presumably a Madonna—was brought into the church and left on the high altar, and says that the letters she was charged with writing could no more have come from her than a scorpion from the mouth of the painting. When Pompilia came to him for help, he says, it was as if the painting had come to life, and the postures through which Pompilia passes, "Her head erect, her face full turned to me, / Her soul intent on mine through two wide eyes," may well reflect Browning's recollection of the Raphael Madonnas in the Pitti Palace.

He defines Guido's character, on the other hand, by associating him with a work by the Bolognese painter, Francesco Albano. In telling the story of the Duke who abducted a peasant girl and had her protesting brother put to death, Guido describes him passing around among his friends Albano's picture of the rape of Europa, for which the girl served as a model. "Florid old rogue Albano," as Browning called him, painted the subject mentioned by Guido several times, in a style that is the perfect expression of the cultivated libertinism whose passing Guido is lamenting.

When Pompilia and her parents are lumped together, says Guido in his hatred,

> *think you see*
> *The dreadful bronze our boast, we Aretines,*
> *The Etruscan monster, the three-headed thing,*
> *Bellerophon's foe! How name you the whole beast?*
> *You choose to name the body from one head,*
> *That of the simple kid which droops the eye,*
> *Hangs the neck and dies tenderly enough:*
> *I rather see the griesly lion belch*
> *Flame out i' the midst, the serpent writhe her rings,*
> *Grafted into the common stock for tail,*
> *And name the brute, Chimaera, which I slew!*

Through this allusion, Browning skillfully characterizes Guido, and links him to his native place. The Chimera of Arezzo is a famous bronze of the fifth or fourth century B.C., thirty-one-and-a-half inches high, which Guido describes accurately enough; it has a lion's head and body, its upturned tail is a snake, and the head of a kid protrudes from one side. In his Preface to *Lives of the Painters*, Vasari reports that it was found in 1554 while the fortifications for Arezzo were being constructed. Browning uses the Chimera in "Old Pictures in Florence" as an image of the harmful effects of monarchy on art, but Vasari mentions it proudly as evidence of the perfection of art among the ancient Etruscans, and the monster has always been regarded with affection by Aretines, who have named the street where it was found after it. In having Guido equate it with the Comparini, Browning shows a mind so filled with hatred that it can regard innocent family relations as grotesque.

Pompilia attends to pictures, for as a child she identifies herself and a playmate as the figures of Daphne and Diana in a tapestry hung in her playmate's house. Just as Caponsacchi sees her as a Raphael figure, she sees him as the Saint George who appears in the Vasari altarpiece in the Pieve. A fleeting allusion she makes to Saint Michael has been identified as a reference to a fresco by Spinello Aretino in the church of San Francesco in Arezzo which is mentioned by Vasari.[36] The pictures she knows are, of course, pious ones, but Browning makes use of quite another kind of painting to characterize her indirectly. "Tertium Quid" explains Pompilia's behavior by positing as a parallel case that of a lady guilty of adultery who says that she would not have behaved as she did if her husband had not repressed her, "curtaining Correggio carefully / Lest I be taught that Leda had two legs." The painting referred to is one of an erotic series depicting the loves of the gods; Pompilia would not have cared for it, and "Tertium Quid's" use of it exhibits his failure to understand her character.

Inferior painters were as useful to Browning in establishing atmosphere as great ones. The first artist mentioned in the poem is Luigi Ademollo, an eighteenth-century painter who did some allegorical subjects in the chapel and halls of the Pitti Palace, and also decorated Sant'Ambrogio, the church for which Fra Lippo promises to paint his *Coronation of the Virgin* in Browning's poem. In *The Ring and the Book* his prints of "scenic backgrounds" are for sale among the cheap goods in the stall where the Old Yellow Book was found. Browning seems to have been equally amused by Ciro Ferri, who is mentioned by Bottini as the artist chosen by the discriminating Governor of Rome to decorate his new palace. Ferri was a seventeenth-century baroque painter, a student of Pietro da Cortona, who distinguished himself mainly by carrying on projects left unfinished by his master in a style remarkably faithful to the original. Browning was familiar with the work of both men from the ceilings of the Pitti Palace, which had been completed by Ferri after Pietro had worked on them for six years. Guido uses as an image of deception a painting by Pietro retouched by Ciro Ferri, and Bottini's taste in art is certainly undermined when he suggests that Ferri has surpassed both Michelangelo and Raphael.

Browning imagines that Pompilia lies dying while a procession of lawyers, priests, and neighbors troops through the room. The baroque painter, Carlo Maratta, hears of her, and comes in to make a sketch of her, praising her features. Considered a great master in his lifetime, Maratta was especially famous for his Madonnas, which even supplanted those of Raphael in popularity, and his inclusion in the monologue of "The Other Half-Rome," who admires Pompilia, supports her connection with the Madonna. It also suggests the superficiality of the public's interest in Pompilia, since Maratta had completely lost his standing by the nineteenth century, and Browning allows Arcangeli to refer to him with admiration.

The wealth of authentic circumstantial detail in *The Ring and the Book* opens a tangible, vital world to the reader's imagination, but its more fundamental effect is the fulfillment of the project first attempted in *Sordello,* that of forming a distinct poetic idiom from the materials of Italian life. Browning's vivid particulars create lifelike scenes, but they also make the scenes articulate, charging them with significance. This effect has been approached from different directions by a number of the critical interpretations. Isobel Armstrong regards the poem's length and complexity as a means of involving the reader in a process of discovery. The poem seeks to base understanding, not merely on communication, but on the task of unraveling its self-modifications and cross-connections, of confronting the difficulties of interpretation as a firsthand experience. Such a poem, she says, must have variety and amplitude, it "must live by the largeness of the world it creates," and the rich background of detail Browning created provides that source of life.[37]

In another analysis, L.J. Swingle has argued that the poem is not merely a renewal of the past in accordance with Browning's poetic theory, but is also an exhibition of the processes through which knowledge of the past is lost. It shows how the truth disappears, how being passes into non-being, leaving only such faint traces as the Old Yellow Book. The poet tells us the truth immediately in Book I, Swingle says, so that we can see how it is progressively obscured. He creates the world of Italy for a similar purpose. It is rendered as an extensive, engulfing physical presence, the "being" for which the Franceschini case stands, a larger and more general existence that has nearly passed into nonexistence under the destructive influence of time.[38]

In their study of *The Ring and the Book*, Altick and Loucks show that the characters, settings, and even the trivial objects that are mentioned embody deceptiveness and ambiguity.[39] This is the impression created by the poem's depiction of Rome and Italy in general. Opulent, powerful, authoritative, the city also exhibits the savagery of its crowds and the dishonesty of its officials. It is intensely preoccupied with the Francheschini case as a subject for gossip and sensation, while remaining utterly blind to its deep tragic resonances. It arouses hopes in the minds of all the characters, then disappoints them. Guido comes to Rome for advancement in his youth, but does not find it. The lovers flee to Rome to gain freedom, but find imprisonment and death. Guido feels that the city exonerates him and approves his cause, but the Pope reverses his view. The Pope himself shakes his head over the conditions of his spiritual capital. Its ancient Christian traditions are marred by the dissension surrounding the body of Pope Formosus, and its artistic traditions by the work of imitators like Ciro Ferri and the *castrato* mentioned by Guido who feigns passion while singing a female part.

Browning, with characteristic optimism, rounds off his presentation of Rome with a hopeful note through Fra Celestino's sermon in Book XII. Preaching in Pompilia's church, Fra Celestino calls upon Rome's remote past to illustrate his point that her fate ought to be a foundation for hope. The catacombs were originally feared as the haunts of a surviving pagan worship, but exploration revealed that they contained the tombs of Christian saints and martyrs. In the same way, he argues, Christianity ought to see the light of hope in the apparent darkness of the time. His lesson, and the immense, complex image of Rome and Italy support the vision of man's life set forth by the Pope. They are corrupt, painful, imperfect, yet they test man's spiritual worth, and provide a setting where souls like Caponsacchi and Pompilia may achieve their true stature.

TEN

The Last Years: Venice and Asolo

It is striking that in spite of his repatriation Browning did not turn to English subjects during the very productive twenty years left to him after *The Ring and the Book*. Instead, he drew his materials from a variety of foreign sources, including ancient Greece, the French (or French-speaking) regions where he and Sarianna usually spent their holidays, and even the Orient. He did not visit Italy again for seventeen years, until the fall of 1878, and Italy now became, with a few exceptions, no more than a minor element of his poetry. But many of his poems, including those on non-Italian subjects, were characterized by the poetic he had developed in writing about Italy. He sought illumination in the thoughts of people of other times and places; he explored the origins of inexplicable, passionate ac- tions, as in *Red Cotton Night-Cap Country;* he approached moral truth indirectly, through the presentation of arguments he did not agree with, as in *Fifine at the Fair;* and he continued to seek sources of vitality in the past, as in *Aristophanes' Apology*. Direct allusions to Italian materials sometimes appear in poems not otherwise con- cerned with Italy: Raphael and Michelangelo are used to illustrate points in *Fifine at the Fair*, and Dante is quoted in *La Saisiaz*.

The first poem containing direct references to Italy written in this period was *Prince Hohenstiel-Schwangau, Saviour of Society*. Brown- ing remained critical of Napoleon III during his reign, and wel- comed his ignominious defeat at Sedan in September 1870. About a year later, while on holiday in a remote hunting lodge in Scotland with Pen, he turned to the prose sketch about Louis Napoleon he had written in Rome in 1860, and completed the long monologue dramatizing the pathetic figure the Emperor had become.

Although Italy occupied only a small part of his career, Browning's Prince looks back to the war he fought against Austria on behalf of Italian independence as his finest work, and an example of a just war. In answer to accusations that he lacked idealism, he describes an Italian landscape, with its plants and ruins, trembling responsively to a wind that carries his words, "Be Italy again!" and recalls a scene in which he argued liberal reforms before a group of timorous reactionary ministers cowering in a dark, dilapidated room on whose wall "Rafael moulderingly bids adieu." He declares that each man is given an individual imprint by God, and defends the attention he has given to the physical needs of the people rather than to abstract political causes by saying, "Mankind i' the main have little wants, not large." These sound like lessons learned in Italy.

Italy also provides him with the instance he uses to remind himself of the final truth that all of his insights may have been self-deceptions. Arguing against those who urged him to beget an heir to carry on his work, he denies that genius is hereditary, and tells of a belief about the priestly office of an ancient temple near the river Clitumnus, whose water was supposed to wash the grey skins of oxen white. The priesthood was believed to pass from father to son, but this was false, says the Prince, for it passed by violence; each aspirant succeeded to it by killing his predecessor. Yet, at the poem's conclusion, in a passage Browning added to a later edition to amend an error of his own, the Prince corrects his story. The place was not Clitumnus, he now recalls, but the lake of Nemi (well known as the site of the murder-ritual later used as the basis of Frazer's *Golden Bough*). The confusion of names was wish fulfilling; the foolish tradition about the water and the oxen deceived him into placing the softened version of the priestly succession there. "Alack," he says, "one lies one's self / Even in the stating that one's end was truth. . . ."

The setting of Browning's next poem, *Fifine at the Fair*, is the region in Brittany where he had spent summer holidays since 1862, but some of its imagery draws upon his memories of Italy; Italian paintings supply the elements of a spiritual vocabulary, and Venice is used as a microcosm of life. Browning's speaker, Don Juan, tries to persuade his wife, Elvire, that his attraction to the gypsy, Fifine, is no more than a superficial interest that does not threaten their marital love. He reminds Elvire of the Raphael he bought from an

Italian nobleman by outbidding an American who had raised the price enormously. For a time, Don Juan recalls, he was overjoyed with his new possession, but familiarity bred a certain amount of indifference, and after a year he was actually capable of turning away from it to look at prints by Gustave Doré. That does not mean that he forgot its true value, any more than his attention to Fifine means that he no longer loves Elvire.

He admires her, in spite of her lack of obvious beauty, he continues, because beauty is a response of the soul, not a property of the object perceived by the senses. This argument is formulated in the line, "What was my Rafael, turns my Michelangelo!" whose full meaning is unfolded in another anecdote. In addition to his Raphael, Don Juan possesses a marble piece so shapeless that it is hard to tell whether it has been carved or has formed naturally. But he insists that he sees evidence on it of Michelangelo's chisel, and that it was intended to be a figure of Eidothea, which remains "partly blent / With stuff she needs must quit." Browning apparently had in mind such unfinished works by Michelangelo as the prisoners intended for the tomb of Julius II, whose vigorous, twisting limbs have been only partially defined, and seem to be emerging from masses of raw stone. The uncompleted Eidothea "whom you shall never face evolved" nevertheless moves the observer, illustrating the power of the soul to provide what is lacking to sensuous perception. Hence, even if Elvire is not a Raphael, obviously pleasing to the sight, she can, like an unfinished but suggestive work by Michelangelo, evoke responses from the soul. (Don Juan's arguments are perhaps weakened by his admission that his attributions of the two works of art he has used to illustrate them are regarded with suspicion.)

Later, he defends Fifine and the mummery of the fair by arguing that false appearances are often essential to the recognition of underlying truth. The passage suggests that this familiar Browning theme is related to the view that Italian life impinges on the theatrical, expressing itself through shows and spectacles that are given equal rank with actual events, the taste for display that Luigi Barzini considers "the fundamental trait of their national character."[1] Don Juan finds confirmation of his argument in Schumann's composition, "Carnival," which inspires a dream vision of carnival time in Venice, and initiates an interplay between appearance and reality.

At the beginning of the dream, he looks down on masked and costumed revelers from the top of the campanile on the Piazza San Marco. From this height he sees the masks that grotesquely distort facial features, but when he is mysteriously transported to the pavement of the square, and mingles with the maskers on their own level, he sees them as human beings, and finds their deviations from nature merely marginal, moving him more "to pity than disgust." He is able to interpret the false surface signs given by speech and gesture as versions of truth, and to see that even such unattractive traits as force and guile are parts of a dialectic of good and evil. This vision requires active analysis and spiritual strength "case-hardened at all points," a robust, belligerent capacity for facing and interpreting life. It is compared to the work of a chemist who isolates individual elements, and then reconstructs the manner in which they combine to produce living forms. The process is the basis of a moral doctrine, but it is also an essential part of Browning's poetic theory, and stands behind his interest in evil, alien figures and the analysis of their psychology.

Why, asks Don Juan, is the vision placed in Venice, "What reason for Mark's Square / Rather than Timbuctoo?" The answer is a repetition of the message in the digression from the third book of *Sordello,* that Venice can serve as a symbol of the world. This time, however, it reflects, not the suffering of humanity, but the mingling of falsehood and truth, show and reality, good and evil, that makes life in general an eternal carnival.

The three long poems published after *Fifine at the Fair, Red Cotton Night-Cap Country* (1873), *Aristophanes' Apology* (1875), and *The Inn Album* (1875), have very little to do with Italy. The first and the third are narratives of violence and intrigue, subjects of the kind Browning had drawn from Italian sources in earlier days. Their comparative ineffectiveness may be due to the absence of the Italian setting and the vitalizing influence it had on Browning's imagination.

Browning's consciousness of Italy had not disappeared, for he turned to Italian materials again for three of the poems in the volume published in 1876, *Pacchiarotto, and How he Worked in Distemper, with Other Poems.* The title poem consists mainly of a fanciful retelling, in jaunty meter and grotesque rhyme, of the misadventures of an obscure Sienese painter, and is an application of the mood and manner of "The Pied Piper of Hamelin" to a subject out of Vasari. The last part of the poem, which describes the appearance before Browning's house of a band of critics offering to clean his chimney, and attacks Alfred Austin as a counterpart of the volatile Pacchiarotto, has little to do with the story of the painter. In his edition of Browning's letters, T.L. Hood cites evidence from the manuscript to show that all of this was a late addition.[2]

Browning drew his material for "Pacchiarotto" from an account added by an annotator to the text of Vasari, and from a brief narrative of Pacchiarotto's life in Filippo Baldinucci's *Delle Notizie De' Professori del Disegno Da Cimabue in Qua*, a work in six volumes published about 1681 which he had used before to supplement Vasari's biographies. There is evidence to suggest that some of the details and emphases in "Andrea del Sarto" and "Fra Lippo Lippi" came from Baldinucci's accounts of these painters, and he is mentioned by name in "Pacchiarotto."[3] In spite of these and other debts, Browning had little respect for Baldinucci.

After a brief ramble through the byways of his documentary sources, Browning turns to his account of Pacchiarotto, who joined a revolutionary group, practiced his oratory by speaking to the faces he had painted on the wall of a grotto, and took part in various disturbances directed against the Sienese authorities. When one of these assemblies was dispersed, he was forced to hide for two days in a tomb in company with a corpse, and afterwards took refuge in a monastery, where the Abbott gave him counsel. From these experiences, Pacchiarotto learns resignation, and declares that he is ready to accept things as they are, to give up reform, and devote himself to his painting. The poem is a comic treatment of the position of the artist in the overheated political atmosphere of an Italian Renaissance city. It might be regarded as an inversion of "Pictor Ignotus," which dealt with a serious artist who suffered the consequences of divorcing himself from contemporary life; "Pacchiarotto" is a high-spirited account of a foolish and superficial artist who brings trouble on himself by taking part in political agitation.

In "Cenciaja," the second of the Italian poems in this volume, we recognize the motive behind the composition of *The Ring and the Book*—that of bringing an obscure episode of the past to light again. Browning drew the story from a British Museum copy of Vatican manuscripts giving the details of criminal cases. Knickerbocker conjectures that he first saw the story in a volume of manuscripts borrowed from Sir John Simeon, decided to use it for a poem, and sought out a similar manuscript in the Museum.[4]

Like "Pacchiarotto" and *The Ring and the Book,* the poem begins with a self-conscious frame, as the poet asks Shelley for permission to explain why the heroine of *The Cenci* failed to gain the pardon she expected from the Pope, quoting—and misquoting—some of the language of Shelley's tragedy. In Shelley's drama, Cardinal Camillo says that the pardon was refused because the Pope had just heard that Paolo Santa Croce had murdered his mother, and felt that such crimes must be stopped. Browning offers "Cenciaja" as a humble footnote that explains this reference by condensing the "verbosity / That lies before me," apparently an allusion to the manuscript. The poem closely follows the language of the document, suggesting that it was written in the British Museum while Browning had his source before him.

The narrative tells how Paolo Santa Croce, after failing to persuade his mother to disinherit his older brother, Onofrio, in favor of himself, decided to kill her. He thereupon sent the older brother a letter defaming her, and asking what he should do, in the hope that the reply would encourage him in the crime he intended to commit. The answer was: act as becomes a cavalier. Paolo thereupon killed his mother and fled. This is as much of the story as concerns the case of Beatrice Cenci. The Santa Croce murder took place on the last day of Beatrice's trial, and the Pope, hearing about it, decided that she must be condemned to death. But Browning goes on to give the rest of the tangled story. In the ensuing investigation, Cardinal Aldobrandini, a nephew of the Pope, found Onofrio's letter among the murderer's effects, arrested him, and had him interrogated for months to learn what he meant by his advice to behave as becomes a cavalier. Ultimately, Onofrio was executed, and rumors sprang up suggesting that dark motives had been at work. The Governor who prosecuted him was made a Cardinal, and it was said that Aldobrandini was jealous of Onofrio because he saw him wearing a ring given him by a lady both admired. The poem returns to its contemporary frame at the end; Browning ironically undermines his chronicler's declaration that the case was a victory for God's justice by alluding to the fact that the new King of Rome is named Victor.

"Cenciaja" is an offhand performance that shows Browning returning to the poetic habits of his Italian period. His interest in the details of the Cenci case sprang, not only from Shelley's play, but from an allusion to Beatrice Cenci in pamphlet 8 of the Old Yellow Book.[5] The poem reflects both his seasoned ability to draw living actions from ancient records, and his insistence on recognizing the evil of human nature and its capacity for perverting justice.

The last poem of Italian interest in the *Pacchiarotto* volume, "Filippo Baldinucci on the Privilege of Burial," like "Holy-Cross Day," tells a tale that shows Italian Jews gaining a moral victory over oppression. It is based on an anecdote from Baldinucci's *Notizie*, with some crucial additions by Browning, and employs Baldinucci himself as a speaker. The poem opens as the narrator, a nephew of Baldinucci, recalls that when he was a child, his uncle warned him that "we must not pelt the Jews," apparently after the boy had done something of the sort. The anecdote which follows originally reflected Baldinucci's contempt for the Jews, and his satisfaction in the trick played upon them. According to the story told in the *Notizie*, the artist Lodovico Buti painted a picture of the Virgin for a wayside chapel that faced the Jewish cemetery near the San Frediano gate in Florence. (The cemetery continued in use long after Buti's and Baldinucci's time, and still survives on the Viale Ariosto.) Browning's speaker faithfully follows Baldinucci's account of the Jews' offer to pay a hundred ducats if the picture were removed, and of the trick, which consisted of moving the offending Madonna, but replacing it with an even more offensive Crucifixion. Baldinucci's story ends with a complaint by the Jews which is rejected, and their silent admission that they had been wrong to try to buy off the religious feelings of the Christians.

Browning, however, adds a significant sequel, consisting of events that reverse the original conclusion, with the implication that Baldinucci deliberately omitted them in his account. He has the burly son of the chief rabbi appear at Buti's shop to buy the oil sketch on which the fresco of the Madonna was based. When he is asked why he wants to keep in his house a picture offensive to his religion, he cites the authority of a Cardinal who, when asked why he owned pictures of pagan deities, replied that the subjects of these works had no meaning in the light of Christian truth, but were valuable only for their technique, "Drawing and coloring are Truth." Slyly adding that he now sees how the Jews were wrong to object to the pictures at the cemetery, he says he will value the painting he has bought "Just as a picture," together with his

"Ledas and what not." The result of this desacralization of relig-
ious iconography, reports "Uncle," was a decline of faith and an
unhealthy tolerance of dissent. He repeats his warning that it is
dangerous "to pelt the Jews," and ends with the lament, "O Lord,
how long? How long, O Lord?" which is Browning's satirical thrust
at Baldinucci's anti-Semitism and a tribute to the resilience of the
Jews.

Browning returned to Italy, after an absence of seventeen years,
in September 1878. His holiday with Sarianna had begun late that
year. In August he wrote from Paris to his friend, Mrs. FitzGerald,
that he was not sure where they would go next although Italy was
a possibility.[6] After "five delectable weeks" in Switzerland, he took
Sarianna, who had never been to Italy, to see some of the scenes of
his first visit, crossing the border on September 23.

He told Mrs. FitzGerald that he wanted to see Asolo again. The
three days he had spent there in 1838 had apparently left him with
a deep subconscious impression, for over the years he had a re-
peated dream in which he was traveling near Asolo with a friend,
saw the town in the distance, and said, "Let us go there!" but his
companion refused, and he was forced to go away disappointed.[7]
His longing was satisfied at last, for on September 28 he wrote to
Mrs. FitzGerald that he and Sarianna were in Asolo. He found it
impossible to tell her what his feelings were after coming back to
"this—to me—memorable place after above forty years absence,"
but he did describe how he showed Sarianna over the town. They
climbed to the Rocca, where Browning rediscovered the echo he
had noticed years before, and brought into *Pippa Passes*. They
walked to Possagno, visited the Canova museum, and returned to
find Asolo in an animated mood on market day. "It confuses me al-
together," wrote Browning.[8] After Asolo, they went to Venice,
made a tour of northern Italy, and returned to London by way of
Paris. Browning spent his long autumn holidays in northern Italy
in eight of his last eleven years. Venice was his headquarters and
ultimately the scene of his death.

The new intervals of Italian life had a slight, but perceptible ef-
fect on the poems he wrote. However, when he dealt with Italian
subjects, he depended on sources in his reading, and on his memo-
ries of earlier Italian experiences rather than on fresh perceptions.
The two volumes of *Dramatic Idyls* published in 1879 and 1880 con-
tain only one such poem, "Pietro of Abano," and there is nothing

else of this kind until *Parleyings with Certain People of Importance* (1887), and his final volume, *Asolando* (1889).

The narrative of "Pietro of Abano," the first poem about Italy written after the visit of 1878, was based on material drawn from books, including the hero's masterwork, *Conciliatur differentiarum*, although Browning had heard of Pietro as a legendary conjuror during his early travels in Italy.[9] A physician and philosopher of the thirteenth and fourteenth centuries who came from a village near Padua, he was able to penetrate the evil intentions of a man who asked to learn his secrets. Browning dramatizes this brilliantly by having Pietro cast a spell in which his visitor lives through years of success gained by the use of his mentor's art while behaving ungratefully to him, and then returns to the present moment. The idea of writing about Pietro seems to have come to Browning's mind after a visit in 1878 to Padua, where the Church of the Eremitani contains a tablet commemorating the philosopher. This locale is the only connection between the main body of the poem and the story about Tiberius throwing dice into the fountain in nearby Abano, a portion added later, as the manuscript shows. The music, which was apparently composed by Browning himself, is an even more gratuitous ingredient flung into an admittedly lighthearted comic fantasy written "for love of that dear land which I so oft in dreams revisit."

Between 1878 and 1881, Browning and Sarianna generally divided their holidays between Venice and other cities in northern Italy. During their first three Venetian holidays, they stayed at the Albergo dell'Universo, which occupied the Palazzo Brandolin-Rota on the south bank of the Grand Canal to the east of the Accademia Bridge. In 1883, 1885, and 1888, however, they were the guests of Mrs. Katherine Bronson, who lived in the Casa Alvisi across the Canal from Santa Maria della Salute, and rented an apartment in the adjoining Palazzo Giustiniani-Recanati to house visitors who stayed with her.

Mrs. Bronson, a wealthy New Yorker who lived in Venice from 1875 to 1895, was wholeheartedly attached to Browning, and he and Sarianna became eminences in residence at the Casa Alvisi, living next door at the Giustiniani, and joining Mrs. Bronson's dinner guests in the evening. Attracted to Asolo by its connection with *Pippa Passes*, Mrs. Bronson bought a small house in the town, and brought Browning there for his last visit. In 1895 she moved to

Bellosguardo, and some years later wrote reminiscences of Browning's visits to her in Asolo and Venice.[10]

The two volumes Browning published after *Dramatic Idyls* in the period when he was spending part of nearly every year in Venice, *Jocoseria* (1883) and *Ferishtah's Fancies* (1884) have no direct relation to Italy, although their Hebrew and Arabian themes may owe something to the oriental elements of the Venetian ambiance. Browning's regime in Venice was that of a man on holiday. He explored the canals in gondolas, took long walks on the Lido where he thought of Shelley, who had described it in "Julian and Maddalo," enjoyed reading the accounts of petty crimes in the newspapers, and went to chapel every Sunday.

In November 1883 he wrote two sonnets on Venetian themes in response to requests. Mrs. Bronson asked him to write something about Rawdon Brown, an Englishman who had found Venice so irresistible that he was unable to leave it, and became a permanent resident for forty years. In his sonnet, Browning has Brown pausing for one last look at the glories of the Venetian sea and sky before his intended departure, then telling his servant to unpack his bags, adding in Italian that he will never leave. Although Browning hardly shared his infatuation with the city, he generously attributes to Brown his own symbolism for Venice—London is death, "Compared with Life—that's Venice!"—and suggests, in the last line, that Browning may be transformed into Brown. In the same month a committee in charge of unveiling a monument to the eighteenth-century comic playwright, Goldoni, asked Browning to contribute some verses to its album. Browning obliged with an impromptu sonnet celebrating Goldoni's expression of the carefree Venetian spirit.

The two Italian figures who appear in *Parleyings with Certain People of Importance* come from sources that Browning had read (or seen) much earlier rather than from his current Italian experiences. While the "Parleying with Daniel Bartoli" is addressed to the author of *De' Simboli*, the Italian work Browning knew from his studies with Cerutti, the poem has little to do with Bartoli, and even less to do with Italy. As DeVane has found, the manuscript shows that "Don" originally read "Sir" and "Daniel," "Doctor," suggesting that the idea of addressing Bartoli may have been an afterthought. The main part of the poem, the story of a pharmacist's daughter who rejects the opportunity to marry a duke in order to save his position, is from an entirely different source, the *Mémoires* of the Marquis de Lausanne.[11]

Browning had always been somewhat impatient with Bartoli, whom he read, as we have seen, mainly for practice in Italian. In a letter to Elizabeth written in March 1845 he criticizes Bartoli for distorting one of his sources, and abusing "God's great gift of speech." Bartoli's method consisted of transforming anecdotes into portentous "simboli" by forcing a moral or religious significance on them, and in the "Parleying" Browning argues that the sainthood of virtuous women is better supported by history than by legends of the kind Bartoli dispenses. Bartoli is addressed in the first five lines of the "Parleying," then forgotten until he is compared with one of the characters in the story. His presence is incidental, but well assimilated. Browning's objection to Bartoli's tales is reasonable, and the fanciful story of Saint Scholastica he improvises, breaking off with a contemptuous "Spare me the rest!" is in Bartoli's true vein.

In "Parleying with Francis Furini," Browning again reprimands an Italian author, but this time his attack is longer and far more vigorous. The "parleying" is a thinly disguised debate on the subject of female nudity in art in which Browning aligns himself with the baroque artist, Francis Furini, in opposition to a contemporary critic of Pen's paintings whom Browning associates with Filippo Baldinucci. Furini comes into it only because he, too, painted nudes and because Baldinucci, in his life of Furini, took a disapproving view of them.

Furini is made to defend "the naked female form" as "God's best of beauteous and magnificent," and also, in a more abstruse argument, to declare that bodily senses of the kind his paintings celebrate are part of a physical reality which exhibits God as its ultimate Cause. There is, of course, no factual basis for attributing these ideas to the kindly, generous, dutiful priest; many of them are thoroughly anachronistic. But Browning's choice of Furini as a defender of Pen's art is appropriate, because his nudes are sensual enough to approach decadence, yet he was known as a painstaking craftsman and a man of virtuous life. Furini achieved a special quality in rendering the subtly shifting flesh tones of the women in his paintings by the ingenious use of ultramarine. Such works of his as

Hylas and the Nymphs in the Pitti Palace, *Cleopatra*, and *Lot's Wife* in the Museo del Fondazione Horne typically show opulent bare figures in a swirl of drapery.

The poem is a clear example of Browning's practice of picking and choosing among the facts offered by his sources, while taking the position that he understood them better than his informants. All of his information about Furini's life and character came from Baldinucci. His opening sketch is based upon Baldinucci's description of Furini as a man "di buona pasta, e amico dell'amico." Furini's claim that he has no evil thoughts while he paints his nudes is based upon a conversation reported by Baldinucci, who says that Furini paid his models exceptionally large fees because he insisted on having young and well-proportioned girls. When Browning's painter is asked whether he does not feel that such subjects expose his soul to danger, he replies that the questioner does not know

> *what the agony*
> *Of Art is ere Art satisfy herself*
> *In imitating Nature.*

Here Browning is following Baldinucci's wording of Furini's explanation that "questi scrupolosi la gran fatica, anzi la mortale agonia, che prova l'artefice nel voler soddisfare a se stesso nel dar verita alla sua fattura" make it impossible for the artist to have other thoughts while he is at work. On the other hand, Browning refuses to accept at face value Baldinucci's report that Furini asked on his deathbed that his nude paintings be burned, snorting "List to the chronicler!" Browning was justified in feeling some contempt for Baldinucci, for the biographer seems deaf to the obvious sincerity of Furini's words, and replies with an evilminded lecture on the harm done by erotic subjects, hypocritically adding that he does not pretend to judge Furini.[12]

In "Furini" Browning's concern with an issue pertinent to his own life and time tends to separate the material from its historical sources. There are some efforts to counterbalance this with allusions to Renaissance artists. Browning ironically has Furini's critics charging that Michelangelo's figures of Night and Morn in the Medici Chapel and the *Creation of Eve* from the Sistine Chapel ceiling are mere expressions of lust. He learned from Baldinucci that

Furini had painted an Andromeda; this was enough to join the argument about female nudity with the theme of rescue that had been a recurrent pattern in his poetry and a part of his attitude toward Italy since he had kept Polidoro da Caravaggio's representation of the subject on his desk in London.

In 1888, the year before his death, Browning's ties with Venice multiplied. Pen, who had first visited Venice with his parents at the age of two, returned to it in September 1885, meaning to set up a studio and pursue his artistic career there. He had fallen in love with the city, to his father's delight, and Browning, apparently at Pen's urging, decided to buy the Palazzo Manzoni, a distinguished example of Venetian architecture situated toward the further end of the Grand Canal, just east of its junction with the Canareggio Canal. Much to his disappointment, however, the owner, an Austrian and an absentee, refused to sell.

Pen remained devoted to Venice and, the year after his marriage to Fannie Coddington in October 1887, he returned to make it a permanent home. Fannie was the daughter of a wealthy American family, and Pen, having failed to fulfill his dream of owning a Venetian palazzo through his father, now succeeded through his wife. By September 1888 he had completed the purchase of the Palazzo Rezzonico, one of the largest and most ornate residences in the city. It confronts the Grand Canal with a formidable facade crowded with arches, pillars, cornices, and the heads of gods and lions. The interior is even more impressive, for an enormous staircase leads to a huge ballroom on the *piano nobile* which is paved with red marble and decorated with ceiling frescoes by Tiepolo. The palazzo was in run-down condition, but Pen bought it in order to exercise his artistic talent in restoring it, and by the spring of 1889 he was able to occupy it and make it his home, in spite of its forbidding size. One of the rooms was turned into an Anglican chapel, and in later years Pen furnished the building with books, portraits, and memorabilia connected with his parents, so that it came to resemble a Browning museum.[13] Later, it became a museum in fact; Pen sold it in 1906, and it is now Venice's Museum of 18th-Century Art.

As Henry James observed, the Rezzonico does not represent the Italy associated with Browning, who was sometimes amused and sometimes impressed by the scale and success of Pen's restorations. The Palazzo's baroque splendors claimed the end of Browning's life, for he spent about six weeks there before his death, sitting in what was called "the Pope's room" in the company of a parrot, and using for his writing a room whose ceiling was decorated with fine allegorical frescoes.

Before Venice, however, there was a thoroughly improbable turn of events. Asolo had remained perfectly obscure, as it was when Browning first saw it, but Mrs. Bronson had bought a residence there, a gatehouse built into the old town wall, called "La Mura." It was an unusual place which overlooked part of the town and the surrounding countryside, commanding a view of hills and valleys romantically dotted with towers and roofs. Sarianna and Browning were invited to join Mrs. Bronson in Asolo, and the poet spent September and October of 1889, his last holiday, in a thoroughly satisfying immersion in the village where he had first touched Italian life.

He found that little had changed in Asolo, except that his old hotel had been demolished, and the silk mills in which girls like Pippa had worked were gone. Places he had mentioned in *Sordello* could be seen from the loggia of La Mura, and on their drives in the country the party visited other sites connected with the poem, as well as Possagno and Bassano. In her account of Browning's visit, Mrs. Bronson reported that he talked of his old Asolo enthusiasms, the thirteenth-century wars and Catherine of Cornaro, examined some of Canova's sketches at Possagno, and climbed to the Rocca again, as he had on his first day.[14] He wrote that the interior of the Rocca had been weeded, that the hawks who lived there had been shot, and that it was difficult this time to locate the right spot for the famous echo.

He told Mrs. Bronson that Asolo seemed to be more beautiful than ever, and made plans to settle down in it. There was a ruined schoolhouse nearby; Browning intended to renovate it, to call it "Pippa's Tower," and to make it his home. Mrs. Bronson describes him discussing the price of the property with the town officials on the loggia of La Mura. Between them, Mrs. Bronson and the poet laid the foundations for a Browning tradition in Asolo that was later kept alive by Pen. Browning never lived to build "Pippa's Tower," but after his death Pen carried out his plans, lived in the house, began a lace industry in Asolo to provide employment for the Pippas of his time, and sold what they made at the Palazzo Rezzonico. Memorials of Browning still survive in Asolo. The street leading from La Mura to the town's main piazza is called "Via Roberto Browning." Both Pen and Wilson are buried in Asolo's cemetery. Part of the palace where the Bishop and the Intendant met in *Pippa Passes* is the Museo Civico; it contains the spinet made in 1522 that Browning had had in Venice, and which he sometimes played in the evenings at La Mura.

The old poet continued to be productive in Asolo. He brought with him poems he had written in London, revised them, and wrote some new ones. One day he told Mrs. Bronson that he had composed a poem in his mind during the drive home from Bassano; this turned out to be "The Lady and the Painter." When he sent the miscellany of poems written during this period to Smith, Elder on October 15, he titled the volume they would form *Asolando*, a fanciful coining derived, as Browning explained, from a nonce word supposedly invented by Cardinal Bembo in which the name of Asolo was made into a verb meaning, according to Browning, "to disport in the open air, amuse one's self at random."

There is a good deal of Italy in this last volume, but it is mainly an Italy shorn of its suggestiveness, a mere source of anecdote and illustration. The three little poems about Italian clerics are slight things and have only a slight relation to Italy. "The Cardinal and His Dog" had been written in 1842 for Willie Macready to illustrate when he was sick, together with "The Pied Piper," but did not find its way to publication until nearly half a century later. Both "The Pope and the Net" and "The Bean-Feast" are based upon anecdotes about Pope Sixtus V which Browning may have read in a biography by Gregorio Leti, but are primarily Browning's inventions. Characteristically, they are not all consistent; in the first, the Pope exposes his pride by removing the net, the emblem of his origin as a fisherman's son, from his coat of arms once he has been elected Pope. In the second, he displays a fitting humility by visiting the poor of Rome in their homes and sharing a lowly meal of beans with them.

"Ponte dell'Angelo, Venice" is based on a carved stone plaque showing an angel which is to be seen on the wall of the Palazzo Soranzano, facing the Ponte dell'Angelo. After reading about it in a book on Venice which Mrs. Bronson had given him, and in a second source mentioned in the poem, Browning made a gondola trip to the site and had his gondolier recount the tale from popular lore connected with the plaque. The poem admirably preserves many details of the story, such as the lawyer's motivation for inviting the Capuchin to dinner, and the revelation of the lawyer's guilt through the blood wrung from the twisted tablecloth.

Browning thought that "Beatrice Signorini" was the best poem in *Asolando*. It reverts to the sort of material he used for his great artist monologues in *Men and Women*, though his information is from Baldinucci rather than Vasari, and the poem is not a monologue, but a narrative that sketches three striking characters instead of thoroughly exploring one. Its source is Baldinucci's account of Artemisia Gentileschi, who was a unique figure, a professional woman painter of the seventeeth century. The daughter of a Roman artist, Orazione Gentileschi, she came to London with her father in 1626, working at the court of Charles I for some years before returning to Italy. Her self-portrait in Hampton Court Palace shows a sturdy woman of thirty lifting a stout arm to the canvas with a brush in hand, and is a candid rendering of a thoughtful, and not especially attractive face. In his poem, Browning remolded an anecdote Baldinucci tells about her, shifting its emphases, and enlarging on the thoughts of the characters, and brought forward the wife, Beatrice, making the exposition of her character the main point of the story.

The poem tells how the baroque painter, Francesco Romanelli, though married to the beautiful and conventional Beatrice Signorini, fell in love with his fellow painter, Artemisia. According to Baldinucci, Artemisia was known as a painter of fruit. Browning changes this to flowers, and has the woman painter give her would-be lover a canvas painted with flowers as a gift for his wife. In the middle of the painting she has left a space where Romanelli is to paint a portrait of the one he loves best. He paints Artemisia there, and shows the picture to his wife. Beatrice expertly criticizes the rendering of the flowers, and then cuts the hated female portrait from the center of the canvas. Her sudden display of violent jealousy as she slashes the canvas is a perfectly convincing exhibition of an unexpected trait of character, and is based squarely on Baldinucci's account. Romanelli, who had thought his wife too passive, is captivated by this emotional display, and feels new interest in her.

At the end of the poem, Browning says he would like to think that Romanelli was a better painter than he is thought to be, and recalls that he had seen some paintings of his that seemed attractive, though they were overshadowed by the work of "the elder race"—the Renaissance artists. It had, in fact, been some time since he could have seen any paintings by the two artists in his poem, and their work has little relevance to it. Romanelli was a student of Ciro Ferri, the artist of the Pitti Palace frescoes, who worked with a smooth, passionless competence that has consigned him to obscurity. Gentileschi, on the other hand, followed the dramatic tradition of Caravaggio, and her work often exhibits a ferocious sadism that is thoroughly out of key with her role in the poem. She painted neither fruit nor flowers, but took as one of her favorite subjects the beheading of Holofernes by Judith, a scene she sometimes depicted with copious amounts of blood.

Browning sent the manuscript of *Asolando* to the publisher on October 21 and at the end of October went to Venice to stay with Pen and Fannie at the Rezzonico. There he pursued his active Venetian life, with many visits, readings of his poetry, and walks on the Lido. On one of these walks he discovered in a church the tomb of Salinguerra, the original of his character in *Sordello.*

An attack of bronchitis forced Browning to take to his bed; he was moved to Fannie's bedroom to be cared for, and died there on December 12. A famous scene took place as a copy of *Asolando* arrived in time for the dying poet to hold it, examine it, and present it to his daughter-in-law. There was some question as to where he should be buried; a grave next to Elizabeth's in Florence seemed logical, but the cemetery there had been closed. Ultimately, a telegram arrived offering burial in Westminster Abbey. First, however, the poet's body had to pass through the irrelevant grandeur of a Venetian funeral. It lay in the gorgeous ballroom of the Rezzonico, and was then carried down the great staircase to the bank of the Grand Canal, where the Golden Barge of Venice, with an angel at its prow and the lion of Saint Mark at its stern, waited to take it down the Canal and across the lagoon to its temporary resting place on the cemetery island of San Michele. A few days later it was sent to England.

In the Prologue to *Asolando,* written after Browning had arrived in Asolo and looked at the familiar scene again, the old poet reports that his visionary powers have faded, and the sights that had seemed intensely evocative in his youth, flaming with meaning like Moses' burning bush, now appear bare and comparatively trivial. The Prologue has been called Browning's "Intimations Ode"; it is also his farewell to Italy, to poetry, and to the world. When he first came to Italy, as he tells us in *Sordello*, he found that its scenes and people seemed charged with significance, and he regarded it as a world that lent itself to his poetic purpose, the pursuit of truth through a tireless attention to external reality. But now that he stands on the verge of mysticism, and the landscape of Asolo has been stripped of the import it once had, he recognizes the ultimate futility of this project, and calmly accepts an insight that has always been latent in his responses to Italy and the life it symbolized: that they are capable of offering humane and esthetic satisfactions, but no lasting spiritual ones.

As we have seen, Browning always admitted that there were depths in the people, landscapes, and religion of Italy that escaped him. The speaker of *Christmas-Eve* finds in his vision of Saint Peter's and its worshipers the experience of a God who is present to others, but absent to him. This absence manifested itself to Browning as he looked about Asolo in his old age. As the Prologue says,

> Italia's rare,
> O'er-running beauty crowds the eye—
> But flame? The Bush is bare.

Poetry, for all its recuperative powers, cannot restore what has been lost. Browning's ironic "Language? Tush!" is an incredibly casual and far-reaching dismissal of the medium he had employed for his vigorous spiritual analyses. Poetry, like Italy, might once have promised to lead to some definitive revelation, but now, in the face of his conviction that "God is it who transcends," the two seem related only to each other, not to anything beyond themselves. Italy is still Browning's metaphor for the world; but it is a world without spiritual content, which tells him only that ultimate truth is elsewhere.

Notes

NOTES TO PREFACE

1. Ian Jack, *Browning's Major Poetry* (Oxford: Clarendon Press, 1973), p. 122.

NOTES TO CHAPTER 1

Browning and the Tradition of Italy

1. Henry James, "The Novel in the Ring and the Book," in *Notes on Novelists with Some Other Notes* (London: J. M. Dent and Sons, 1914), p. 318. This essay was originally delivered as a speech before the Royal Society of Literature on 7 May 1912, and published in the *Transactions* of the Society, Vol. 31, 2nd series, Part 4 (1912). It also appeared in the *Quarterly Review* 217 (1912): 69–87.

2. Browning made this remark to Hiram Corson in "the early eighties." See Lilian Whiting, *The Brownings: Their Life and Art* (London: Hodder and Stoughton, 1911), p. 246.

3. Edmund Gosse, *Robert Browning: Personalia* (London: T. F. Unwin, 1890), p. 86.

4. *Elizabeth Barrett Browning: Letters to Her Sister, 1846–1859*, ed. Leonard Huxley (New York: Dutton, 1930), 24 November 1846, p. 5.

5. John Stuart Mill, "On the Application of the Terms Poetry, Science and Philosophy," *Monthly Repository* 8 (1834): 323–31. The quotation appears on p. 324.

6. *Learned Lady: Letters from Robert Browning to Mrs. Thomas FitzGerald 1876–1889*, ed. Edward C. McAleer (Cambridge, Mass.: Harvard Univ. Press, 1966), 17 March 1883, p. 157. The discussion that follows is indebted to Harold Bloom, *The Anxiety of Influence* (New York: Oxford University Press, 1973).

7. Browning refers to Caravaggio in a letter to Miss Haworth, 30 December 1841 *(Letters of Robert Browning Collected by Thomas J. Wise,* ed. Thurman L. Hood. New Haven: Yale Univ. Press, 1933), and in his poem, "Waring," where he is called "great Caldara Polidoro." The engraving is mentioned in a letter to Elizabeth, *The Letters of Robert Browning and Elizabeth Barrett Barrett, 1845–1846,* ed. Elvan Kintner (Cambridge, Mass.: Harvard Univ. Press, 1969), [26 February 1845], 1: 27. It is reproduced in John Maynard, *Browning's Youth* (Cambridge, Mass.: Harvard Univ. Press, 1977), pp. 160–61. For a study of the Andromeda theme in Browning, see W. C. DeVane, "The Virgin and the Dragon," *Yale Review* 37 (1947): 33–46.

8. *Browning to His American Friends,* ed. Gertrude Reese Hudson (New York: Barnes and Noble, 1965), to the Story family, 20 August 1861, p. 76.

9. *Dearest Isa,* ed. Edward C. McAleer (Austin: Univ. of Texas Press, 1951), 19 May 1866, p. 238.

10. *Letters of Elizabeth Barrett Browning,* ed. Frederic G. Kenyon, 2 vols. (New York: Macmillan, 1897), to Mrs. Jameson, 23 November 1846, 1: 309.

11. See Robert Armstrong Pratt, "Geoffrey Chaucer, Esq. and Sir John Hawkwood," *ELH* 16 (September 1949): 188–93.

12. *Letters of Percy Bysshe Shelley,* ed. Frederick L. Jones (Oxford: Clarendon Press, 1964), 23 March 1819, 2: 85.

13. *Ibid.,* December 20 (?), 1818, 2: 67.

14. *Ibid.,* to Peacock 6 April 1819, 2: 93–94.

15. George Stillman Hillard, *Six Months in Italy* (London: John Murray, 1853), 2: 26. Other details in these two paragraphs are from the notes by J. R. Hale in *The Italian Journal of Samuel Rogers* (London: Faber and Faber, 1956).

16. Frances Power Cobbe, *Italics: Brief Notes on Politics, People and Places in Italy in 1864* (London: Trubner and Co., 1864), p. 2.

17. Luigi Barzini, *The Italians* (London: Hamish Hamilton, 1964), p. 57.

18. Wallace K. Ferguson, *The Renaissance in Historical Thought: Five Centuries of Interpretation* (New York: Houghton Mifflin, 1948), p. 132.

19. Nathaniel Hawthorne, *Passages from the French and Italian Notebooks* (Boston and New York: Houghton Mifflin, 1891), p. 280.

20. William Hazlitt, *Notes of a Journey Through France and Italy* (London: Hunt and Clarke, 1826), pp. 221–22.

21. *Dearest Isa,* 19 May 1866, p. 239.

22. D. H. Lawrence, *Collected Letters,* ed. Harry T. Moore (London: Heinemann, 1962), to Ernest Collings, Gargnano, 7 January 1913, 2: 180.

NOTES TO CHAPTER 2

The First Italian Tour: Sordello *and* Pippa Passes

1. *The Letters of Robert Browning and Elizabeth Barrett Barrett, 1845–1846,* ed. Elvan Kintner (Cambridge, Mass.: Harvard Univ. Press, 1969), [3 March 1846], 1: 509. The Giorgione work Browning mentioned has since been attributed to another artist. Similarly, two paintings attributed to Gerard de Lairesse, whose *Art of Painting* influenced Browning, are now thought to be the work of G. Hoet.

2. See John Maynard, *Browning's Youth* (Cambridge, Mass.: Harvard Univ. Press, 1977), pp. 304–7. Did Browning study—or intend to study—Italian at London University when he entered it in 1828? W. Hall Griffin and H. C. Minchin's *Life of Robert Browning* (London: Methuen, 1910) says that his name was listed among the students of Italian (p. 90), and there is a similar report in Henri Brocher, *La Jeunesse de Browning et le poème de Sordello* (Geneva, 1930). However, H. Hale Bellot ("Browning as an Undergraduate," *TP and Cassell's Weekly,* 26 February 1927, p. 617) says that he was enrolled only for German, Greek, and Latin, and Maynard's discussion of the period Browning spent at London University says nothing about Italian (pp. 447–49).

3. The allusion to Sordello is fleeting, and does not occur in section XI, as DeVane has it, but in Simbolo IX, "Il Cane Bronzo nel Campidoglio in Atto di Sanarsi una Ferita Leccandola." It reads: "I recall the very gentle description which Virgil gives, with the pen of Dante, to Sordello, of the place where he lives underground. . . ." Bartoli then quotes the passage from the *Purgatorio,* and praises its understatement, saying nothing further about Sordello.

4. Mrs. Sutherland Orr, *Life and Letters of Robert Browning* (Boston and New York: Houghton Mifflin, 1891), p. 135. Was Byron his example? The preface to the first two Cantos of *Childe Harold* begins: "The following poem was written, for the most part, amidst the scenes which it attempts to describe."

5. This itinerary is taken from a holograph Diary, consisting of two leaves and covering the period from April 3 to June 26, which is in the University of Toronto Library. The entries are brief, never more than one line long, often giving no more than the names of the towns visited, or the weather and position at sea. The many blank dates apparently indicate days when Browning did not travel. In the entry for June 17, he mistakenly calls Castelfranco "Castel Vecchio."

6. *Letters,* ed. Kintner, [11 September 1845], 1: 189.

7. *Ibid.,* [13 July 1845], 1: 122–23.

8. The phrase originally read "an empty palace-step." For the 1863 edition of his poems, Browning made many revisions of this kind, and also added the explanatory page headings for *Sordello.*

9. *New Letters of Robert Browning,* ed. William Clyde DeVane and Kenneth L. Knickerbocker (New Haven: Yale Univ. Press, 1950), to Miss Euphrasia Fanny Haworth, Thursday night [May 1840], p. 18.

10. *The George Eliot Letters,* ed. Gordon S. Haight (New Haven: Yale Univ. Press, 1954–55), to Mrs. Richard Congreve, 4–6 April 1860, 3: 288.

11. Moncure D. Conway, *Autobiography* (London: Cassell, 1904), 2: 18–19, and Michael Mason, doctoral dissertation, Oxford University. I am indebted to Michael Mason for calling my attention to this wrapper.

12. He decided, says Betty Miller, "to make a love for suffering humanity become, thenceforward, the motivating force in Sordello's life" *(Robert Browning: A Portrait* [London: John Murray, 1952], p. 67). J. Hillis Miller regards Browning's identification with others as an extension of the sympathetic identification with objects found in Romanticism, an immersion of the self that corresponds with Keats's principle of the chameleon poet *(The Disappearance of God* [New York: Schocken Books, 1965] p. 106).

13. See Trevor Lloyd, "Browning and Politics," in *Robert Browning*, ed. Isobel Armstrong (Athens, Ohio: Ohio Univ. Press, 1975), p. 146. Lloyd says: "Browning . . . seems to have picked up a good many of the *Repository*'s views, at least at an intellectual level, before they burst upon him emotionally and artistically during his visit to Italy; the political message of *Sordello* is so much along lines Fox would have approved that it is not really necessary to look further for its origins. . . ."

14. A thorough study of this subject is to be found in S. W. Holmes, "The Sources of Browning's *Sordello*," *Studies in Philology* 34 (July 1937); 467–96.

15. W. J. Fox, a review of *The Village Poor-House*, *Monthly Repository*, NS 6, No. 67 (August 1832); 536–44.

16. Fox, "The Poor and Their Poetry," *Monthly Repository*, NS 6, No. 63 (March 1832); 190.

17. We can see how Browning's inventiveness leaped to seize these opportunities in his treatment of the 1194 battle of Vicenza. He had read about it in Verci, Sismondi, and other sources, and had made it a key element of his poem, organically involving it in several different ways. Ezzelino the Monk, who shared power in Vicenza, was bested in political maneuvering and expelled, but he resisted and set fire to the city, creating a scene of dreadful carnage. Browning, without any historical justification, places the separation of Salinguerra from his son at this battle. In the poem, Salinguerra believes that his wife and child have been lost in the flames; but they were rescued, and while the mother died soon afterwards, Sordello, the child, survived to be raised by Adelaide. All of this remains secret until Palma reveals it (having been told of it by Adelaide), creating one of the poem's turning points. This same battle is the subject of a long soliloquy by Salinguerra. The atmosphere of chaos and horror is recreated through the details that he recollects. But the main function of the soliloquy is to characterize Salinguerra as he exposes the feelings the various episodes of the battle aroused in him.

18. Gyorgy Lukács, *The Historical Novel*, trans. Hannah and Stanley Mitchell (London: Merlin Press, 1962).

19. *Letters*, ed. Kintner, [21 December 1845], 1: 336. The passage translated is *Purgatorio*, V, 52–57.

20. Quoted in T. J. Wise, *A Browning Library* (London, 1925), p. 56, from a letter to Pen Browning, Asolo, 15 September 1889.

21. Quoted in Lilian Whiting, *The Brownings: Their Life and Art* (London: Hodder and Stoughton, 1911), letter to Mrs. Bronson, 10 June 1889, p. 282.

22. George Stillman Hillard, *Six Months in Italy* (London: John Murray, 1853), 1: 150 ff. In spite of Browning's disapproval, this must have been one of the most popular of all Italian travel books. It had its twenty-third American edition in 1883.

23. In the first edition, the stage direction places these girls "on the steps of MONSIGNOR's brother's house." But the two steps before the door of this house are small and shallow, unsuited for this gathering. Perhaps better recall led Browning to write unspecified "steps" in the 1849 edition, thus making it likely that they were sitting on the long, broad flight across the piazzetta from the house.

24. Orr, *Life and Letters*, to Miss Haworth, Tuesday evening, 1838, p. 139. When he examined some of Canova's sketches on this last visit to the Asolo area in 1889, Browning observed, "He would have been a greater man in a greater period" (Katherine Bronson, "Browning in Asolo," *Century Magazine* 59 [April 1900]: 223–31).

25. *Ruskin in Italy,* ed. Harold I. Shapiro (London: Clarendon Press, 1972), letter of 10 July 1845, p. 141.

26. There is evidence of Browning's strong interest in Catherine in the fact that two pictures connected with her were sold with the Browning Collections in 1913: a pastel drawing by Titian of "the Cornaro family" in Lot 14, and a portrait of Catherine attributed to "Venetian School" which is included in Lot 55. This portrait is probably not authentic, and the whole question of Catherine's portraits is a difficult one. There are two genuine portraits by Gentile Bellini, one in the Museum of Fine Arts in Budapest, and one among the figures in the Miracle of the Holy Cross in the Accademia in Venice (Harold E. Wethey, *The Paintings of Titian,* p. 196). There is a persistent tradition that Titian painted a portrait of her, and numerous paintings exist which Browning may have seen and believed to be Titian's Catherine, but all have been discredited, and it is possible that the picture once existed, but is now lost. The *Rittrato Ideale di Caterina Cornaro* No. 909 in the Uffizi Gallery in Florence, is generally considered a copy of a lost original by Titian (Rodolfo Pallucchini, *Tiziano*

[Florence, 1969], 1: 344. Berenson thinks it is a collaboration, Titian being responsible for the hands and head, but not the costume. The portrait labeled as a portrait of Catherine in the National Gallery in London (No. 536), which shows a stout, smiling woman leaning with one hand on a parapet bearing a profile of her head in relief is an authentic Titian, but is not of Catherine, and is now known as *La Schiavona* (Wethey, p. 139).

27. In "P. R. B. Journal" for 16 May 1849, W. M. Rossetti recorded that Gabriel was "redesigning" the picture, and on the twentieth that he was making "considerable progress" with it (*Pre-Raphaelite Diaries and Letters,* ed. William Michael Rossetti, [London, 1900]). The completed painting is in the museum in the brewhouse at Eton College. Elizabeth Siddal also illustrated *Pippa Passes,* in a drawing showing the innocent Pippa, carrying a branch and passing three girls who sit cringing on a step as she goes by, with some medieval towers in the distance. D. G. Rossetti reported that Browning was "delighted beyond measure" when he was shown this picture. See Rossetti's *Letters to William Allingham,* ed. George Birkbeck Hill (London, 1897), pp. 161–62; the picture appears facing p. 161.

NOTES TO CHAPTER 3

The Second Italian Tour

1. *Robert Browning and Alfred Domett,* ed. Frederic G. Kenyon (London: Smith, Elder, 1906), 22 May 1842, p. 35.

2. *Ibid.,* 8 November 1843, p. 96.

3. *Robert Browning and Julia Wedgwood: A Broken Friendship as Revealed by Their Letters,* ed. Richard Curle (New York: Frederick A. Stokes Co., 1937), 19 November 1868, p. 147.

4. Louis S. Friedland, "Ferrara and 'My Last Duchess, ' " *Studies in Philology* 34 (1936), 656–84. The Duchess was identified with Alfonso's duchess in Helen A. Clarke, *Browning's Italy* (New York: Baker and Taylor, 1907), pp. 287–88. For a thorough discussion of historical details connected with the poem, see R. J. Berman, *Browning's Duke* (New York: Rosen, 1972).

5. C. P. Brand, *Torquato Tasso* (Cambridge: Cambridge Univ. Press, 1965), Ch. 8, "The Legend of Tasso's Life," pp. 205–225.

6. This picture is in the Victoria and Albert Museum. There is a miniature portrait of Lucrezia in the Museo Mediceo by Bronzino or his studio that shows a young woman with a peculiar, tearful squint, a high forehead with a widow's peak, a humorless mouth, and a scar or birthmark on her left temple. She is elegantly dressed, with oval pearl earrings, a bonnet trimmed with enormous precious stones, and a high collar that rises up the back of the neck in an elegant crest. It is a picture of a victim in finery, corresponding well to Browning's poem, except that there is no sign of kindness or generosity in the face. (It is numbered 161 in this collection of miniatures of the members of the Medici family.) Another portrait in the Kunsthistorisches Museum of Vienna showing a Medicean princess resembles this sitter, but presents her in an entirely different mood. It is a portrait of a sophisticated, attractive young woman in fine clothing and jewelry with a slight smile. The birthmark is obscured by good use of shadows. These and other representations are reproduced and discussed in Berman, *Browning's Duke*, pp. 103–14.

7. Unpublished letter dated 26 February 1845, extracted in Griffin Collection, British Museum Library, Add. MS 45560.

8. *The Letters of Robert Browning and Elizabeth Barrett Barrett, 1845-1846*, ed. Elvan Kintner (Cambridge, Mass.: Harvard Univ. Press, 1969), [28 June 1846], 2: 822.

9. *New Letters and Memorials of Jane Welsh Carlyle*, ed. Alexander Carlyle (London: John Lane, 1903), 2: 38–39.

10. *Letters*, ed. Kintner [15 April 1845], 1: 46–47. The page of the letter containing the sketch is reproduced facing p. 46. It shows the tower mentioned in the poem.

11. *Ibid.*, [4 January 1846], 1: 356–57. He adds this after warning her, if she should ever to go Italy, not to pull at the tail of a lizard seen hanging out of a hole in the wall; it would simply snap off.

12. Mario Praz, *The Flaming Heart* (Garden City: Doubleday, 1958), p. 27.

13. Two historical figures have been proposed as originals for Browning's Bishop, neither of them connected with Santa Prassede. For an evaluation

of these claims, see Barbara Melchiori, *Browning's Poetry of Reticence* (Edinburgh: Oliver and Boyd, 1968), pp. 21–22.

14. The poem, of course, refers to St. Praxed as a man. William J. Rolfe and Heloise E. Hersey, the editors of a volume of *Select Poems* of Browning (New York: Harper's 1887), reported that the poet, in a letter to them dated 10 July 1886, had confirmed their opinion that the Bishop's mistake about St. Praxed's sex is due to "the dying man's haziness" and is a self-exposing error (p. 195). But Barbara Melchiori has pointed out the obvious implausibility of the notion that the bishop would make this mistake about the patron saint of his own church, and it does remain more likely that the error is Browning's rather than the Bishop's.

15. William Lyon Phelps, *Robert Browning: How to Know Him* (Indianapolis: Bobbs-Merrill, 1915), p. 194.

16. John D. Rea, in "My Last Duchess," *Studies in Philology* 29 (1932); 120–22, points out that "elucescebat" occurs in Ireneo Affo, *Vita di Vespasiano Gonzaga* (1780), a biography of a figure who may have been the original of the Bishop.

17. *The Works of John Ruskin*, ed. E. T. Cook and A. Wedderburn (London: George Allen, 1903–12), 20: 33.

18. Wallace K. Ferguson, *The Renaissance in Historical Thought: Five Centuries of Interpretation* (New York: Houghton Mifflin, 1948), p. 132.

19. J. B. Bullen, "Browning's 'Pictor Ignotus' and Vasari's 'Life of Fra Bartolommeo di San Marco,' " *Review of English Studies*, NS 23 (1972: 313–19.

20. See also David J. DeLaura "The Context of Browning's Painter Poems," *PMLA* 95 (May 1980); 372–73, which plausibly argues that Browning's distortions of the painter's character were a response to the praise of Fra Bartolommeo's religious withdrawal in Alexis Rio's *De la Poèsie chrétienne*, and to Rio's general emphasis on pious painters who were indifferent to public approval and followed the traditional principles of religious art.

NOTES TO CHAPTER 4

From Wimpole Street to Pisa

1. *The Letters of Robert Browning and Elizabeth Barrett Barrett, 1845–1846,*
ed. Elvan Kintner (Cambridge, Mass.: Harvard Univ. Press, 1969), [16 November 1845], 1: 271. The editor points out that another word has been
written over the word usually read as "England," so that it is not legible.
However, no better possibility than "England" has been suggested.

2. *Ibid.,* [30 April 1845], 1: 50.

3. *Ibid.,* [3 May 1845], 1: 54–55.

4. *Ibid.,* [16 September 1845], 1: 196.

5. *Ibid.,* [22 June 1846], 2: 806–8.

6. The facade of the Duomo was not completed until 1871–87, so that
Browning never saw the building in its finished state. He wrote to Furnivall in 1882 that the idea of a Moorish facade had no historical basis, but
was "altogether a fancy of my own." *Letters of Robert Browning Collected by
Thomas J. Wise,* ed. Thurman L. Hood (New Haven: Yale Univ. Press,
1933), 23 January 1882, p. 208.

7. Frances Trollope, *A Visit to Italy* (London, 1842), 1: 90–92.

8. *From Robert and Elizabeth Browning,* ed. William Rose Benet (London:
John Murray, 1936), to Henrietta, 7 January 1847, p. 53.

9. Sir Joseph Archer Crowe and Giovanni Battista Cavalcaselle, *A New
History of Painting in Italy* (London: John Murray, 1864), 1: 126.

10. *Ruskin in Italy,* ed. Harold I. Shapiro (London: Clarendon Press,
1972), 18 May 1845, p. 67.

11. Leigh Hunt, *Autobiography,* ed. J. E. Morpurgo (London: Cresset
Press, 1948), p. 341.

12. Unpublished letter to Mrs. Jameson, [4 February 1847], from the
typed manuscript of the Kenyon edition of Elizabeth's letters in the British
Library, p. 172. Portions of this manuscript were omitted from the published letters.

13. *The Life, Letters and Friendships of Richard Monckton Milnes, First Lord Houghton*, ed. T. Wemyss Reid (London: Cassell, 1890), letter of 31 March 1847, 1: 385.

NOTES TO CHAPTER 5

Florence, 1847–1851

1. *The Letters of Robert Browning and Elizabeth Barrett Barrett, 1845–1846*, ed. Elvan Kintner (Cambridge, Mass.: Harvard Univ. Press, 1969), [18 June 1846], 2: 800.

2. Unpublished letter to Miss Mitford, 30 January 1849, Kenyon typescript, British Library, pp. 343–44.

3. An excellent study of the English community at this time is Giuliana Artom Treves, *The Golden Ring: The Anglo-Florentines 1847–1862*, trans. Sylvia Sprigge (London: Longmans, Green, 1956), originally published as *Anglo-fiorentini di cento anni fa* (1953). For Browning, see especially Ch. 5, "Casa Guidi."

4. Thomas Adolphus Trollope, *What I Remember* (London: R. Bentley and Son, 1887), 2: 172.

5. Henry James, *William Wetmore Story and His Friends From Letters, Diaries, and Recollections* (Boston: Houghton, Mifflin and Co., 1903), 1: 112, 120.

6. Unpublished letter to Miss Mitford, 30 January 1849, Kenyon Typescript, p. 343.

7. James, *William Wetmore Story*, letter of 19 March 1862, 2: 117.

8. *Ibid.*, 2: 283.

9. *Letters*, ed. Hood, to Richard Hengist Horne, 3 December 1848, p. 21.

10. *Dearest Isa*, ed. Edward C. McAleer (Austin: Univ. of Texas Press, 1951), 19 July 1862, p. 110.

11. T. A. Trollope, *What I Remember*, 2: 195–96.

12. *Ruskin in Italy,* ed. Harold I. Shapiro (London: Clarendon Press, 1972), 17 June 1845, p. 118.

13. *Ibid.,* to his mother, [25 June 1845], p. 129.

14. This was also a reflection of contemporary taste. See Leonee Ormond, "Browning and Painting," in *Robert Browning,* ed. Isobel Armstrong (Athens, Ohio: Ohio Univ. Press, 1975), pp. 188–89.

15. T. A. Trollope, *What I Remember,* 2: 131–37. Mrs. Stisted, inevitably, was the author of a book of impressions about Italy, *Letters from the Bye-ways of Italy* (1845).

16. *New Letters of Robert Browning,* ed. William C. DeVane and Kenneth L. Knickerbocker (New Haven: Yale University Press, 1950), to Miss Euphrasia Fanny Haworth, 29 June 1847, p. 43.

17. *Letters,* ed. Hood, 2 July 1849, p. 25.

18. *Letters of Elizabeth Barrett Browning,* ed. Frederic G. Kenyon (New York: Macmillan, 1897), 2 April [1850], 1: 441.

19. *Ibid.,* to Miss Browning, 14 November 1852, 2: 93.

20. *Letters,* ed. Hood, 16 January 1853, p. 38.

21. *Letters of Elizabeth Barrett Browning,* ed. Kenyon, 17 March [1853], 2: 108.

22. The main source of information about Jarves is Francis Steegmuller, *The Two Lives of James Jackson Jarves* (New Haven: Yale University Press, 1951). After many vicissitudes, his collection was exhibited in Boston and New York, and was ultimately sold to Yale University, where it waited until the twentieth century before obtaining the recognition it deserved.

23. James, *William Wetmore Story,* letter from Story to Lowell, 10 August 1853, 1: 266–70.

24. *Letters of Elizabeth Barrett Browning,* ed. Kenyon, [May 1854], 2: 168–69.

25. *Letters of the Brownings to George Barrett,* ed. Paul Landis (Urbana: Univ. of Illinois Press 1958), 2 May [1852], p. 183.

26. *Dearest Isa,* 18 October 1862, p. 131.

27. Henry James, "The Novel in the Ring and the Book," in *Notes on Novelists with Some Other Notes* (London: J. M. Dent & Sons, 1914), p. 318.

28. *Dearest Isa,* 22 May 1867, p. 267.

NOTES TO CHAPTER 6

Old Pictures and Browning

1. Francis Steegmuller, *The Two Lives of James Jackson Jarves* (New Haven: Yale Univ. Press, 1951), letter from James to C. E. Norton, August 1859, p. 171.

2. Dante Gabriel Rossetti, *Letters to Willliam Allingham, 1854–1870,* ed. George Birkbeck Hill (London: T. F. Unwin, 1897), pp. 160–61.

3. This unpublished letter is quoted in Julia Markus, " 'Old Pictures in Florence' Through *Casa Guidi Windows*," *Browning Institute Studies* 6 (1978): 54–55. The letter implies that the picture has just been discovered, but it had turned up some time earlier in the enormous collection of Cardinal Fesch, an uncle of Napoleon, which was auctioned between 1841 and 1845. Browning mistakenly gives its original location as the Church of San Spirito. In 1886 he made another mistake, writing to Hiram Corson that the iconography of the picture was the Last Supper; this letter is reproduced in facsimile both in Corson's *Introduction to the Study of Robert Browning's Poetry* (Boston: D.C. Heath 1898), and in Lilian Whiting, *The Brownings, Their Life and Art. The Death of the Virgin* is now in the Kaiser Friedrich Museum in Berlin.

4. Leonee Ormond, "Browning and Painting," in *Robert Browning,* ed. Isobel Armstrong (Athens, Ohio: Ohio Univ. Press, 1975), p. 201.

5. For the suggestion that the Padua frescoes, which often show figures reacting to each other, are indebted to sacred dramas, see Eugenio Battisti, *Giotto,* trans. James Emmons (Skira, 1960), pp. 96–99. Battisti's contention that all of the Padua frescoes are "founded on a dialogue, on an exchange of sharp and significant glances," and thus reflect dramatic situations, opens an aspect of the paintings that would have intrigued Browning.

6. For details about these developments, see Camillo von Klenze, "The Growth of Interest in the Early Italian Masters," *Modern Philology* 4 (October 1906): 207–65.

7. *Tuscan Athenaeum* 1 (13 November 1847): 22.

8. Henry James, *William Wetmore Story and His Friends From Letters, Diaries, and Recollections* (Boston: Houghton, Mifflin and Co., 1903), 1: 9.

9. For the relation between the two poems, see Markus, " 'Old Pictures in Florence' Through *Casa Guidi Windows*," pp. 43–61.

10. David J. DeLaura, "The Context of Browning's Painter Poems," *PMLA* 95 (May 1980): 382–83. My discussion is heavily indebted to this valuable article.

11. "The Ancient Refectory of Santa Croce," *Tuscan Athenaeum* 1 (24 December 1847): 75. Mrs. Jameson also visited this building and saw the looms.

12. "The Frescoes of Florence," *Tuscan Athenaeum* 1 (4 December 1847): 48.

13. Sir Joseph Archer Crowe and Giovanni Battista Cavalcaselle, *A New History of Painting in Italy* (London: John Murray, 1864), 1: 260ff.

14. Quoted in Steegmuller's *James Jackson Jarves*, p. 126.

NOTES TO CHAPTER 7

Men and Women

1. Henry James, *William Wetmore Story and His Friends From Letters, Diaries, and Recollections* (Boston: Houghton, Mifflin and Co., 1903), 2: 225–27.

2. Letter of 10 August 1855 from "Lettres inédites de Robert Browning à Joseph Milsand," *Revue Germanique* 14 (September 1923): 422–25.

3. Browning, "Essay on Shelley," *Complete Poetical Works* (Boston: Houghton Mifflin, 1895), p. 1009.

4. DeVane thought Browning attributed a "psychological realism" to Lippo on the basis of a passage in Filippo Baldinucci's *Notizie de Profes-sori del Disegno* (*Browning's Parleyings* [New Haven: Yale University Press, 1927], pp. 172–73). However, this has been adequately refuted, and Browning's transfer of Masaccio's realism to Fra Lippo explained in two articles by Johnstone Parr: "Browning's *Fra Lippo Lippi*, Baldinucci, and the Milanesi Edition of Vasari," *English Language Notes* 3 (March 1966): 197– 201; and "Browning's *Fra Lippo Lippi*, Vasari's Masaccio and Mrs. Jameson," *English Language Notes* 5 (June 1968): 277–83.

5. Giorgio Vasari, *Lives of the Most Eminent Painters, Sculptors and Archi-tects*, trans. Gaston De Vere (London: Philip Lee Warner, The Medici Soci-ety, 1912–14), 2: 189.

6. Anna Jameson, *Memoirs of the Early Italian Painters* (Boston: Houghton Mifflin, 1895), pp. 72, 71. First published as a series of essays in the *Penny Magazine*, and as a volume in 1845.

7. Bernard Berenson, *Italian Painters of the Renaissance* (London and New York: Phaidon, 1968), 2: 14.

8. *The Letters of Robert Browning and Elizabeth Barrett Barrett, 1845–1846*, ed. Elvan Kintner (Cambridge, Mass.: Harvard Univ. Press, 1969), [11 September 1845], 1: 190.

9. David J. DeLaura, "The Context of Browning's Painter Poems," *PMLA* 95 (May 1980): 378–79.

10. See Charles Thomas Flint, "The Painting of St. Laurence in 'Fra Lippo Lippi'; Its Source at Prato," *Studies in Browning and His Circle*, 6 (Fall 1978), 45–51.

11. See the criticism of Vasari in John Shearman's *Andrea del Sarto* (Ox-ford: Clarendon Press, 1965), 1: 9–10.

12. Jameson, *Early Italian Painters*, p. 175.

13. Julia Markus, " 'Andrea del Sarto (Called "The Faultless Painter")' and William Page (Called 'The American Titian')," *Browning Institute Studies* 2 (1974): 1–24.

14. Shearman, *Andrea del Sarto*, 1: 126, 125.

15. *Dearest Isa,* ed. Edward C. McAleer (Austin: Univ. of Texas Press, 1951), 18 August 1862, p. 119.

16. Laurence Lerner, "Poetry," in *The Victorians,* ed. Laurence Lerner (New York: Holmes and Meier, 1978), pp. 26–28.

17. See Johnstone Parr, "The Site and Ancient City of Browning's Love Among the Ruins," *PMLA* 68 (1953): 128–37.

18. William Wetmore Story, *Roba di Roma* (Boston: Houghton Mifflin, 1889), 2: 341.

19. Betty Miller has identified "the tune the children were singing last year in Venice" which Browning transcribed in an 1839 letter to Miss Haworth with "the toccata of Galuppi's" the young Florence Nightingale heard sung in Italy, but her reasons are not clear. In his notes to *Men and Women* (London: Oxford Univ. Press, 1972), p. 320, Paul Turner suggests that a manuscript harpsichord piece found in the library of the Brussels Conservatoire and labeled a "Toccata" may be the one Browning had in mind. But he agrees that the poem probably refers to the style of Galuppi's music in general rather than to a particular composition.

20. Unpublished extracts from the Diary of Alfred Domett, Griffin Collection, British Library, Add. MS 45559.

21. George Stillman Hillard, *Six Months in Italy* (London: John Murray, 1853), 2: 137.

22. George Santayana, "The Poetry of Barbarism," in *Interpretations of Poetry and Religion* (New York: Charles Scribner's Sons, 1900), pp. 188–216. Barbara Melchiori, "Browning in Italy," in *Robert Browning,* ed. Isobel Armstrong (Athens, Ohio: Ohio Univ. Press, 1975), pp. 173–78.

23. Unpublished letter to Arabel, 24 December and Christmas Day 1846, Berg Collection, New York Public Library.

24. Barbara Melchiori, "Browning and the Bible: An Examination of 'Holy-Cross Day'," in *Browning's Poetry of Reticence* (Edinburgh: Oliver and Boyd, 1968), pp. 90–113.

25. Story, *Roba di Roma,* 2: 424.

26. *Ibid.,* 2: 440–41.

27. Vicenzio Golzio, *Raffaello*, (Città del Vaticano, 1936), p. 182.

28. *Ibid.*, p. 217.

NOTES TO CHAPTER 8

Pauses of the Pen

1. *Letters of Elizabeth Barrett Browning*, ed. Frederic G. Kenyon (New York: Macmillan, 1897), to Miss Browning, [Rome, End of March 1861], 2: 436.

2. *Letters of Robert Browning Collected by Thomas J. Wise*, ed. Thurman L. Hood (New Haven: Yale Univ. Press, 1933), 23 January 1856, p. 44.

3. Rossetti, *Letters to William Allingham*, ed. George Birkbeck Hill (London, 1897), p. 163.

4. David J. DeLaura, "Ruskin and the Brownings: Twenty-Five Unpublished Letters," *Bulletin of the John Rylands Library* 54 (Spring 1972): 314–56.

5. *The Works of John Ruskin*, ed. E. T. Cook and A. Wedderburn (London: George Allen, 1903–12), 36: xxxiv-xxxv.

6. *Letters of Elizabeth Barrett Browning*, ed. Kenyon, to Miss Browning, [March] 1861, 2: 436.

7. *Life of Frances Power Cobbe* (London: R. Bentley and Son, 1894), 2: 17.

8. *Letters of Elizabeth Barrett Browning*, ed. Kenyon, February 1857, 2: 257.

9. *Ibid.*, 9 April [1857], 2: 258.

10. *Ibid.*, 14 September 1857, 2: 272.

11. William Irvine and Park Honan, *The Book, The Ring and the Poet: A Biography of Robert Browning* (New York: McGraw-Hill, 1974), p. 354.

12. *Letters*, ed. Hood, to Leigh Hunt, 6 October 1857, pp. 48–49.

13. Nathaniel Hawthorne, *French and Italian Notebooks*, 8 and 9 June 1858, pp. 292–96.

14. Extract from the Diary of Alfred Domett, 28 February 1877, Griffin Collection, British Library.

15. William Lyon Phelps, "Robert Browning as Seen by His Son," *Century Magazine* 85 (January 1913): 419.

16. *Letters of Elizabeth Barrett Browning*, ed. Kenyon, to Miss Blagden, 7 January [1859], 2: 303.

17. *Dearest Isa*, ed. Edward C. McAleer (Austin: Univ. of Texas Press, 1951), from Mrs. Browning, 15 February [1859], pp. 32–34.

18. *Ibid.*, [27 March 1859], pp. 39–40.

19. *Letters of Elizabeth Barrett Browning*, ed. Kenyon [about May 1859], 2: 314.

20. *Ibid.*, 27 March [1859], 2: 308.

21. W. C. DeVane, in his *Browning Handbook* (New York: Appleton-Century-Crofts, 1955), p. 359, quotes letters from Elizabeth and Browning as evidence that Browning wrote an early poem and destroyed it.

22. *Dearest Isa*, 9 September 1859, p. 47.

23. *Letters of Elizabeth Barrett Browning*, ed. Kenyon, to Mr. Chorley, 25 November [1859], 2: 351–52.

24. *Letters*, ed. Hood, to H. F. Chorley, [1860], p. 56.

25. *Dearest Isa*, 3 December 1860, p. 67.

26. *Letters*, ed. Hood, 30 June 1861, p. 62.

27. Henry James, *William Wetmore Story and His Friends From Letters, Diaries, and Recollections* (Boston: Houghton, Mifflin and Co., 1903), 2: 66.

28. *New Letters of Robert Browning*, ed. William C. DeVane and Kenneth L. Knickerbocker (New Haven: Yale University Press, 1950), July 1861, pp. 139–40.

29. Phelps, "Robert Browning as Seen by His Son," p. 417.

30. *Letters*, ed. Hood, 30 June 1861, p. 62.

NOTES TO CHAPTER 9

London and The Ring and the Book

1. *Dearest Isa,* ed. Edward C. McAleer (Austin: Univ. of Texas Press, 1951), 26 July 1862, p. 114.

2. *Browning to His American Friends.* ed. Gertrude Reese Hudson (London: John Murray, 1965), 21 January 1862, p. 95.

3. *Dearest Isa,* 19 September 1862, pp. 122–23.

4. Henry James, *William Wetmore Story and His Friends From Letters, Diaries, and Recollections* (Boston: Houghton, Mifflin and Co., 1903), letter of 17 July 1863, 2: 142.

5. *Dearest Isa,* 18 August 1862, p. 117.

6. *Ibid.,* 19 September 1862, p. 124.

7. *Ibid.,* 18 October 1862, p. 128.

8. *William Allingham: A Diary,* ed. H. Allingham and D. Radford (London: Macmillan and Co., 1907), p. 181.

9. Until recently, this ring was confused with one of the pair that Isa had given the Brownings in 1858, which Browning wore on his watch chain. It is actually an entirely different ring. For a full explanation and a photograph, see A. N. Kincaid, "The Ring and the Scholars," *Browning Institute Studies* (1980): 151–59.

10. A facsimile and translation of Browning's source, together with notes and comment, has been published as *The Old Yellow Book, Source of Browning's The Ring and the Book,* ed. Charles W. Hodell (Washington, July 1908), publication No. 89 of the Carnegie Institution of Washington. A second translation by John Marshall Gest was published in 1927 by the University of Pensylvania Press, Philadelphia. This version alters the order of the material, organizing it into chapters bearing on particular issues in the case. The Hodell volume includes a translation of the Secondary Source, a pamphlet entitled "The Death of the Wife-Murderer Guido Franceschini, by Beheading," which is the document Isa sent Browning in 1862, and an eighteenth century manuscript found in a Roman library called the Third Source and titled "Trial and Death of Franceschini and His Companions, etc." Hodell thought that Browning did not know the Third Source, but it

has been argued that it is the document mentioned in Browning's letter to W. C. Cartwright of 18 May 1865, and that the poem owes certain details to it. See Kay Austen, "The Royal Casanatense Document: A Third Source for Browning's *The Ring and the Book*," *Studies in Browning and His Circle* 4 (Fall 1976): 26–44. A manuscript related to the Secondary Source, but independent of it has been translated in E. H. Yarill, "Browning's Roman Murder Story: As Recorded in a Hitherto Unknown Italian Contemporary Manuscript," introd. William O. Raymond, *The Baylor Bulletin* 42 (December 1939). *Curious Annals,* ed. Beatrice Corrigan (Toronto: University of Toronto Press, 1956), presents translations of a number of documents from other lawsuits initiated by Guido, and some additional papers connected with his trial discovered in a library in Cortone. The introduction to this volume contains the most complete and dependable account of the actual events. It reveals, for example, that Pompilia's mother was not a prostitute, as she is in the poem, but a respectable woman named Corona Paperozzi.

11. "Essay on Shelley," *Complete Poetical Works* (Boston: Houghton Mifflin, 1895), p. 1009.

12. *Robert Browning and Julia Wedgwood: A Broken Friendship as Revealed by Their Letters,* ed. Richard Curle (New York: Frederick A. Stokes, 1937), 19 November 1868, p. 144.

13. Letter of 20 February 1883 to Furnivall cited in John Munro's introduction to Frederick J. Furnivall, *A Volume of Personal Record* (London: N. Frowde, 1911), p. lxx.

14. John Stuart Mill, "On the Application of the Terms Poetry, Science and Philosophy," *Monthly Repository* 8 (1834): 323–31.

15. These specifications are from the "Essay on Shelley," *Complete Poetical Works,* p. 1008.

16. Quoted in Katherine Bronson, "Browning in Venice," *Century Magazine* 63 (February 1902): 575.

17. *Robert Browning and Julia Wedgwood,* 19 November 1868, p. 145.

18. Introduction to Furnivall's *Volume of Personal Recollections,* p. lxxi.

19. *The Old Yellow Book,* ed. Hodell, p. 212.

20. See William Coyle, "Molinos: 'The Subject of the Day' in *The Ring and the Book*," *PMLA* 67 (1952): 308–14.

21. *Robert Browning and Julia Wedgwood*, 1 February 1869, p. 163.

22. Shelley, Preface to *The Cenci*, in *The Complete Poetical Works of Percy Bysshe Shelley*, ed. Thomas Hutchinson (London: Oxford Univ. Press, 1945), p. 277.

23. *Robert Browning and Julia Wedgwood*, "Monday afternoon," [1869], p. 175.

24. See William Wetmore Story, *Roba di Roma* (Boston: Houghton Mifflin, 1889), 2: 517–18.

25. James, "The Novel in The Ring and the Book," in *Notes on Novelists with Some Other Notes* (London: J. M. Dent and Sons, 1914), p. 317.

26. Sir Frederick Treves, *The Country of the Ring and the Book* (London: Cassell, 1913) is a valuable source of topographical information and has many fine photographs. The theater, according to a typewritten report in the Archivo Statale in Arezzo, was "dirritto fino al sommo della Piazza," that is, the Piazza Grande, which is at the rear of the Pieve. In 1624, the Fraternità dei Laici, whose palace was opposite, gave a large sum to restore it, but by 1701 it was again "in pessimo stato." Its site can be determined from the fact that it was occupied in 1925 by the Assize Court, whose name is still carved over one of the doors of the Logge.

27. Professor Griffin's photographs are in the Print Room of the British Library, No. 250a, Boxes 14–17.

28. In his invaluable *Commentary Upon Browning's Ring and The Book* (London: Oxford Univ. Press, 1920). pp. 279–81, A. K. Cook explains that Browning took the Via Paulina mentioned in a statement by Francesca in *The Old Yellow Book* for the site of a second home owned by the Comparini; actually, Via Paulina was the old name of the Via del Babuino, which intersects the Via Vittoria at the corner where the Comparini house stood. As Cook demonstrates, it follows that the house where Pompilia was raised, and the house where she was murdered are one and the same, and "a certain villa smothered up in vines" in the "Pauline district" to which Guido and his bravos steal in the poem is entirely Browning's invention. Treves was responsible for this clarification, but was apparently too compunctious to point out Browning's error.

29. Treves, *The Country of the Ring and the Book*, pp. 97–100.

30. *Ibid.*, p. 120.

31. *Ibid.*, pp. 135–37. Treves reports that in his time (1913) it was used as a depot for prison wardens. But the "Guide to the Criminological Museum of Rome" (1977) has it still in service as a prison in 1924. In 1977 it was occupied by the offices of the United Nations Social Defense Institute, a radical change from its earlier function.

32. Corrigan, *Curious Annals*, p. 101.

33. T. A. Trollope, *What I Remember* (London: R. Bentley and Son, 1887), 2: 206–7.

34. Story, *Roba di Roma*, 2: 532.

35. Richard D. Altick and James F. Loucks II, *Browning's Roman Murder Story: A Reading of "The Ring and the Book"* (Chicago: Univ. of Chicago Press, 1968), p. 23n.

36. Cook, *Commentary*, p. 153.

37. Isobel Armstrong, "The Ring and the Book: The Uses of Prolixity," in *The Major Victorian Poets: Reconsiderations*, ed. Isobel Armstrong (London: Routledge and Kegan Paul, 1969), p. 180.

38. L. J. Swingle, "Truth and *The Ring and the Book:* A Negative View," *Victorian Poetry* 6 (Autumn-Winter 1968): 259–69.

39. Altick and Loucks, *Browning's Roman Murder Story,* Ch. 3, "The World's Illusion," pp. 82-111.

NOTES TO CHAPTER 10

The Last Years: Venice and Asolo

1. Luigi Barzini, *The Italians* (London: Hamish Hamilton, 1964), p. 90.

2. *Letters of Robert Browning Collected by Thomas J. Wise*, ed. Thurman L. Hood (New Haven: Yale Univ. Press, 1933), p. 362.

3. See W. C. DeVane, *Brownings's Parleyings* (New Haven: Yale Univ. Press, 1927), pp. 167–76 for a review of Browning's use of Baldinucci.

4. Kenneth Leslie Knickerbocker, "Browning's *Cenciaja*," *Philological Quarterly* 13 (October 1934): 390–400.

5. A letter to Buxton Forman in *Letters*, ed. Hood, dated 27 July 1876, pp. 174–75 implies that Browning also consulted the source of the quotation in the Old Yellow Book, Farinacci's *Dissertation on the Statutes of the Cities of Italy*, edited in 1838 by George Bowyer, a good example of his thorough investigation of minor points.

6. *Learned Lady*, ed. Edward C. McAleer (Cambridge, Mass.: Harvard Univ. Press, 1966), 9 August 1878, p. 54.

7. The dream is described in a letter of 10 June 1889 quoted in Katherine Bronson, "Browning in Asolo," *Century Magazine* 59 (April 1900): 920. It is also mentioned in *William Allingham: A Diary*, ed. H. Allingham and D. Radford (London: Macmillan and Co., 1907), p. 248; and Lilian Whiting, *The Brownings: Their Life and Art*(London: Hodder and Stoughton, 1911), pp. 282–83.

8. *Learned Lady*, 28 September 1878, pp. 68–69.

9. *The Letters of Robert Browning and Elizabeth Barrett Barrett, 1845–1846*, ed. Elvan Kintner (Cambridge, Mass.: Harvard Univ. Press, 1969), [8 February 1846], 1: 443–44.

10. For Mrs. Bronson, see Henry James, "Casa Alvisi," in *Italian Hours* (New York: Grove Press, 1909), originally published in *The Cornhill Magazine* in February 1902.

11. DeVane, *Browning's Parleyings*, p. 62.

12. Filippo Baldinucci, *Notizie de' Professori del Disegno da Cimabue in Qua* (Milano: Società Tipografica de' Classici Italiani, 1812), pp. 266–67. Furini has spoken of "those scruples, the great labor, even the mortal agony that the artist experiences in the effort to satisfy himself in giving truth to his creation."

13. Whiting, *The Brownings*, pp. 263–64.

14. Bronson, "Browning in Asolo," pp. 923–31.

Index